# GERMANY AND ITS EVOLUTION
## IN MODERN TIMES

# GERMANY AND ITS EVOLUTION
# IN MODERN TIMES

BY

## HENRI LICHTENBERGER

*Maître de Conférences à la Sorbonne*

TRANSLATED FROM THE FRENCH BY

## A. M. LUDOVICI

NEW YORK

## HENRY HOLT AND COMPANY

1913

PRINTED BY
HAZELL, WATSON AND VINEY, LD.,
LONDON AND AYLESBURY,
ENGLAND.

# CONTENTS

## INTRODUCTION

# BOOK I
## ECONOMIC EVOLUTION

### CHAPTER I

#### THE DEVELOPMENT OF THE SYSTEM OF CAPITALISTIC ENTERPRISE

### CHAPTER II

#### THE EFFECTS OF THE SYSTEM OF ENTERPRISE UPON THE OLD FORMS OF INDUSTRY

v

## CHAPTER III

### THE EFFECT OF CAPITALISTIC ENTERPRISE UPON AGRICULTURE

## CHAPTER IV

### SOCIAL EVOLUTION

# BOOK II

## POLITICAL EVOLUTION

## CHAPTER I

### THE PROBLEM OF GERMAN LIBERTY AND UNITY

# CONTENTS vii

## CHAPTER V

### THE GERMAN EMPIRE AND HER
### HOME POLICY

## CHAPTER VI

### MODERN POLITICAL IDEALISM

# BOOK III

## THE EVOLUTION OF RELIGIOUS AND PHILOSOPHICAL THOUGHT

### CHAPTER I

#### THE RENAISSANCE OF CATHOLICISM IN GERMANY AT THE BEGINNING OF THE NINETEENTH CENTURY

### CHAPTER II

#### THE PROGRESS OF CATHOLICISM DURING THE NINETEENTH CENTURY

# CHAPTER III

## THE PROTESTANT SPIRIT

# CHAPTER IV

## THE PROTESTANT CHURCH

# CHAPTER V

## FREE THOUGHT

# CONTENTS                                    xi

# BOOK IV

# *EVOLUTION IN ART*

## CHAPTER I

### THE VALUE OF ART

## CHAPTER II

### ROMANTICISM, REALISM, AND IMPRESSIONISM

# CONTENTS

## CHAPTER III

### SYNTHETIC ART

## CONCLUSION

# INTRODUCTION

THE great fact which strikes us when we compare
the present day with the ages that have preceded it
is the enormous growth in human power which took
place during the course of the last century. It is
possible to have some doubts about the " progress "
of humanity, in the sense that it is very far from
certain that the man of to-day is happier, wiser, or
even in a safer position than he was formerly. On
the other hand, it is perfectly clear that the sum-
total of human power in the face of nature has
increased enormously. The conquest and subjuga-
tion of elemental forces by the intelligence of man
made a tremendous stride during the nineteenth
century. Man no longer regards the Universe in
the same way or with the same feelings as he once
did. Even his mental outlook has been profoundly
modified, and, to use an expression which is con-
tinually recurring in the works of German critics,
it has developed in the direction of "subjectivity."

The Middle Ages were filled above all with a deep
sense of our *helplessness* in the face of forces far more
powerful than ourselves. If we examine the state
of mind which prevailed, even towards the beginning
of the fifteenth century, we find that the most fundamental difference between ourselves and the men of
that period was the fact that they had no conception

of causality. We live under the firm conviction
that every circumstance, without exception, can be
explained as the effect of one or more causes. We admit the existence of an inexorable bond of causation
between all phenomena—a rule which admits of no
exceptions ; and we force ourselves throughout the
whole range of our experience to grasp clearly the
chain of cause and effect. Even when we cannot
find this relation, we are convinced that it exists
and that greater scientific knowledge would enable
us to discover it. It is this fundamental conviction
which was above all lacking in the man of the Middle
Ages. His knowledge of the outside world was still
very limited in range, and, unlike his modern brother,
he had not got at his disposal an enormous number
of systematised experiences, which had been classified and organised. His intelligence in the presence
of every fact and event did not imperatively demand
a causal explanation. In order to get his bearings
and to find his way in the midst of the chaos of
phenomena, he was content at every turn to reason
by analogies which were more or less haphazard and
superficial, and not to pursue a course of rigorous
induction. It is not surprising, therefore, that in
addition to a very restricted group of phenomena,
in which experience had taught him to trace a
certain regularity, he gladly postulated the existence
in our very midst of a far vaster realm of miracles,
which was independent of natural laws, and which,
at any moment could break the normal chain of
events. Nor is it surprising, either, that, in the
absence of firmly established positive science, and
by reason of the insignificant sum of experience that
can be acquired by a single individual, the traditional wisdom bequeathed from the past should have

exercised powerful authority over him. Indeed, there is nothing astonishing in the fact that a religion founded on a belief in miracles and based on the authority of long tradition should have dominated the spirits and imposed itself with irresistible force upon men's intelligence as well as their will.

How different is the mental attitude of the modern man!

Whilst the intellect of the Middle Ages bowed willingly before the authority of tradition, and saw miracles in everything, and the hidden, arbitrary, mysterious influence of superior powers in the world of phenomena, modern thought becomes ever more resolutely *self-reliant*. The intellectual horizon of mankind spreads to vast distances ; the sum-total of human experience, classified and docketed, grows greater every day. Science and the scientific instinct developed along parallel lines. Belief in the absolute determinism of phenomena has slowly taken the place of faith in the supernatural ; rigorous inductive reasoning has supplanted reasoning by analogy. At the same time, there has sprung up, chiefly during the last three centuries, a wider and more complete knowledge of the universe based upon reason and experiment. Through the great discoveries of Simon Stevin, Galileo, Newton, Descartes, Leibnitz, Euler, d'Alembert, and Laplace, mathematics and mechanics were placed upon a firm basis during the seventeenth and eighteenth centuries. Towards the end of the eighteenth century the empirical sciences in their turn leave the stage of blind groping. Lavoisier inaugurated the era of modern chemistry, Galvani and Volta that of electricity. And during the nineteenth century a vast conception of the mechanistic unity of the world was gradually elaborated. Human intelligence learnt to consider all the physical forces of nature in turn—mechanical processes, heat, light, sound, and electricity—as so many different expressions for one and the same fundamental power which manifests itself in every natural phenomenon, but remains unchanged in essence. It thus proved the unity of the forces of nature, and established the fact that everywhere and in every shape force obeys a fundamental cosmic law—the law of the conservation of energy and of the constancy of force and matter in the universe. Pushing its conquests yet further afield, it attempted at last to extend these laws to organic nature. In one of the simple, elementary substances—carbon—it unveiled the marvellous material which determines the formation of an infinite variety of organic bodies, and which, consequently, represents the *chemical basis* of life (Haeckel); it finds in the simple, solitary cell, the elementary organism which by successive combinations gives birth to all the tissues composing vegetable or animal organisms. With the theory of evolution, prophetically foreshadowed by Goethe at the end of the eighteenth century and scientifically formulated in 1859 by Darwin, it extended the mechanistic theory to the realm of biology and proclaimed that the universe as a whole was nothing more than an eternal evolution of matter.

But reason did not rest satisfied with postulating an explanation of the universe based upon the principle of causality ; it was not content with theory alone—it became practical, it acted, it created. In proportion as it acquired a sounder knowledge of the laws which govern phenomena, it learnt to subdue the forces of nature, to train them and make them work for its own profit. At the same time as it founded science, it also instituted a rational method of dealing with technical processes.

These, in the old days, were essentially empirical. The artisan knew, through having learnt it from his predecessors, how to set about obtaining a given result or product. His master had transmitted to him, through the channel of practical work, the knowledge gained by experience and the various processes by means of which a certain article was produced. And, in his ignorance of the laws of nature, he applied these formulæ without knowing, as a rule, how or why they gave the desired results. Sometimes a lucky fluke provided him with a clue to a new process by which he could gain his end with greater speed and certainty, and in such a case he enriched by some new rule the technical code, which he bequeathed to the generation to follow. But this code still remained a collection of empirical formulæ fortuitously discovered and not a well-co-ordinated body of reasoned and scientifically correct knowledge.

Now the distinguishing feature of modern technical processes is precisely the gradual substitution of rational knowledge for empiricism and of scientific methods for traditional formulæ. Thus scientific knowledge has, as its corollary, a profound modification of all technical processes, which gradually assume an entirely new complexion. What is the goal towards which natural science is tending ? It is essentially directed towards reducing differences of *quality* to difference of *quantity*, towards finding a mathematical formula for giving an adequate explanation of some natural fact, and finally towards bringing down all the phenomena of organic life to

*b*

the increasingly complex movements of primordial elements, which, in essence, are the same as those which constitute inorganic bodies. Similarly, modern technical processes in all their various forms— mechanics, thermophysics, chemistry, electricity, etc. —tend everywhere to eliminate living agents and to substitute dead elements in their stead ; to replace, for instance, human or animal motive power by steam or electricity, workers made of flesh and bone by instruments of iron and steel and by machinery ; natural organic products such as wood, vegetable colours, and manure, by artificial inorganic products like coal and iron, aniline dyes, and chemical manures. Thus technical processes become ever more exact, impersonal and independent of time and space ; they no longer depend upon capacity, whether natural or acquired—manual dexterity, keensightedness, hearing, taste, or smell—among various classes of men ; they operate with the rigorous, impartial, unswerving accuracy of a machine ; they are not obliged to submit to conditions of time and place, to which the natural growth of animal or vegetable organisms is subject, but produce the results they wish to obtain by means of an artificial combination of elements and forces which are always at their disposal. They are no longer more or less delicate arts, whose secrets it would be possible to lose, but definite acquisitions, for all time and all nations, of the knowledge common to all mankind.

Thus the development of science and of technical processes based upon reason increased the power of man and his dominion over nature to inordinate proportions. And under these circumstances we also find a profound change in his entire attitude towards life and the world.

In the Middle Ages, as we saw, man felt himself essentially a dependent creature. In all the departments of his material or spiritual life he obeyed either God or tradition. In the domain of religion, the Bible or the Church gave him for all great metaphysical problems a definite and complete solution inspired by God Himself, which he was expected to accept without reservation or discussion. Morality was imposed upon him as a divine ordinance which he should humbly obey. The organisation of society, founded upon ancient tradition, was also invested with a semi-sacred character. In all the important acts of his life, man *obeyed* a command given by a power whose will was infinitely above his own, and to whom a humble and resigned submissiveness was the only possible attitude.

Now, it is precisely this submissive attitude towards an outside authority which is modified as man gains consciousness of his own power. For centuries Christianity provided men of the western world with a cosmology—an explanation of historic evolution, an interpretation of the meaning of life and a rule of conduct ; for centuries they had inscribed Faith at the head of their Table of Values. But as rational knowledge grew, together with the power of organisation which such knowledge confers, man learned self-confidence. Science now rose up as a rival to Faith. Proud of her magnificent victories, Reason aspired to usurp the place of Religion in all departments of human life. She in her turn raised her eyes towards the first place upon the Table of Values. Since the seventeenth and eighteenth centuries the rationalistic movement has resulted in gigantic synthetic constructions, such as the systems of Descartes, Spinoza, and Leibnitz, in which Reason, elevated to the tribunal of the supreme judge of truth, sets herself the task of constructing, by the light of her own illumination alone, and independent of all authority, of all tradition and all revelation, an order of the Universe. At the beginning of the modern era, German thought, in the persons of Kant and Fichte, announced, with no uncertain voice, the great principle of Free Will. This disturbed the connection which was hitherto regarded as existing between religion and morality. The old order of ethics, which attributed the principles of morality to the Divine Will and curbed the human will by the ordinances of God, was, for Kant, a heteronomous morality, founded upon the principle of authority, which he repulsed with all the force at his command. In maintaining that " Pure Will," or will determined by pure Reason, and swayed exclusively by the law she lays down for herself, is the principle of all true morality, and by proclaiming that there is no authority in the world which can command human Liberty, that man is his own lawgiver, and that in obeying the moral law it is the voice of his own Reason to which he listens, Kant accomplished, in the domain of ethics, a task which in its bearings was truly colossal and inaugurated a new era in the history of moral consciousness. Through him the human race became definitely conscious of its autonomy.

The idea of human autonomy was from that time forward proclaimed with ever-increasing strength. Humanity learned to believe ever more and more firmly that the thinking and active " subject " recognises no power above himself before whom he should bow. The modern man has a growing conviction that he should not obey, but command and organise. He resolutely faces the problem of the

rational exploitation of the universe, and he labours
at the scientific organisation of life in all its aspects
—moral, economic, social, and political.

In its most extreme and paradoxical form, the
subjectivism of our day proclaims with Nietzsche
that " God is dead," denies not only the transcendental deity of the theologian, but also the immanent
God of the metaphysician, urges mankind to remain
" faithful to this world," to put resolutely aside
all interest in a Beyond, and to understand that he
should be a " creator of values," that outside himself
there is no " objective " truth, morality, or metaphysics to which he should submit, but that in all
independence he should be a law unto himself.
There is nothing in the world but centres of force in
a state of perpetual evolution and of unceasing
action and reaction upon each other. The Will to
Power, to ever-increasing power, which subjects
to its dominion an ever greater sum of energy, is
the fundamental fact of the life of the universe.
The severance from the point of view prevalent in the
Middle Ages is complete. Then we had the believer
who felt himself surrounded by mystery and miracle,
and submitted meekly to the authority of tradition,
whether religious, moral, or scientific. To-day we
find the stern Titan, who no longer recognises any
law or any master above him, but sees in the ceaseless Will to Power, the eternal destiny of man,
mankind, and the whole world.

When I contrast the old belief in authority with
modern subjectivism, I do not wish in any way to
assert that either of these two conceptions of life is
intrinsically superior to the other, or that one of
them should necessarily supplant the other, or that
history shows us a progressive evolution, continuous

though indefinite, towards rationalistic subjectivism. All that I wish to say is this—that mankind during modern times, and especially during the nineteenth century, has felt within himself the tremendous growth of the belief in the organising power of the human intellect and will, that he has applied his energy with remarkable intensity to the conquest of "power," whether scientific or technical, economic or political, and that the effort to inaugurate the universal rule of scientific and free reason is, perhaps, the greatest fact of the nineteenth century. But it is also true that the "religious" instinct, which made the spirits of the Middle Ages bow before the mystery of God, which led them to reverence in tradition the manifestation of the Divine Will, which impelled them to adoration and submission to a universal order—in short, to an attitude, not of command, but of reverent humility before the riddle of the world—this instinct has not, even in our days, ceased from making its voice heard. The modern man works with all his might to conquer the world through intelligence and conscious will. And he has pride in his strength. But he also retains a consciousness of the strict limitation of his power over matter. He still reveres the terrible and infinite powers which close about him and upon which he feels his dependence. And, especially in Germany, he willingly esteems and respects, in addition to the rules of conduct dictated by reason, that unconscious wisdom which finds expression in great religious, moral, political, and social traditions.

The history of Germany in the nineteenth century is therefore doubly interesting. Of all the nations of Europe, the German people is one of those among whom scientific reason and organising will have displayed the most extraordinary prowess and modern subjectivism has blossomed most luxuriantly. But it is also one among whom the " religious " spirit, respect for tradition and authority, has retained the greatest strength. German thought has been a powerful helper in the development of the positive sciences and in the elaboration of a rational explanation of the universe. German force has organised itself in a manner as methodical as it is formidable ; it has clung with incomparable energy to the conquest of power, both economic and political ; and it has made Germany, together with England and the United States, one of the most *expansive* nations of the world. German Reason, therefore, has proved herself a force of the first magnitude and a peerless instrument of power. But she has not posed as an absolute and intolerant sovereign, and has always sought to work as amiably as possible with the forces of the past. She has endeavoured, in the realm of religion, to make a compromise with traditional beliefs, to " fulfil " Christianity rather than fight it to the death. And in the domain of politics, instead of founding a uniformly rationalistic state, she has displayed great consideration for tradition, has shown a respect for monarchical authority, and has been careful not to violate vested interests, or to precipitate too hurriedly the evolutionary process which bears modern nations towards democracy.

Does this constitute a strength or a weakness ? This is indeed a question. Some will admire the continuity of the political and religious evolution of Germany ; they will regard it as a priceless advantage for a nation not to have made a clean slate of the past ; they will consider it probable that she will continue to develop along the same lines, without any violent shakes or blows, seeking and finding, in the means between the two extremes of democracy and Socialism, or feudalism and clericalism, a formula acceptable to the great majority. Others, on the contrary, will think that the Germany of to-day— a military and feudalistic state, an empire with a sternly realistic outlook, thirsting for power and wealth, and disdainful of all democratic and humanitarian idealism—is an anachronism in modern Europe, and cannot fail—perhaps in the near future—to undergo grave, and maybe violent, transformations.

I, for my part, have no pretensions to giving an original verdict on questions so hotly disputed. Without pretending that it is possible in a matter of this kind to attain complete objectivity, I shall at least try to describe as impartially as I can, and with the least possible obtrusion of my own personal feelings, a collection of phenomena which are of extraordinary interest to us. For some time past German science has, in numerous works by single individuals and several collaborators, taken upon itself the task of making up the balance-sheet of the last century. Some of these works—from which I shall quote in particular Lamprecht's admirable *History of Germany*—are of the highest importance. I thought it would be interesting to present to the French public, in as simple a shape as possible, some of the general results of this vast field of inquiry.[1]

[1] The most important are : *Das XIX Jahrhundert in Deutschlands Entwicklung*, hg. v. P. Schlenther, Berlin, Bondi, 1898, ss. ; *Die Allgemeinen Grundlagen der Kultur der Gegenwart*, hg. v. P. Hinneberg, Berlin u. Leipzig, Teubner, 1906, ss. ; *Am Ende des Jahrhunderts*, Berlin, Cronbach, 1898, ss. ; *Das Deutsche Jahrhundert in Einzelschriften*, hg. v. G. Stockhausen, Berlin, Schneider, 1901 ; H. St. Chamberlain, *Die Grundlagen des XIX Jahrhunderts*, München, Bruckmann, 1889. It seemed to me, moreover, impossible, without making my book too heavy, to give either a biblio-

By very reason of the profound differences which at present separate France from the Germany of to-day, it would be useful for us to force ourselves to form, without passion, a clear image and a general idea which shall be as precise as possible of the tendencies of that nation. My only object, in this study, is to trace the bold outlines of this picture as faithfully and sincerely as I can.

graphy of the works I have consulted, or to quote, in any detail, the authors to whom I refer. Among the works from which I have derived most profit, I must mention in the foremost place the three volumes which Lamprecht published as supplements to his *History of Germany* under the title of *Zur jüngsten deutschen Vergangenheit* (Freiburg, 1902–1904), then the German works of Sombart, Ziegler, Treitschke, E. Marcks, Lenz, Zwiedineck-Südenhorst, F. Mehring, Paulsen, Trœltsch, Nippold, Brück, Windelband, Ueberweg-Heinze, Külpe, R. M. Meyer, Bartels, Gurlitt, Muther, Meier-Graefe, Riemann, etc., and finally the French works by Andler, Basch, Denis, Goyau, Lévy Brühl, Albert Lévy, Matter, Milhaud, Pariset, Rouge, etc. It goes without saying that I might enlarge this list considerably. But I do not see what use such a catalogue would be to the French reader. I merely wish to point out that the ideas I develop in this volume are not my own exclusive property. This essay, I repeat, has no other object than that of giving a summary of the researches lately made on the subject of the culture of modern Germany by historians without whom my book would never have been written.

c

# BOOK I
## ECONOMIC EVOLUTION

# CHAPTER I

## THE DEVELOPMENT OF THE SYSTEM OF CAPITALISTIC ENTERPRISE

THE great fact which dominates the economic and social history of Germany, as well as that of the whole of Europe, during the nineteenth century, is the growth of capitalism, or, to use a term more generally favoured by German political economists, the system of "enterprise" (*Unternehmung*).

Former ages never felt to the same extent as the nineteenth century that greed for unlimited gain which is characteristic of the modern speculator of every category. In the pre-capitalistic era, each individual, from the lowest to the highest in the social scale, aimed only at earning enough to ensure him the means of sustenance (*Nahrung*) and a mode of life in keeping with the customs of his class. This was the ideal of the country gentleman, of the *Junker*,[1] who, as a rule, did not aim at that intensive cultivation of his property which would make it yield the absolute maximum of production, but only asked from his lands sufficient maintenance for his rank, the right of living like a lord on his estate for part of the year, of hunting in the autumn, paying a visit to the capital of the kingdom or province during the bad

---

[1] The landed proprietor, whose class is the dominating one in Prussia. It is from this class that all officers and higher officials are drawn.—TR.

3

season, and providing a dowry for his daughters and supplementing the income of a son in the army.   The ideal of the artisan and of the " master " was a similar one.   He expected his trade to support him, together with his family and the journeymen and apprentices, who lived under his roof and formed part of his household.   He never dreamt of extending his output indefinitely, but only aspired to the life of a self-supporting producer, who faithfully satisfied the ordinary demands of a very limited number of clients, whom no man had the right to lure away from him.   And, like the craftsman, the tradesman had no other object than that of earning a livelihood by disposing of his goods among a more or less restricted circle of customers with whose tastes and traditional needs he was familiar.

Under these conditions, the general tendency of the age was to protect the position which a man had won, or inherited, against the results of unrestricted competition and the encroachments of neighbours, who were either too greedy or too enterprising.   The landed proprietor was bound not to allow his lands to lie fallow, or to reduce the number of his tenures or the sum-total of the peasant families for whom he provided a livelihood on his estate ;  he was even liable to help them in time of difficulty.   In return, he was certain of always having at his disposal, through the institution of serfdom and forced labour, the service which was necessary for the cultivation of his property. In a similar way, the artisans were protected by their guilds, which, although they were fast dying out, still existed in rough outline at the beginning of the nineteenth century.   These guilds had the effect of creating, in every town, a sort of monopoly, based either upon law or upon usage, in favour of the

" masters " of the various trades, and of limiting the competition between the masters themselves in such a way as to prevent the appropriation of raw material and labour by a few individuals and to hinder the diversion of custom.

This idea of a " competency " gradually gave way to that of " free enterprise." From the end of the eighteenth century protestations resounded on every side against the barriers which barred the path to private initiative. The old organisation of the rural community, which, by the partition of an estate and the inextricable mingling of the allotments, made all the inhabitants of a village dependent upon each other and forced them to cultivate their land according to a traditional plan laid down by the elders of the place for use throughout the entire area of cultivation, was set aside. The people rebelled against the feudal system of a landed aristocracy, which placed the peasant in a position of absolute subjection to his lord and denied him the opportunity of ever winning economic independence. They complained of the countless obstacles placed by the guilds in the way of the natural growth of industry and commerce; but, above all, they protested against the tutelary administration of the enlightened despotism, which, in the eighteenth century, reserved for itself all initiative in economic matters and regulated, down to the smallest detail, the life and productive powers of the nation. The physiocrats in France, and Adam Smith in England, proclaimed the blessings of *laisser-faire*, and a similar spirit inspired William of Humboldt, in his celebrated pamphlet on the " Limits of State Interference " (1795), to raise an energetic protest against a bureaucratic system which made man into a machine, cast officials in the moulds of slavery, and stifled all independent action in the masses.

At the beginning of the nineteenth century, after the annihilation of Prussia at Jena, these ideas tended to gain the upper hand among the patriots, who set themselves the task of raising their native land from the dust. In their opinion, the weakness of Prussia relative to the French Empire was due to the fact that, whilst in France the Revolution had roused the whole nation to take a share in public life, enlightened despotism and the feudal system had crushed out every trace of spontaneity in Prussia. They accordingly set themselves the task of awakening the national conscience, of breathing life into the sluggish mass which constituted the Prussian State, and of transforming it into an organism in which every limb was alive and co-operated freely in the work of the whole system. They persuaded the king to carry out from above the Revolution which the French people accomplished from below.

It was imperative for the nation to be set free from feudal and administrative tutelage. Absolute rule, which was incapable, on its own resources, of making good the evils caused by the war, or of providing any effective relief for the various grievances of private individuals, abdicated its economic prerogatives and decided to " suppress every obstacle which had hitherto been able to prevent any individual from attaining that degree of prosperity to which his powers entitled him to raise himself." In every department of the administration, Stein endeavoured to introduce the principle of autonomy. Stein, and afterwards Hardenberg, attempted to raise the condition of the rural population by abolishing serfdom, allowing the redemption of forced labour, setting the tenant free from his lord's estate, and the peasant from the village community, and by favouring the formation of a class of independent peasantry who possessed their own land. In the towns they enfranchised the Third Estate by proclaiming the freedom of industry and commerce, destroying the guild system, and granting parochial self-government on a liberal scale. In spite of the resistance of the feudal party, which succeeded for many years in preventing this agrarian reform from being carried into execution, and, in the final liquidation of the feudal system, managed to secure enormous material advantages, the old order crumbled away after a hopeless defeat. The State renounced the right of directing the economic life of the nation. On a large number of cardinal points it left a clear field for private initiative, and unchained the spirit of enterprise, whose ambition had till then been thwarted by the feudal system and the guilds. The era of unrestricted competition was inaugurated. A new class of speculators now sprang into existence and grew rapidly, at first among the landed proprietors, and afterwards among the industrial and trading classes as well. They were men in whom the spirit of enterprise had become incarnate, and who were actuated only by the desire to develop their economic power indefinitely. It is this class which from that moment took the lead in the economic movement ; and in a very short time unrestricted competition, by utilising for its own ends the marvellous progress in science and technical processes, which we have just sketched, succeeded in overturning and transforming with incredible rapidity the manner of life of the whole nation.

Let us trace the principal phases of its evolution during the course of the nineteenth century.

At the beginning of the century, Germany was a rather poor agricultural country, but little developed from the economic point of view. It is estimated that the Empire itself had at that time a population only of about 25 millions, of whom three-quarters, at least, lived in the country, and two-thirds were engaged in agricultural pursuits. There was very little industry and commerce. Means of communication were few and bad : Prussia in 1816 possessed only 523 miles of high-roads, and they were execrable ; the post was slow, inconvenient, and costly. Moreover, the Treaties of Vienna sanctioned the political and economic partition of Germany. As soon as peace was declared, thirty-eight lines of customs frontiers paralysed all internal commerce, and, to use List's well-known description, produced " much the same result as if one decided to bind up the various members of the human body in order to prevent the blood from circulating from one to the other." Every industrial impulse was, consequently, for the time being, impossible. Moreover, the economic life of the nation was still somewhat primitive. The line of demarcation between agricultural and industrial pursuits remained very indistinct. The peasant still fashioned a large number of the utensils, clothes, and articles of all kinds which he required; and, conversely, many artisans and journeymen had, in addition to their trade, a little corner of ground which they cultivated themselves. Agriculture alone had been developed, and was even in a prosperous condition. Important demands for agricultural products arose in England owing to the growth of industry and the increase of urban centres ; while

Holland and the Scandinavian countries also became importers of corn. Now Germany at that time happened to be in a position to export part of her agricultural products, and was consequently able to sell a fairly large quantity of them, especially corn, abroad. This favourable state of things gave the landowners the opportunity of improving their methods of culture ; agricultural processes were perfected under the able guidance of Thaer, and the price of land went up. At that moment, for various reasons, a number of important towns sprang into existence in the north of Germany, in consequence of which the spirit of enterprise awoke, and we find the growth of fairly active speculation in agricultural land.

Throughout the first half of the century this state of things changed very little, but it is possible to trace the birth of circumstances which a little later on were to bring about the economic awakening of Germany. The first factor was the population, which, in consequence of the agricultural prosperity, increased by leaps and bounds : between 1816 and 1845 the number of inhabitants rose from 25 millions to 34½—that is to say, an increase of 38·7 per cent.— the highest that was ever reached during the century. Secondly, the establishment of the *Zollverein* during the 'thirties had the result of creating in Germany a territory of 8,253 square miles which was free from all internal customs and contained a population of at least 25 million inhabitants. The rhythm of exchange began to grow more rapid and the means of communication more frequent. New roads were made, and under the energetic sway of Nagler, the Postmaster-General, the postal service became quicker and more reliable. In 1835 the first railway line in Germany was built between Nuremberg and Fürth, and at the end of ten years—in 1845—there was a network of 2,131 kilometres of railroad. At the same time, the first and still feeble indications of the new spirit of enterprise made their appearance in the domain of industry. The great mining industry gradually freed itself from the old forms which fettered its flight, and every day saw the growth of its own importance. In connection with certain branches of the textile industry, and especially in the spinning and weaving of cotton, factories grew more numerous and tended to monopolise the entire production. But, generally speaking, the period between 1820 and 1850 did not produce any decisive economic progress. About 1820, agriculture even underwent a crisis which lasted nearly ten years, and made itself felt by a depression in land values and numerous bankruptcies. German industry also found great difficulty in struggling against the crushing competition of England, which, in default of sufficiently high protective tariffs, inundated Germany with cheap goods. Thus the country went through a period of difficulty and discomfort, and complaints were everywhere rife about want of money and hard times.

But directly after the great crisis of 1848 everything changed. As the scale of commerce for several years turned in favour of Germany, money began once more to flow in and accumulate there. The price of agricultural products, and consequently the value of land, showed a steady rise. The triumph of reactionary principles, moreover, seemed to herald a period of internal peace. The whole country, sick of political struggles and the fruitless agitations they involved, flung itself from that moment with redoubled energy upon the conquest of material prosperity and wealth. The spirit of enterprise and the love of speculation were not confined, as they had been at the beginning of the century, to a small fraction of the public, but invaded the lowest layers of the nation, and once for all took possession of the business world. During the twenty years which separated the crisis of 1848–49 from the Franco-German War, modern capitalistic Germany was formed. We now find a great increase in credit banks, such as the *Bank für Handel und Industrie zu Darmstadt* (founded in 1853) and other similar institutions whose business consisted in collecting the financial means necessary for the organisation of great industrial speculations or means of transport, and of thus stimulating to the highest possible pitch the spirit of enterprise which gave them birth and which kept them alive. Joint-stock companies, which, in a sense, make speculation democratic and associate the most modest resources with great capitalistic enterprises, sprang from the earth on every side and multiplied with extraordinary rapidity. It is estimated that in Germany, between 1853 and 1857, the issue of shares in new banks alone amounted to 200 million thalers, and railway shares to 140 million thalers, whilst a similar increase was shown in issues of a different nature, such as railway or industrial bonds, shares in insurance companies, mining ventures, steam navigation, machinery, sugar refineries, cotton mills, etc. The years inaugurating the second half of the century formed the first lap in the marvellous economic development which was to place Germany at the head of the industrial nations of Europe. It was during this period that the network of great railways joining the principal towns of Germany to each other and the outlying districts to the centre was built. At the same time, mining and weaving industries assumed a definitely modern complexion, whilst in the domain of agriculture, scientific processes of cultivation were every day more widely employed.

The four years following the war of 1870 are known in the economic history of Germany by the name of *Gründerjahre.* The fructifying rain of wealth due to the millions of the war indemnity produced a luxuriant and disordered crop of capitalistic enterprises. A veritable debauch of speculation filled Germany. The economic phenomena which had followed the crisis of 1848 appeared once more, but exaggerated beyond all bounds. There was a formidable inundation of economic activity in all quarters and a headlong rush for fortune. It is sufficient to quote one figure to illustrate the extraordinary intensity of this movement. The twenty years between 1851 and 1871 (first half) had seen the birth of 205 joint-stock companies with a capital of 2,404 millions of marks. The four years between 1870 (second half) and 1874 witnessed the sprouting of 857 with a capital of 3,306 millions of marks. As is only to be expected, a reverberating crash was the result of this orgy of speculation.

After this violent crisis of growth, the economic development of Germany assumed a more normal pace, and during the last thirty years she has made giant strides along the path of progress. It is true that German agriculture is in the toils of serious difficulties. In spite of the remarkable technical progress made during the second half of the century, it entered upon a critical period, which came slowly into existence, manifested itself clearly about 1875, and has not even yet passed away. But in the domains where the spirit of capitalistic enterprise is most conspicuous, such as banking, transport, industry, and commerce, German industry has accomplished marvels. The great law of the "concentration of capital," in virtue of which modern enterprise tends to accumulate capital in ever greater masses, to increase indefinitely the dimensions of factories, mills, and institutions of all kinds, to collect ever-growing armies of workers in them, and to produce ever more and more enormous bulks of merchandise, is proved in the case of Germany in the most astounding manner. During a relatively short lapse of time, one can trace the extraordinary development in that country of credit banks,[1] of means of communication

[1] A few figures will illustrate better than any theoretic explanations the progress achieved by Germany in the organisation of credit and the tendency towards concentration in financial matters. In 1846 there were, in Prussia, 1,100 persons engaged in finance and in the employment of 442 establishments, which gives a proportion of 658 employees to 442 employers. In 1895 there were 17,896 persons employed in 2,763 establishments, which gives 15,133 employees to 2,763 employers, or an average of about 6 men to each master. The first great credit banks in Germany, the *Darmstädter Bank* and the *Diskontogesellschaft*, were founded, the former in 1853 with a capital of 6·8 millions of marks, the latter in 1856 with a capital of 37·2 millions of marks. At the beginning of the twentieth century, the principal German bank, the *Deutsche Bank*, was carrying on business with a capital of 257 millions of marks (including the reserve funds) ; and the seven largest credit banks possessed, in 1905, in subscribed and reserve capital, a total of nearly 1,400 millions of marks. The average daily circulation of bank-notes increased from 120 millions of marks about 1850 to 1,316 millions of marks in 1900 and 1,485 millions in 1905. The circulation of bills in the *Königliche Bank* of Berlin in 1820 was about 1½ millions of marks ; the total sum of bills discounted at the *Reichsbank* reached, in 1905, nearly 9,000 millions of marks. In the principal banks of the Empire, the annual average of the sum-total of discounted bills reached 5·26 thousand millions of marks per annum from 1876–80, 20·4 thousand millions of marks from 1896–1900, and 28·6 from 1901–1905. At the same time, the

and transport business, railway, river, and sea traffic, postal, telegraphic, and telephonic [1] services,

total annual amount of the transfer operations in deposit accounts rose from 3,500 millions of marks in 1875 (*Preussische Bank* and *Hamburger Bank*) to 164,000 millions of marks in 1900 in the *Reichsbank* and 222,000 millions in 1905, whilst the sum-total of settlements carried out by the agency of the Clearing Houses, founded by the *Reichsbank*, rose from 12·1 thousand millions of marks in 1884 to 29·5 thousand millions in 1900 and 37·6 thousand millions in 1905. (The majority of the figures I give have been either supplied or verified by the Board of Financial Investigation of the *Crédit Lyonnais*, to whom I take this opportunity of expressing my gratitude for their courtesy.)

[1] Let me once more quote some typical figures. The network of roads in Germany increased from 30,000 kil. in 1857 to 96,000 kil. in 1900; the railroads from 469 kil. in 1840 to 54,164 kil. in 1905; her revenues are over 500,000 millions of marks; her maritime fleet rose from a tonnage of 500,000 about 1850 to 2 million tons in 1900 and 3½ million in 1905; she has thus become the second maritime power of the world, with a fleet inferior only to the English Navy. At the same time, there is a noticeable increase in the size and power of vehicles and in the number of passengers and amount of goods they transport. Large four-horse waggons used to carry at most 5 or 6 tons of merchandise; when the railways were first opened, an engine drew 40 waggons of 2 tons apiece—that is to say, 80 tons—whilst at the present moment it draws 100 waggons of 10 tons—that is to say, 1,000 tons. The large boats which bear the traffic of the Rhine carried 400 tons in 1840, 800 in 1880, 2,000 in 1900. The average tonnage of the ships in the Port of Hamburg rose from 187 tons between 1841 and 1845 to 1,233 for the year 1900; the steamship *Wilhelm II.* alone is a vessel of 19,500 tons—that is to say, half the tonnage of the whole fleet of Hamburg about 1840, which consisted of 211 ships with a tonnage of 39,670; the engines of the Great Eastern about 1850 rose to 3,000 horse-power, whilst those of the large steamers of to-day reach 40,000 h.p. The circulation of travellers and goods has increased in similar proportions. In 1834 the stage-coach service carried about 1 million passengers; in 1905 it carried over 3 millions by road; but to this number we must add the 1,000 million passengers who travelled by rail in 1905, besides the 761½ millions of townspeople who used the tramways and those who patronised the 15,410 cabs on the streets of the towns (1899). It is estimated that in 1846 there were, within the confines of the *Zollverein*, 38,349 horses in use for the transport of passengers and goods whose total power was computed at 130

and large industries of every description. The total annual production of the mining and metal industries in Germany, which about 1800 represented a gross value estimated at about 25 millions of marks, reached in 1900 a value of about 4,000 millions of marks.[1]  Chemical industry, which was still insignifi-

---

millions of kilometric tons ; the power in use in 1900 on the network of railways is estimated at about 37,000 millions of kilometric tons, which is equivalent to the work done by about 11 million horses.  The traffic in the Port of Hamburg, which in 1831 amounted to a tonnage of 232,000, rose to 8 million tons in 1900 and 9½ million tons in 1905 ; for the aggregate of German ports, it has increased from 6,228,000 tons in 1873 to 18 million tons in 1900 and 22·4 million tons in 1905.  Comparative statistics of the river and canal traffic show an enormous increase during the last quarter of the century : it is reckoned that the total traffic of the five principal ports (Duisburg, Ruhrort, Mannheim, Berlin, Magdeburg) rose from 7,761,000 tons in 1882 to 28,813,000 tons in 1903, whilst at the same time the import and export trade in the Rhine ports rose from 6,400,000 to 36,100,000 tons.  Lastly, correspondence has developed to colossal proportions.  Whilst about 1851 the average was about 3 letters a head, it is estimated that every German received on an average 58·57 letters or cards in 1900 and 72·26 in 1904.  The total number of postal packages of all kinds has reached nearly 7,000 millions a year.  In 1850, 35,000 telegraphic messages were sent, in 1904, 46 millions ; and the telephone, which in 1881 served 7 localities with 1,504 call offices, served, in 1904, 22,792 localities with 515,300 public and private call offices.

[1] The progress lately achieved by the mining and metal industries will be realised from the following figures.  In 1880 the output of coal was about 50 million tons and of cast iron 2·7 million tons.  In 1905 the figures are respectively 121 million tons and almost 11 million tons.  As a producer of iron and steel, Germany since 1903 has outstripped England and is second only to the United States.  Motor-power has increased in similar porportions.  About 1840 there were barely 500 motors in the whole territory of the *Zollverein* ; in 1873 the sum-total of motor-power already exceeded a million horse-power; in 1895 it reached 3·4 million, and it is estimated that since that time it has increased again by 90 or 100 per cent.  Mulhall has made a calculation of the total power (human, animal, or mechanical) in use in Germany, and taking as his unit the force necessary to raise a weight of 1 ton

cant towards the middle of the century, increased
rapidly, especially during the last twenty years of
the nineteenth century, and actually produced an
output the total value of which was estimated at
1,250 millions of marks in 1905.  Electrical industry,
the latest result of the great creative impulses due to
the spirit of capitalistic enterprise, increased with
extraordinary rapidity after 1880 and especially
after 1895, triumphantly surmounted a formidable
crisis during the opening years of the twentieth
century, and carries on its work to-day with a capital
of nearly 625 millions of marks, and represents, if we
include the capital involved in electric installations,
a gross value of about 2,500 millions of marks.  Thus,
at the beginning of the twentieth century, German
industry has risen to an unprecedented degree of
power and prosperity, of which those who are engaged
in it are justifiably proud.  Animated by an extraordinary creative activity, it increases its enterprises
with a rapidity and a boldness which baffle the
imagination.  The years between 1895 and 1899
especially formed a period of peculiarly great economic
activity.  During these five years, the net sum-total
of stocks issued exceeded 10,000 millions of marks, of
which over 1,250 millions consisted of bank shares,
and over 2,250 millions of industrial stock.  And if the
first years of the twentieth century were inaugurated
by a fairly serious crisis, the business market shows
clear signs to-day of complete recovery.  Whereas in
1900 the sum-total of stocks issued (in shares, bonds,
and loans) was estimated at 1,500 millions of marks;
in 1905 it was over 3,000 millions.

On the whole, therefore, the result of the last few

to a height of 1 foot, he has estimated that in 1840 there were
310 units of power per head, in 1860, 415, and in 1895 about 900.

years has been a brilliant triumph for German industry and commerce. Fifteen years ago Germany ranked fourth among the commercial powers, and gave precedence to England, France, and the United States. To-day, whilst France has sunk from the second to the fourth place, Germany, outstripping both France and the United States, has won the second place. The sum-total of her commerce rose, in 1905, to 12·7 thousand millions of marks, of which seven consisted of imports and 5·7 thousand millions of exports.[1] She is even threatening the traditional commercial supremacy of England. The gross value of her industrial productions is estimated, according to American statistics, at over 2,900 millions of dollars, which is 650 millions above that of France (2,245 millions) and inferior only to that of England (4,100 millions) and the United States (7,000 millions).

[1] The corresponding figures are : England 19·3, the United States 11·8, and France 7·6 thousand millions of marks.

# CHAPTER II

## I

AFTER having described the system of capitalistic enterprise, and depicted its chief manifestations, we must now consider how it has modified the old forms of economic activity, domestic industry, the craftsman's work, and agricultural life.

The importance from the earliest times until quite recently of home industries among rural populations is well known. Until about the middle of the last century, the German peasant differed very little from his prototype of ancient days, who, with the help of his household, was almost entirely self-supporting. Even when the nineteenth century was in full swing, the German peasant did not limit himself to producing the simple necessities of life, but, in addition, utilised his leisure moments to fashion for himself the various things he required. He was his own baker and his own butcher. He used to spin and weave the wool or the flax required for his clothes and linen. He was able to build and repair his own house with its wooden framework, its loam-coated walls, and its thatched roof, and was enough of a blacksmith and wheelwright, if occasion demanded, to make and keep in repair his agricultural implements

18

and carts of all kinds.    When he was not in a position
to make what he wanted himself, he had recourse to
the help of workmen and tradespeople—the tailor,
the cobbler, the carpenter—whom he generally had
to work under his own supervision in his own house.
Only in very exceptional circumstances was he
obliged to turn to outside aid and buy in the market
or the town articles or provisions which he was
unable to produce by his own industry.    Generally
speaking, the peasant was still able to supply himself
with all the essentials he required, and he was almost
entirely independent of the fluctuation of prices or
the working of the law of supply and demand.

During the second half of the century, this
patriarchal state of things underwent a rapid modification.    Workers confined themselves more and more
exclusively to one speciality and produced this, no
longer merely for their own use, but for the market,
and with the proceeds bought the various necessities of life.    Political economists quote as a typical
example the case of the peasant woman of Hagsfeld,
in the province of Baden, who declared she no longer
even had the time to do the family washing herself at
home, but sent it to the steam-laundry at Karlsruhe.
It is true that every German housewife has not yet
come to such a pass, and in many of the rural districts, both urban and rural, domestic work is held in
high esteem.    Nevertheless, it plays, on the whole, an
ever smaller part in the economic life of the middle-
classes and peasantry.    If industry on a large scale
has reached ever-increasing dimensions, and if the
proportion of the population engaged in industrial
pursuits has grown enormously during the course of
the last century, one of the chief reasons for this
development is to be found precisely in the dis-

appearance of domestic work. Articles once made in leisure hours round the family hearth are to-day manufactured wholesale by specialists. Consequently, the apparently prodigious growth of industry can be at least partially explained by the gradual specialisation of economic activity. The peasant confined himself more and more rigorously to purely agricultural pursuits ; he gave up home industry and supplied his wants in this sphere, by means of an ever-increasing class of industrial craftsmen who had nothing whatever to do with agriculture.

Where home industry still survived, it completely changed in character, owing to a series of consecutive transformations. The peasant who used to employ the leisure moments which his work in the fields allowed him, in the exercise of some supplementary trade worked for himself and not with the object of selling his goods to the general public. Little by little, however, we find him labouring with an eye to the market. He joined some friends in working a mine ; he became a weaver or a worker in metal or wood. He thus turned into an industrial worker on a small scale and circulated his wares by means of pedlars. Then his condition changed ; from being an independent craftsman he gradually sank to a position of dependence upon the big town merchant from whom he received his raw material and the implements necessary for his work. He thus, in fact, became simply the paid servant of a master, who found it profitable to allow his employees to work at home instead of collecting them into shops and factories. The craftsman, moreover, was at first protected to a certain extent by the State, which subjected the employers to the minutest regulations of an officious fiscal legislation, exercised a strict supervision over them, and prevented them from sweating their under-lings. This form of home industry was fairly flourishing at the beginning of the nineteenth century.

In the mountainous and barren districts of Central Germany, and especially in Silesia, the Erzgebirge, the Frankenwald, the Hartz Mountains, and West-phalia, a large part of the population was engaged in the textile industry. But this form of home industry was also condemned to disappear before the progress of industry on a large scale. It was im-possible for the single craftsman who carried on his trade by hand to compete with mechanical work produced by the help of machinery and by workers collected in a factory. In order to meet this crush-ing competition, the contractors, who gradually freed themselves from State supervision, had no alternative but to reduce the salaries of their work-people, whom they thereby condemned to the direst poverty and sometimes even to the horrors of starvation. Every one has heard of the terrible straits to which the Silesian workers found them-selves reduced during the 'forties, and their sufferings and revolts have been immortalised by Gerhard Hauptmann in his famous play *The Weavers*. The final result was almost always the disappearance of home industry. In every case where it had once existed—in the mining and textile industries and in various minor branches of the metal industry—whole-sale manufacture, concentrated in a mill or factory, gained the upper hand once for all.

Whilst home industry thus died out more and more completely in the rural districts, we find it, on the other hand, reviving under a new form in the large towns, such as Berlin and Stettin, Frankfort, Nuremberg and Stuttgart, Munich and Barmen-

Elberfeld. In these places, during the second half of the century, a flourishing industry sprang up for the production of clothes and linen. These industries are now concentrated in the hands of a few great firms, who employ a large number of hands working either at home or in small workshops under the supervision of sub-contractors. But we all know the price paid for this prosperity and the ludicrous salaries which the large manufacturers and their middlemen can impose upon the unfortunate men and women whom they sweat and condemn only too often to poverty or prostitution. Home work, which is so difficult to supervise or regulate, thus entails the most glaring abuses, and its history in every country is, without a doubt, one of the most shocking chapters in the evolution of capitalism.

## II

Just as the growth of capitalism proved fatal to home industry, it also completely destroyed the " trades " guilds.

The old-fashioned " master " was a sort of manufacturer on a small scale, who combined in his own person the functions of capitalist, employer, qualified craftsman, and tradesman. He was an independent producer, who worked on his own account, together with the members of his family and a few journeymen and apprentices, who formed part of his household. Under these conditions his ambition could not soar very high. He did not aspire to extend his sphere of action indefinitely or to exploit his underlings unduly. Moreover, the guild system, which still survived in rough outline at the beginning of the nineteenth century, would not have allowed him to develop his business beyond certain limits. This system had the effect, in short, of securing to each master a sphere of activity in which he was scarcely troubled at all by outside competition, but which, on the other hand, he himself could not extend. By establishing in every town a sort of monopoly in favour of the masters, by limiting the number of masters in each district, by forbidding the cornering of raw material, by defining the number of journeymen and apprentices which each master might employ, and by punishing the diversion of custom, it protected the " master " against the competition of outside rivals or of his fellow guildsmen in the same town, whilst at the same time it prevented him from raising himself above a very modest pinnacle of prosperity.

The guild system, which was fast falling into decay at the beginning of the century, disappeared completely about the middle of the nineteenth century. The first crisis took place during the 'forties. The old regulations gradually fell to pieces. Complaints grew louder on every side : the apprentices and journeymen rebelled against the guild rules, and the limits assigned to each guild in the division of labour were no longer regarded ; everywhere privateers (*Bönhasen*) sprang into existence, and were, as a rule, not prosecuted. In vain did the labour parliament which met at Frankfort in 1848, side by side with the national parliament (middle of July to middle of August 1848), protest at its first session against industrial freedom—in vain did it demand the restoration of the guild regulations of the Middle Ages. The tide which was hurrying the whole epoch towards a system of unrestricted competition could not be stemmed. The old order crumbled away in

spite of the fruitless efforts of legislators to save it.
The whole of the labouring class, the whole of that
lower middle class, which had been so modest, hardworking, thrifty, and respectful of tradition, saw the
customs of centuries swept away, and was violently
shaken by a crisis which attacked the very foundations of its existence. The masters, the most ambitious and the most easy-going alike, tried harder
every day to free themselves from the guild regulations. They accepted the system of competition,
increased the number of their apprentices and
journeymen, introduced division of labour, created
specialisation, and organised their system of employment to the best advantage without regard for old
customs. In short, they became small contractors,
made a position for themselves in the new order of
society, and succeeded, thanks to their activity and
business instinct, in maintaining their economic
activity. Those of a less energetic frame of mind
clung to the old routine, and were hurried more or
less speedily to final disaster, in the midst of fruitless
lamentations over the bad times, the decay of the
old customs and ancient privileges. Many lost
heart, gave up business, and became petty officials,
or found employment on the railways or in some
industrial or commercial enterprise. Others, more
particularly in Swabia and the Palatinate, emigrated
in large numbers, and went to seek their fortunes
beyond the seas, especially in South and South-West
America. And lastly, many who were less enterprising, were content to leave town for the country,
where, in spite of the jeers of their urban brethren,
they ended by taking root and making a suitable
position for themselves. The artisan and craftsman
class, transformed in this way by the influence of the

spirit of enterprise, roughly maintained its position for a quarter of a century longer.

Nevertheless, about 1880 there began to be discerned the indications of a fresh crisis, which was more terrible and severe than the first, and threatened to deprive workers once for all of the last vestiges of economic independence. This crisis was not, like the first one, caused by the entrance of new psychic elements into the working class—it was due to the crushing competition which the single worker in every branch of economic activity had to meet on the part of colossal industrial enterprises.

In short, wholesale production, concentrated in a factory or a mill, established its superiority more and more firmly every day, and steadily gained ground. In every domain and every branch of human industry, the small producer and the independent craftsman found themselves gradually wiped out by the very force of circumstances. The retreat from the old position was manifested everywhere, not only in the large and small towns, but even in the country, where the peasant grew more and more accustomed to buying cheap ready-made articles supplied him by large firms. Every profession found itself faced by a similar menace. The progress of colossal industries was not equally swift in every department : it was rather more rapid in the clothing industry, for example, and in furniture ; somewhat slower in food stuffs and the building trade. But there is nothing to show that this process will end before it has secured the triumph of capitalism at every point.

Practically speaking, craftsmen belonging to nearly every kind of trade—carpenters, cobblers, tailors, masons, thatchers, etc.—had already fallen under the more or less disguised dominion of some capitalistic contractor, and were thus really in a position quite as dependent as that of the factory hand, although nominally they were still free. Thus builders were dependent on the contractor who could provide them with work, carpenters were at the mercy of the furniture dealer, who bought the articles they made at a low price, and tailors depended upon the clothier who gave them orders. In the most favourable circumstances, the worker could become a capitalist on a small scale—a sort of cross between the old master and the wholesale manufacturer ; he could still earn an honest livelihood as a baker, a butcher, a bespoke tailor, a locksmith, a cabinet-maker, etc. But he always ended by having to face the competition of large industries. Sometimes these entirely monopolised the production of an article and only left repairs to craftsmen (as in the bootmaking trade). Sometimes they produced nearly every article and only left to the craftsmen installations, alterations, and repairs (the locksmith's trade). Sometimes they monopolised the production of certain articles in such a way that they were made partly in the factory and partly in the shop or by hand (joinery). Lastly, they sometimes appropriated to themselves the fabrication of a small number of special articles and allowed the old arrangements to continue more or less as before (butchers and bakers).

On the whole, the class of independent craftsmen was rapidly dying out. It is true that according to statistics there was still an aggregate of about two million craftsmen. It is also true that there was even an absolute increase in their number ; thus, between 1834 and 1895 the number of craftsmen in Prussia showed an increase of nearly 450,000. But the number of craftsmen in proportion to the total population seems to have diminished a little—in Prussia it dropped, during the period above mentioned, from 4·1 per cent. to 3·7 per cent. ; whilst in social importance the working class fell much lower than statistics can show. The craftsman, who was once a free agent, was now only free in name, and his condition, except in rare cases, differed very little from that of the ordinary member of the masses.

# CHAPTER III

## THE EFFECT OF CAPITALISTIC ENTERPRISE UPON AGRICULTURE

THE effect which the rise of the spirit of enterprise had upon the development of German agriculture is far less striking than that produced in the domain of industry during the same lapse of time. It has even been pointed out that, superficially, Germany, judging from the distribution of agrarian property, changed very little during the last century. About 1800 there existed, and still exist to this day, districts where large estates predominated (the country east of the Elbe), others where there were large numbers of peasant proprietors (Schleswig, Hanover, Westphalia, Brunswick), and yet others where moderate-sized and small estates were the rule (the region south-west of the valley of the Rhine). Moreover, the most varied types of undertakings subsisted peacefully side by side, without any particular one showing signs of definitely gaining the upperhand in the near future. But it was none the less certain that German agriculture had undergone a series of fundamental internal transformations, of which I will endeavour to trace the principal features.

In the first place, agricultural products had increased enormously. This result was due chiefly to the fact that the surface of the ground had been more fully utilised since the development of husbandry, which had considerably reduced pasture and fallow land. In this connection, it is estimated that the ground occupied by fields and gardens was a quarter, perhaps even a third, as much again as it was during the previous century. This, however, was due principally to the perfection reached in technical processes. Scientific knowledge about the conditions necessary for the growth of vegetable produce, and especially the great discoveries of Liebig in the domain of agricultural chemistry, had the result of substituting rational methods for the old rules-of-thumb. The old plan of triennial distribution gave way to that of the rotation of crops, which in its turn was supplanted by the system of intensive cultivation through the aid of chemical manures. The old primitive instruments used by the peasants in the Middle Ages were gradually replaced by complicated agricultural machines of all kinds—steam ploughs and engines for sowing, weeding, and thrashing— whose numbers multiplied particularly rapidly after about 1880. The culture of paying crops was developed at the expense of those which were less remunerative. Side by side with agricultural concerns, factories sprang up, where the products of the soil underwent a transformation into industrial commodities: the beetroot grower, for instance, became a sugar-refiner as well, the potato planter a distiller. The methods of afforestation and the rearing of cattle were gradually brought to perfection, and the results obtained became every day more fruitful. The output per acre continued to increase. The number of head of cattle of all kinds grew to considerable proportions, the stock was improved, and the average weight of the animals went up. In short, it is estimated that the sum-total of agricultural production has increased at least two, if not threefold, during the last hundred years.  As, moreover, the number of rural labourers has not multiplied in similar proportions, it seems evident that, owing to the progress made in technical processes, the productivity of agricultural labour has increased enormously during the last century.  It is not possible, however, yet to decide to what extent it has done so, or whether at the present time this capacity for production is tending to increase or diminish, and whether, therefore, the working of the law of the gradual exhaustion of the soil is making itself felt in Germany or not.

But if, both in agriculture and industry, we find that progress has been based upon the employment of more rational technical processes, their respective modes of development are nevertheless exceedingly different.  Whilst in industry, as we have pointed out, capital became concentrated in ever more colossal enterprises, this law did not make its action felt in the domain of agriculture, where we do not find that large enterprises tend to expand indefinitely.  On the contrary, they seldom reach more than modest dimensions, and cultivated properties of over 2,500 acres are the rarest exceptions.  Neither do we observe that small or moderate-sized concerns are fatally inferior to the large ones.  Not only do the former survive, but a diminution—very slight, it is true—in large properties may even be discerned.  Moreover, we do not see in agricultural enterprises that tendency towards specialisation which is so characteristic of industry.  On the contrary, it would seem that to-day a greater variety of produce is obtained by any one concern than was the case a hundred years ago. It is impossible to hold the theory that the capitalist who works a large estate can produce more cheaply than the ordinary cultivator, and that wholesale production is consequently an economic necessity in agriculture. It is, therefore, incorrect to say that just as small industries are stifled by large ones, the peasant, finding it impossible to struggle against the competition of great landed proprietors, is hastening to irretrievable disaster.

Nevertheless, the new spirit shows itself in agricultural life as well, by a series of characteristic symptoms.

The most important of these is the revolution which took place during the first half of the nineteenth century in the management of agrarian property, by which private cultivation was substituted for collective cultivation.

About 1800 a country village was still a sort of collectivist settlement. Each peasant or member of the community was given a *Hufe,* or privilege of having a share in the general possessions of the village, such as cultivated land, rivers and ponds, roads and lanes, meadow-lands and forests. By virtue of this principle, every member of the association had the right to possess property enough to employ his own activity and to draw from it the products necessary for the sustenance of himself and his family. The *Hufe* thus included : a farm and its appurtenances, which was the private property of the peasant ; the right of using the unapportioned part of the commonty, or *Allmende,* as it was called ; and lastly a certain amount of arable land. But this arable land was never leased to one man alone. At the time when the village was founded, the total area of arable land (*Flur*) had been divided up into a certain number of sections—thirty to forty—each containing ground of about the same quality ; and in each of these sections every peasant family had been allotted a *Morgen* or *Joch*—that is to say, as much land as a yoke of oxen could plough in one morning. Under these circumstances, and in spite of the modifications which had taken place, the arable land belonging to a village was still, at the beginning of the nineteenth century, divided into hundreds, and sometimes thousands, of allotments, and each peasant owned a large number of these plots scattered over the whole territory of the village. Now, this partition of arable land (*Gemengelage*) necessarily resulted in a collective system of cultivation. As the allotments were all mixed up together, and an owner had no means of access to his property except through his neighbour's field, the entire area of cultivation was worked according to a plan laid down by the elders of the village. By the law of *Flurzwang* each peasant was bound to grow a particular plant in a given piece of land, and to begin to till the ground or to gather in the harvest at fixed dates. In short, his right to possess the land he cultivated was defined by a series of exceedingly strict obligations which prevented him from organising the culture of his property as he liked, and subjected him, on a large number of points, to the decisions of the whole community.

Nevertheless, the peasant, in the course of centuries, nearly always fell into economic or social dependence upon the overlord or large landowner. This dependence was represented, at the beginning of the nineteenth century, by two kinds of obligations. The peasant paid rent, either in money or in kind, to the overlord, in his capacity as master of the soil (*Grundherr*). In districts where this was the only imposition, nothing was altered in the typical organisation of the village which has already been described. Secondly, the peasant was bound to give his lord, in his capacity as owner of the domain, gratuitous labour for the cultivation of his private property (*Frondienst*). In such cases, the overlord was the owner of pieces of land scattered about in the midst of those belonging to his peasants or tenants, who were bound to cultivate, in addition to their own fields, the plots belonging to the lord. Agricultural labour was managed, through the whole area of cultivation, by the head of the rural community—the *Schulze*—who was the lord's agent. The rights which the tenant had over his land were consequently quite precarious, and the overlord practically considered himself the co-proprietor of all rural holdings. Though he no longer had the power of appropriating the land of the peasants to his own use, nor of allowing his fields to lie fallow, he still, at least, possessed the right of replacing one tenant by another, and consequently of turning a peasant out of his holding, of transferring him to another holding which was either better or worse than the old one, or even of reducing him to the position of a day labourer. Bound by the system of forced labour, chained to the soil by the prohibition to leave his lord's territory without the consent of his master, without any right of appeal against the arbitrary will of the overlord and his agents, the peasant, under these circumstances, was nothing more than a hard-worked beast of burden, who would have made good his escape if he had not been bound to the land by the ties of serfdom.

3

Now the liquidation of feudal property took place throughout Germany during the first half of the nineteenth century. The process varied in rapidity and thoroughness in different districts. It began, as a rule, during the first few years of the century, only to be completed after the revolution of 1848 under the pressure of new economic and social conditions.[1] But everywhere it had the definite result of emancipating the peasant from the control of the overlord, or of the rural community, and making him the absolute and independent owner of his own property. Let us examine a little more closely the consequences of this change for the landlord and the peasant.

As far as the large landowner was concerned, the transition from the old order of things to the new was carried out without much difficulty. The owner of ancestral estates had long before 1800 become a commercial man who ran his estate by means of the unpaid work provided by forced labour. It is true that the agrarian reforms deprived him of gratuitous labour. But, in the first place, he received a large compensation in kind, either in land or in money paid for the redemption of taxes, forced labour and liabilities, in consideration of which he consented to give to the peasants the liberty of which he had formerly deprived them without indemnity. Secondly, he was not slow to discover that free labour, on the whole, was a good exchange for the old forced labour he had had the right to demand from his tenants.

[1] In Prussia there were four distinct stages in this process of liquidation: First, Stein's edict of October 7, 1807, abolishing serfdom; second, Hardenberg's *Regulirungsedikt* and *Landeskulturedikt* of September 14, 1811; third, the *Gemeinheitsteilungsordnung* of July 7, 1821; and fourth, the edict of March 2, 1850, which once more set in motion the reforms which had been stopped by the opposition of those whom they hit.

It is true that he had to pay for it, which he had not done before. But, on the other hand, he got more profitable work ; as early as 1809 Thaer calculated that two free labourers did as much work as three forced ones. Moreover, once their wages were paid, the master was free from all responsibility towards them, and did not have to trouble his head about procuring them a livelihood. So that, under the new system, it was possible for him, when work was pressing, to hire a whole army of labourers, whom he could dismiss at a moment's notice without having to consider what would become of them when he no longer required their services.

The liquidation of feudal estates under these circumstances only had the result of developing among the landowners a class of capitalistic contractors. At the beginning of the nineteenth century, a landowner did not regard his property merely from the point of view of the profit he could derive from it. He saw in it the hereditary cradle of his race and the basis of his social power, as well as the source of his competency. His *primary* object was to get from the land the products necessary for the sustenance of himself, his family, and his tenants ; only after this had been secured did he aim at a surplus destined for sale and to bring in money. Now everything changed. In the first place, the large landowner is not necessarily of noble birth. Whilst at the end of the eighteenth century no burgess was allowed to possess titled property, it is an ascertained fact that about 1800, in the eastern provinces of Prussia alone, 7,086 estates out of 11,065 belonged to commoners who could only have acquired them by the payment of money. In the second place, the landed proprietor, when he lost his seigniorial rights, ceased to have any jurisdiction over his people, and, consequently, found himself in the same position with regard to the labourers he hired as the manufacturer was in respect to his workmen.   The natural tie which once united the overlord to his property was thus considerably weakened.   The modern landlord came to regard his estate more and more as a source of revenue, as capital which should be rationally exploited and the highest possible rate of interest secured—property which could be leased to a farmer in order to avoid the trouble of personal administration, or sold to a new owner as soon as a favourable opportunity occurred.   If, in spite of all, the remembrance of the old order has survived even in our own day ; if a few old titled estates are still managed as they were in patriarchal times, and if in many cases the change to capitalism has been far from complete, many landowners, on the other hand, have become true business men, who have deposit accounts at the Reichsbank, keep their books as accurately as a trading firm, and administer their domains according to the principles of a rational utilitarianism which is utterly devoid of all sentiment.

As far as the peasant was concerned, agrarian reform meant emancipation either from the dominion of the overlord or from that of the village community.   On the one hand, the tenant became, on the payment of rent, the owner of his own farm and free to dispose of his property and his person as he pleased ; whilst the peasant, on the other, was liberated from his obligations to the village community.   The *All-menden* were divided among those who had a claim to them ; the rights of usage were redeemed ; the *Gemengelage* was abolished by consolidating the various allotments belonging to one owner into the property of a single tenant or into a small number of fair-sized plots. Thus we find the revival of the primitive system of a class of peasant proprietors free from all seigniorial or municipal control, at liberty to manage as they please and on their own responsibility the property which they possess in their own persons and share with no one. What is the result of this transformation for the rural population ?

The individualisation of property has, without a doubt, been a good thing for the intelligent and industrious peasant. It has allowed him to free himself from routine, to get the best he can out of his property, to derive advantage from the progress of technical science in agriculture—in short, to become a contractor on a small scale. And as the redemption of rights of usage put him in possession of a little capital, he found himself able to make some necessary improvements in his land. The bound made by German agriculture during the nineteenth century, the large increase in the output of the soil, and the rapid growth of population prove that the liquidation of feudal property really provided the means of progress for at least one section of the peasant class.

For others, on the contrary, it was practically disastrous. The small tenant, who was only allotted a little bit of land not large enough to provide him with a livelihood, and the incapable or unlucky peasant who did not succeed in managing his property well, found themselves much worse off. The destruction of the strong tie which once bound the inhabitants of a village to each other, or the tenants to their landlords, had the effect of exposing every day to the most rigorous consequences of the law of com-

petition a number of poor people for whom it was
impossible to be self-supporting by their own unaided
efforts.

It is true that the peasant, unlike the small shop-
keeper or industrial worker, did not toil merely with
the object of selling his goods, but to a large extent
with a view to his own needs. He thus to some
degree escaped the most disastrous results of capitalistic competition. In fact, in theory there is no
reason why a peasant family which once lived on its
own property and produced all it required should
not still be self-supporting to-day. If it works for
its own requirements, and not to produce an article
destined for sale, obviously it can be independent
of the current price of corn, and has nothing to fear
from the competition of a better equipped producer
or a more clever husbandman, for the simple reason
that it does not compete with any one. But all this
changes from the moment the peasant requires
money, and is consequently obliged to sell all or part
of his harvest. If he is ill equipped or unskilful, and
if in consequence his work is not highly productive,
he must of necessity come to a point when he can
no longer produce enough to earn the sum of money
he requires ; or, with the same result to himself, he
will be obliged to sell his goods at a price which,
whilst it is still sufficiently remunerative to his rivals,
means ruination to him. Now the peasant, under
present conditions, must have money. Even if he
could succeed in producing all he consumes, as he
did in the good old days, and even assuming that he
could keep himself out of debt, a capitalistic State
takes good care to put him under an obligation,
without his permission, by forcing him to take his
share in the public expenses. Taxation is the factor

that spells ruination to the peasant. Willy-nilly, he must work for the market ; he must make good the inferiority of his primitive equipment and his superannuated methods of culture by exceedingly heavy toil. Whilst he is exceedingly hard upon himself, he exploits unmercifully those whom he employs on his small estate—his wife and children, his man-servant, his maid-servant, and his day labourers. In spite of all, he only keeps his head above water with difficulty ; he is at the mercy of the slightest accident, a bad harvest, or an illness. Despite the most desperate efforts, the moment irrevocably arrives when the unfortunate man is obliged to mortgage his estates. This is the prelude to the inevitable catastrophe, because, in addition to his old difficulties, he is now obliged to pay the interest on his debts : before he can sit down to table himself he must satisfy his creditors. It is true he no longer, as he once did, runs the risk of being turned out of his property by fraud or violence ; but he has not gained much by the change, for from the day that he becomes insolvent he has his land taken away from him as before—and, moreover, under the full sanction of the law, which is a very poor consolation. The rural populations, who used to live without moving for centuries, now find themselves rudely uprooted and dispersed. Numberless tenants evicted from their little bit of land, and peasants ruined and bankrupt, are obliged either to emigrate or to go to the towns, where they swell the ever-increasing army of unskilled industrial labourers.

The condition of rural workers is even worse—the owners of diminutive holdings, small farmers and cotters, or simple day labourers—who try to make a living by their toil. The chief cause of their hardships is that the large landowner who gives them work does not need their services all through the year, but only during the agricultural seasons, which have been very much curtailed by the use of machinery. It is to his interest, therefore, to encourage a large number of labourers during a short space of time when a maximum of work is done, and to dismiss most of them immediately afterwards. Consequently these unfortunate people have alternate periods of killing work—fifteen to eighteen hours a day in the height of the season—and enforced leisure. Settled workers have not even the hope of seeing an improvement in their lot. For they are exposed to the ruinous competition of swarms of casual labourers, chiefly foreigners—either Poles or Russians—who congregate in every district where there is work, and are eagerly welcomed by the landowners, as these unfortunate people are docile and incapable of resistance, content with ludicrously low wages, and go away as soon as they are no longer required.

The individualisation of property has not only had the most serious consequences for the material condition of the rural populations, but it has also had a profound effect even upon the mind of the peasant. Once upon a time, a very strong tie bound a peasant family to the property handed down for cultivation from father to son. The family seemed to feel a *common* obligation to devote their labour and care to this property. According to the district, the land either remained undivided among all those who had a claim to it and cultivated it in common, or else it passed into the hands of a privileged heir (either the eldest or the youngest son), who became the head of the family and generally kept his brothers and sisters in his service. The men and maid-servants

were not treated as hirelings, but as members of the
family, and also, to a certain extent, shared in this
devotion to the land.  Now all this has changed.
The peasant family is disintegrating, and an eye to
the main chance has taken the place of the instinct
of solidarity.  The younger brothers, instead of remaining on the family property, go out to seek their
fortunes in the industrial world or else emigrate.
In fact, statistics for the years between 1882 and
1895, alone, show a decrease of about 500,000 under
the heading of " members of the family engaged in
agricultural pursuits " (382,872 in 1895 compared
with 866,413 in 1882)—a deficit which was partly
made good by an increase in domestic servants, both
male and female, whose number grew from 1,589,088
to 1,718,885.  The peasant proprietor thus became
a contractor, who tried to get as much as possible
out of his workmen, whilst the servants, on their
side, aimed at obtaining the best possible terms from
their masters.  Now, the general growth in these individualistic tendencies was a grave menace to the
existence of peasant proprietors.  It either resulted
in the infinite partition of land, under a system by
which it was divided among all the heirs, or else in
debt, in the cases where one heir inherited the whole
property and found himself obliged to pay a money
compensation to the rest.

We thus witness in the domain of agriculture also
a conspicuous development in the spirit of enterprise.  The type known as the *business man* gradually grows more and more common among the class
of large landowners, peasants, and farmers.  But
whilst the commercial speculator found his business
extraordinarily prosperous, especially at the end of
the last century, the agriculturist, on the contrary,

has been struggling for over thirty years in the toils of a formidable crisis, the end of which is apparently not yet in sight. The question is, how did this crisis arise ?

The period between the 'thirties and 1870 was one of remarkable prosperity for German agriculture.

About 1800 Germany was in a position not only to feed her own people, but also to sell her surplus produce abroad. But the growth of population was so rapid and the consumption of food-stuffs developed to such colossal proportions that, in spite of the increased power of production due to the progress made in the technical processes of agriculture, Germany soon ceased to be able to satisfy the needs of her own market herself. Towards the middle of the century, her import of rye began to exceed her export, until, about 1880, in consequence of the growth in her imports, Germany not only found herself dependent upon the foreigner for cereals of all kinds—wheat, barley, and oats—but was also obliged to import domestic animals of every sort—sheep, cows, and horses. This, obviously, created a condition of things favourable to agriculture. And, indeed, from about 1830 onwards, agriculture enjoyed over forty years of prosperity, during which it is reckoned there was a general rise in all agricultural produce varying from 60 per cent. in corn to 148 per cent. in beef. This rise naturally entailed a corresponding increase in the value of land. It is estimated that farms more than doubled in value, whilst the price of land was three or even four times as great as it had been.

From about 1880 this state of things began to change. Germany—and for the matter of that the whole of Western Europe, as is well known—began to feel the effects of the competition of new countries which produced corn in large quantities at a low price—countries like Russia, Roumania, the United States, India, Uruguay, and Argentina. In consequence of the growth of international intercourse and the gradual diminution in the cost of transport by rail and sea, corn could be sold in the German market at ever lower prices. A period of depression therefore set in; between 1896 and 1900 prices fell, according to the different kinds of corn, $13\frac{1}{2}$ to $23\frac{1}{2}$ per cent. as compared with the rates between 1876 and 1880. This was accompanied by a corresponding depression in the value of farms and land. Now, this lowering in market value and prices had most terrible results for the German agriculturist, especially by reason of the debt with which landed property was weighed down in consequence of it. Mortgages, indeed, increased in enormous proportions during the course of the century. Proprietors borrowed money in order to carry out improvements calculated to increase the output of the land; or heirs, if they wished to keep their property whole, were obliged to compensate their co-inheritors by a sum of money. Or else speculators, expecting a rise in the market, calculated that in the long run they would profit more by working heavily mortgaged estates, of which they could obtain possession by the outlay of a small initial capital. In short, for a host of reasons, landed proprietors found their debts growing without limit. In Prussia alone, between 1883 and 1896, this increase reached a total of nearly 2,500 millions of marks. It is obvious that to the owner of a heavily mortgaged estate a decrease of income quickly causes inconvenience, and means complete ruin as soon as the returns from his land are less than the interest he is obliged to pay his creditors every year.

Thus the competition of new countries and the indebtedness of landed property produced an agricultural crisis which was further aggravated by other minor circumstances, and especially the difficulty experienced by large landowners in securing the necessary labour. This crisis was rendered somewhat less severe by a series of measures tending either to raise the price of agricultural produce or to give assistance to the agriculturist : the protectionist policy inaugurated in 1879 by Bismarck, for instance ; the lowering of railway rates in favour of the home producer, which enabled him to meet foreign competition more successfully ; the improvement of education in agricultural matters, and the organisation of a system of credit in that department. But even to-day the crisis cannot be regarded as ended. German agriculture maintains its existence by means of protective tariffs and thanks to the solicitude of the Government for the interests of the landed nobility and the rural classes. It is very far indeed from following in the ambitious footsteps of German commerce, and political economists are reduced to expressing the hope that the gradual " industrialisation " of agriculture may perhaps, in the future, succeed in imparting fresh vigour to it.

In the meantime, it is certain that agriculture has lost much of its importance in the life of the nation. About 1830 it is estimated that four-fifths of the population was engaged in agricultural pursuits. About 1860 the proportion was only three-fifths; in 1882 it was very little more than two-fifths (42½ per cent.); and in 1895 it falls below this figure (35·7 per cent.). Whilst agriculture is obliged, owing to the

lack of labour, to employ every year, during the busy
season, bands of foreign workers, chiefly of Polish
extraction, to supply the deficiency of German
labour, the percentage of the population living by
industry and commerce daily increases.   In Prussia,
for the year 1843, it was 25·3 per cent., for 1895 nearly
50 per cent.   This figure is greater for the whole of
Germany, and has reached 50·6 per cent.   Before
our eyes a large proportion of the rural population
is emigrating to the towns or abroad, and Germany
is becoming an industrial country.   Lamprecht
quotes statistics which show that about 1900 the
annual agricultural produce was worth 6,000 millions
of marks, whilst small and large industries produced
twice that amount ; and that the revenue derived from
agricultural enterprises reached 3,000 millions, whilst
that drawn from industry and commerce was 13,500
millions.

An investigation into the balance of trade proves,
in a striking manner, the change which has taken
place in this respect.   It is a well-known fact that
since between 1885 and 1888 the imports of Germany
have exceeded her exports, and to such an extent
that in 1900 her imports reached 5,833 millions of
marks, whilst her exports only reached 4,555 millions,
thus showing an excess in the imports of 1,278
millions of marks.   Now, what do these figures
prove ?   First of all, that Germany is to-day an
industrial country, no longer living on the produce of
her own soil, but on the industry of her inhabitants.
Political economists have calculated that if Germany
wished to produce from her own soil the food-stuffs
and raw material necessary for her own consumption
and her own industry, she would require a territory
at least twice or three times as large as that of the

present Empire, and this exclusive of tropical products, such as spices, coffee, and cotton, which her geographical position prevents her from growing. It is thus obvious that the present population of the German Empire could not exist if it were not in a position to procure an enormous quantity of foreign goods, the production of which would require an extent of territory which Germany does not possess. How does she secure this ? In the first place, by exchanging one product for another, either by selling abroad in her turn certain products of her own soil, and above all the articles manufactured by her industry. Secondly, by making good the difference between her expenditure and her income by the help of two main sources of revenue—that provided by her maritime commerce and that by capital invested abroad. The estimate for 1899 of the profits realised by German maritime transport is about 250 millions of marks, whilst the revenue derived during the same year from capital invested abroad was valued at 1,000 millions of marks. These two sums together reach a total which almost covers the deficit of 1,278 millions of marks shown by the balance of trade during 1900. The extraordinary rapidity with which the change was accomplished is proved by the fact that as late as 1880 the balance of trade showed a credit of 86 millions of marks, whilst in 1888 it showed a debit of only 67 millions, which reached 1,278 millions in 1900 and rose in 1905 to 1,253 millions.

It is thus quite clear that the population of Germany cannot exist on the produce of her own soil alone. It lives by industry, maritime commerce, and acquired wealth. An agricultural country at the beginning of the last century, Germany is on the

way to becoming a colossal industrial and capitalistic state. And this transformation has not been
realised without inspiring many Germans with feelings of regret and anxiety. They are asking themselves whether the change from a rural to an urban
manner of life, from labour on the land to industrial
toil, will not entail disastrous consequences for the
physical and moral well-being of the race. And they
perceive a possible, if not an actual, danger in the
fact that Germany is growing less and less able to
nourish her own population, and finds herself obliged
to rely ever more completely for her livelihood on
her external trade, and consequently upon foreign
purchases.

# CHAPTER IV

THE system of enterprise has not only considerably modified the condition of production—it has also fundamentally changed the social structure of the nation.

At the beginning of the nineteenth century there were, roughly speaking, three distinct classes in Germany—the " nobility," including in addition to the aristocracy proper, the old patrician families of the free towns ; a rather vague " intermediate " class, consisting, on the one hand, of the cultured *élite* of the nation, and, on the other, of everybody who possessed a moderate competency, high and petty officials, manufacturers and merchants—in short, the greater part of what is to-day called the middle class ; and, lastly, the " people " formed by the artisans, the rural populations, and the proletariat which was coming into existence at that time. Until about the middle of the century, the line of demarcation between the various types was exceedingly faint. On the one hand between the wealthy member of the upper middle class and the noble, and on the other between the member of the lower middle class and the labourer, the difference was practically indistinguishable. The capitalistic middle class did not yet exist as an order of society. The proletariat was regarded as a collection of the

48

unclassed remnants of society, and it was considered
the business of the Government gradually to include
it in the other social categories and thus to put
a stop to the multiplication of its members.

In the second half of the century, with the rise of
capitalistic enterprise, this state of things changed
rapidly.  On the one side, we see a huge army of
labour coming into existence, in which social outcasts
of every description are found shoulder to shoulder
with craftsmen in domestic industry, the majority of
skilled artisans ruined by the competition of the
large manufacturers, the bulk of agricultural labourers
and evicted peasants.  And at the other extremity
of the social ladder there sprang up a class of " contractors," into which everybody who in one way
or another had some interest in capitalistic enterprise
congregated, from the old landed proprietors belonging to the ancient nobility, or the kings of
commerce and finance, down to workmen who had
grown wealthy, small merchants, and the managers
of large industrial firms.

The proletariat—that is to say, the class of people
who, according to Sombart's definition, only make
a livelihood by earning a salary paid in money, are
engaged for a particular job, and can be dismissed
on the shortest notice, or even summarily—was not
numerous until about 1850.  It is true that from the
end of the eighteenth century there existed a labouring class living in a state of dependence upon capitalistic enterprise.  It is, no doubt, also true that this
class increased slowly between 1820 and 1840 in
proportion to the development of enterprise in
Germany.  But it did not yet show any marked
features, and there was scarcely any clear line of
demarcation discernible between the common work-

4

man and the artisan or petty tenant. It was only
during the 'fifties and 'sixties, when the old forms
of industry underwent a violent crisis, that the
German proletariat, which from that day forward
never ceased to multiply, really came into existence.
And this phase of its evolution seems also to have
been its most painful one. The terrible uncertainty
of life for the proletariat is well known ; the absolute
dependence of its members upon the employer, who
can at any moment deprive them of their work and reduce them to want ; the dangers they run on account
of the crisis in supply and demand to which industry
is periodically subjected ; the ever-increasing difficulty
for the workman to raise himself to the position
of a master ; the degradation of labour due to the
development of machinery, which has made man
merely an appendage to the machine, and thus condemns him to a stupefying toil from which he can
derive no satisfaction. We all know the terrible
drama of proletarian pauperism : the shameless exploitation not of the workman alone, but of his wife
and family ; the indefinite extension of the working
day, the overcrowding in unhealthy surroundings,
the starvation wages, the crises of unemployment,
which reduce whole districts to despair. Germany
has not been more successful in escaping these evils
than any other industrial nation. The most that
can be said is that she has perhaps suffered less in
proportion than England, because the rise of capitalism came later in Germany, and the abuses of
the new system met, as soon as they appeared, with
a more determined opposition on the part of the
public conscience.

At all events, it is certain that " class feeling "
developed fairly rapidly in the German working man.

During the last thirty years of the nineteenth century, the proletariat increased [1] in numbers, and at the same time organised itself into a political party. Worked out in the brains of philosophers, who dreamed of turning to the advantage of society as a whole the discoveries of inventors, and who saw in the community of wealth, or in the nationalisation of the means of production, the only cure for the ills of the people, the Socialistic ideal gradually became the popular ideal. At the same time, the instinctive chaotic revolt of labour against oppression and poverty gave place to the methodical organisation of the proletarian forces in their struggle against capitalism. Fichte and Hegel, and afterwards Feuerbach and Young Germany, Moses Hess and Karl Grün, and finally Marx and Engels, gradually developed the materialistic theory of history and the doctrine of collectivism. From the beginning of 1848, the *Communistic Federation*, which combined the popular and the intellectual elements of the new party, launched forth its celebrated *Manifesto*, which formulated in all its essential features the programme of Socialism and urged the proletariat of every country to combine for the class struggle. In 1863, under the leadership of Lassalle, the *General Association of German Workmen* was founded, which concentrated the forces of the labouring class into a party which was independent of the progressive section of the middle classes. From that moment, the Socialist Party, which was at first split up for some years into " Lassallians " and " Internationals," but was unified in 1875 at the Congress of Gotha

---

[1] Sombart calculated that in 1895 the proletariat consisted of about 35 millions—that is to say, about 67½ per cent. of the whole population of the Empire.

under the title of *German Socialist Labour Party*, made uninterrupted progress. In 1871 it secured 113,000 votes in the Reichstag elections ; in 1881, 312,000 ; in 1890, 1,427,000 ; in 1896, 2,107,000 ; and almost 3,200,000 in 1907 [1] ; and it now has a larger number of constituents than any other party. It is true that these do not consist entirely of orthodox Socialists, but also include a large number of malcontents of all kinds, who, by voting for the Socialist candidate, merely wish to register, in the most emphatic manner possible, their disapproval of the actual state of affairs ; but it is none the less certain that the party as a whole is composed of the proletariat themselves, and that this class, concentrated in a large party, subjected to a severe discipline and animated by a strong *esprit de corps*, forms an imposing bulk which grows every day more conscious of its own power.

For a long time the labour movement in Germany was chiefly political. Unlike its brethren in England, the country of powerful trade unions and prosperous co-operative societies, the German proletariat was rather slow to form any organisation in the economic field. Nevertheless, it has to-day made a great advance in this domain also. Outside the Socialist Democratic Party, but sharing its ideas, strong unions have sprung up, whose influence has grown considerably, especially during the last ten years, and whose actions are generally in unison with those of the Socialist Party. No doubt non-Socialist unions also exist. The *Hirsch-Duncker Professional Associations*, founded in 1868 by the Progressive Party, and the Christian syndicates inaugurated a few years ago by the Catholic Centre Party, do not

[1] The number in 1912 was estimated at 3,800,000.—Tr.

place themselves upon the basis of class antagonism, but, on the contrary, assert the unity of interests between the employer and the employed, or recognise the equal rights and duties of capital and labour respectively.  But these associations have not anything like the importance of the *Free Syndicates*,[1] which, even if they are neutral in theory and exact no profession of political faith from their members, are in reality composed of a huge majority of Socialists. Under these circumstances, in spite of the inevitable hitches and temporary rivalry between " politicians " and " syndicalists," the unions nearly always work in harmony with the Socialist Democratic Party. Now, these unions, which were founded with the object of protecting the professional interests of the working man, have given proofs of great vitality, more especially during the last few years.  Menaced in their very existence by powerful employers' syndicates in Germany, they have not only resisted disorganisation, but have even imbibed fresh force from the attacks levelled against them.  Their papers announce with pride that the lock-outs decreed by the employers' syndicates in response to strikes have at present only had the effect of strengthening the solidarity of labour and attracting fresh recruits to the armies of Trade Unionism.

With the organisation of a large political party divided into strong associations of the various trades, the proletariat of Germany is fighting energetically to win a more tolerable existence for itself.  And apparently these efforts have not been altogether

---

[1] Statistics show that towards the end of 1895 the *Hirsch-Duncker Associations* numbered 120,000 members, the *Christian Syndicates* 250,000, and the small group of *Independent Syndicates* 75,000 ; whilst the *Free Syndicates* had over 1,300,000 members.

fruitless.  Pessimism with regard to social matters seems to have made way for an at least comparatively optimistic frame of mind.  The Socialists are marching forward full of confidence to the conquest of political and economic power.  They also look more and more for the realisation of their hopes, not to some great social upheaval, but to a slow process of pacific evolution which will transform the capitalistic order of society *from within*.  The gloomy resignation of early days has given place to a pugnacious spirit.  A very pronounced desire for culture and art has been added to an interest in the mere material necessities of life.  A number of political economists, moreover, regard the economic future of the country with less suspicion.  They quote with satisfaction the general rise in the revenues, a slight relative decrease in numbers in the poorest class, the rise of wages, the improvement in the conditions of life among the people,[1] and the diminution of emigration.[2]  They draw attention to the increased security given to the working classes by insurance against accidents, invalidity, old age, and illness.[3]

[1] Statistics show that during the last thirty years of the nineteenth century, the consumption of cotton, per head of the population, was trebled, whilst the consumption of beer, corn, meat, eggs, and milk almost doubled.  This improvement, certainly to a large extent, benefited the working classes.  Statisticians also note, to the credit of the proletariat in Germany, that during the same period the consumption of alcohol and tobacco remained almost stationary.

[2] The number of emigrants, which between 1881 and 1885 reached an average of 170,000 persons per annum, fell to 22,000 in 1900 and rose to only 28,000 in 1905.

[3] Insurance against accident is enjoyed by nearly 19½ million workmen, and the insurance companies paid claims amounting to 126·7 millions of marks during 1904.  Insurance against invalidity and old age paid, in the same year, claims amounting to 150 millions of marks, and during the total thirteen years that it has been in

They point out that among the bulk of the proletariat there are signs of a growing tendency to differentiate, and that above the mass of incapable, unfortunate, or fallen members of society and the crowd of " unskilled " labourers, a body of " skilled " artisans is coming into existence whose standard of life is improving every day. All these symptoms seem calculated to inspire the hope that the terrible problem created by the colossal growth of the proletariat will find a solution by means of pacific evolution instead of violent upheavals.

At the same time as the system of capitalistic enterprise created at the foot of the social ladder the great class of the proletariat, it also profoundly modified the upper and intermediate sections of German society.

Generally speaking, modern social evolution tends to substitute, for the old categories founded on differences of social function, new subdivisions based simply upon differences of income. It wipes out or modifies the differences between the countryman and the townsman, between the peasant, the tradesman, and the industrial worker, who are on the same level of material wealth. For those who roughly enjoy the same competency, it creates more or less uniform habits and conditions of life. And if, among the innumerable social types which constitute the upper and middle classes—small contractors and small town and country tradesmen, the head employees of large concerns of all kinds, the late survivals of the old middle class, the cultured minority engaged in the liberal professions, officials and officers, the aristo-

working, almost 855·6 millions of marks. In 1903 the insurance against illness dealt with almost 11 million cases, and the claims paid during that year amounted to over 213 millions.

cracy of commerce or of birth—there are certainly profound distinctions, the difference is much more one of income than of special occupation or the observance of certain traditional manners and customs.

There is also noticeable, on the other hand, a drastic destruction of recognised tables of values. In the place of the old aristocracies of birth and of culture, there has sprung up a commercial and industrial aristocracy whose fundamental criterion for distinguishing rank and merit is a capacity for business and for success. It is unnecessary to remark that this evolution is very far from having reached its highest development and that the majority of the old groupings still subsist more or less intact in the very midst of modern society. This accounts for the fact that people of the middle class who are engaged in the " liberal professions," especially the clergy, schoolmasters and professors, the members of the Civil Service, or officers in the army, have scarcely been touched by the spirit of enterprise. Nevertheless, this new spirit is gradually insinuating itself into almost every department of life, and is little by little dissolving the ancient hierarchies. Even the aristocracy, who, on principle, declared that it was impossible for them, without demeaning themselves, to take part in modern economic life, the commerical character of which was repugnant to them, have not escaped the contagion. And, as a matter of fact, the nobility, in their capacity as landed proprietors, have also been caught in the wheel of the capitalistic system. And in their case this has happened under unfavourable conditions, because agricultural enterprise gives returns which are, as a matter of fact, far inferior to those provided by industrial or com-

mercial speculations. So much is this the case, that
some thinkers have wondered whether the economic
basis upon which the power of the nobility is
founded in these days is solid enough to allow of
their maintaining their preponderating political
influence and their social prestige much longer.
At all events, the new commercial aristocracy is
growing every day more strong and self-confident
by the side of the aristocracy of birth. After
having for a long time—until about the 'eighties
—tried as far as possible to ape the old nobility
and to adopt their customs and way of life, they
seem at present to aim more at asserting their
own independence and maintaining their own individuality. They are in the midst of a process of
forming themselves into a separate caste, with their
own special characteristics and ranks, and owning
allegiance to a small oligarchical coterie engaged in
high finance.

. . . . .

We have now seen pretty clearly the general results of that tremendous rush for economic power
which was characteristic of the nineteenth century.
By utilising and exploiting the marvellous discoveries
of science and the improvements in technical processes, by working without ceasing to progress in
scientific knowledge in order to create new sources
of profit, the spirit of enterprise introduced an
organised method into the rational exploitation of
the forces of nature, of the wealth of the land, and of
human labour. And it has reached these prodigious
results by the proclamation of the principle of unrestricted competition and the right of every man
to develop as he pleases his various faculties and his
capacity for work, and by destroying the traditional

institutions which were opposed to the free expansion
of individual energy, which curbed unbridled and
insatiable ambition and assigned to each man a
clearly circumscribed sphere of action from which it
was almost impossible for him to escape.  The result
attained is certainly wonderful.  The nineteenth
century produced an enormous increase in the
power of man over matter, and it succeeded in achiev-
ing a gradual " rationalisation " of life.  It developed
the production of material wealth to colossal proportions.  It solved the problem of making Germany
capable of providing a tolerable livelihood for 60
million souls, whilst at the beginning of the century
only 25 million could live on the same extent of
territory, and that under conditions certainly far
harder than they are to-day.  It transformed a poor
agricultural country into a formidable factory provided with the most perfect industrial and commercial equipment, living on the industry of its
workers and on the income from its acquired wealth.
Germans are proud, and justly proud, of the capacity
for application, for energetic perseverance, for scientific rectitude, for order, and above all for discipline,
which have allowed them to take, in the general
unloosing of competition, one of the foremost places
among the industrial nations of the modern world.

But they also acknowledge that this tremendous
upheaval has not taken place without bringing many
an evil in its train.  They are filled with anxiety at
the thought that Germany is no longer in a position
to feed her people with the produce of her own soil,
and ask themselves whether the gradual industrialisation of national life will not produce lamentable
results from the point of view of the physical and
moral balance of the race.  They are depressed at

the sight of the constant increase in the pace of life, and the ever swifter and more rapid motion which hurries men and things onward and envelopes in its vortex all that has anything to do with the system of enterprise. They deplore the insecurity of life to which the system of unrestricted competition, with its anarchical method of production, its periodical crises, and its perpetual instability, has exposed all who are engaged in it, whether they belong to the proletariat or the capitalist class, whether they are masters, employees, or ordinary workers. They draw attention to the fact that man ends by becoming a slave to the things he creates. Modern industry and commerce impose on the consumer a limited number of products which tyrannically beg his favour. And so well does it succeed, that all variety in private life is clearly dying out and making way for an ever-increasing uniformity of requirements, which are satisfied, and at the same time determined, by wholesale production. In short, many Germans feel very little edified by the results which the great principle of the sub-stitution of quantity for quality has given with regard to the development of the race. They con-template without enthusiasm the artificial man of to-day, their contemporary townspeople, the off-spring of the asphalt of large cities, with no direct contact with Nature, without traditions and without a past, without any real personality—an abstract type, middling and mediocre, the product of present-day urban civilisation. And they ask themselves, not without some feeling of trepidation, whither this evolution is tending. Will it end in a violent catas-trophe, or in slow decay, till the advent of those " last men "—a vast host of sand fleas, over-cautious

and over-cautioned creatures, without hopes and
without ideals, which the ardent imagination of
Nietzsche foresaw ?

If, in spite of all this, they are on the whole confident in the future, it is because they expect, in
one shape or another, a fundamental transformation
in the system of capitalistic enterprise. And it is
not Socialists alone who hope either for the advent of
collectivism by means of revolution or for the gradual
peaceful " socialisation " of the country. Men who
absolutely repudiate all upheavals, and who frankly
admire the economic and political achievements of
the last century, are also of the opinion that the era
of unrestricted competition is drawing to its close.
Lamprecht, for instance, far removed as he is from
believing in the social cataclysm predicted by orthodox Marxism, is none the less certain that a profound
change is slowly preparing itself. The fact that a
new order of things is imminent seems proved to him
by a host of signs—such, for instance, as the development of associations of credit and of production, the
growing extension in State enterprises, the increase
of trade unions on the one hand and of employers'
syndicates on the other, the development of co-
operative societies, and, also, the spread among the
working and thinking classes of social doctrines which
grow more practical and less Utopian every day, the
incessant progress of insurance, both public and private, and the great measures for the protection of
labour carried out by the State. All these symptoms
seem to indicate that the principle of free enterprise
is being gradually discredited on all sides, that there
is a growing tendency to limit competition, and
that Germany is slowly advancing towards a less
anarchical method of production and a system which

will give more individual security. *Free* enterprise
and *unrestricted* competition are thus being gradually
supplanted by a system of *organised* enterprise and
of *regulated and restricted* competition (*Gebundene
Unternehmung*) which will give more permanence and
stability to the social hierarchy, organise a new
aristocracy of labour and commerce, and also secure
for the proletarian masses a less precarious and more
humane manner of life. It is on the advent of this
era of economic and social solidarity that the picked
intellects of Germany seem to build their hopes to-
day.

# BOOK II

*POLITICAL EVOLUTION*

# CHAPTER I

## THE PROBLEM OF GERMAN LIBERTY AND UNITY

### I

THE rise of the system of free enterprise, which during the course of the nineteenth century resulted in such an astonishing intensification of human labour and in such a marvellous development of economic activity, could not fail also to have a decisive influence upon the political evolution of Germany.

Free enterprise, which tends towards unlimited economic expansion, has, as its first logical corollary, a desire for the attainment of political power. Its fundamental principle is quantitative production, it creates ever more enormous bulks of merchandise, and thus tends to accumulate stocks of goods which are larger than the requirements of the consumer's immediate demand. It consequently finds itself driven to seek every conceivable means of circulating its goods, it is obliged to extend its field of operation as much as possible, and after consolidating its natural economic domain—Germany itself—to seek outlets for its produce in foreign lands, and to demand free trade everywhere and liberty of access to all the markets of the world. In short, it aims at enlarging its sphere of influence indefinitely, and in order the better to secure its supremacy and defend itself against foreign competition, it is irresistibly

5                              65

impelled to build its economic power upon a foundation of political strength.

Thus German policy during the nineteenth century
aimed at unity and imperialism and endeavoured to
win political solidarity, to restore the Empire and
then develop a system which would result in union.
But it did not rest content with this.  It gradually
came to consider the German Empire, founded
on the victories of 1866 and 1870, as the solid
kernel of a far more extensive Pan-Germanic " Im-
perium."  This Greater Germany embraces the entire
sphere of German interests throughout the world.
It includes not only the home territory, but the
countries in which the German element plays a
more or less leading part—as it does in Austria, the
Baltic provinces of Russia, Switzerland, Holland,
and Flemish Belgium.  It extends to the German
colonies, which emigrants have planted all over the
world, and binds together all the material and spiritual
interests of Germany in the four quarters of the
globe.  Germany thus grew accustomed to extending her gaze far beyond her own political frontiers,
and from a *national* State she became an *expansive*
State.  She grew familiar with the idea of imperialism,
which considers a nation something more than an
ethnical entity tied down to a limited area, and regards it as a ceaselessly active force which is ever striving to extend its sphere of influence and struggling
without relaxation throughout the whole world and
in every corner of the globe against the energies of
rival peoples whose powers of expansion form a
barrier to its own might.  Germany thus found herself dragged into building a fleet and becoming a
maritime Power ; she founded a colonial empire and
took an ever more energetic share in the world's

politics. And accordingly she ranks to-day, together with England and the United States, as one of the most resolutely "expansive" nations of the modern world.

At the same time as Germany was carrying out the process of her unification and organisation against the foreigner, she was also transforming her own institutions. This internal evolution also took the form of a struggle for power between rival parties, each of which aspired to take that share of influence in the national organisation to which might gave it right. And during the course of the nineteenth century this conflict assumed an ever more realistic and practical character. If the parties were, as a matter of fact, in the beginning founded upon distinctions of principle, they tended gradually to change into social groups, and ended by really becoming associations based upon interest. At the beginning of the nineteenth century men fought for the principle of authority or for the religion of liberty. At the beginning of the twentieth century we find the representatives of agriculture, industry, and commerce, workers and Catholics, forming powerful societies, in which they eagerly discuss their business, and in the last resort submit their disputes to the arbitration of the monarch, who, standing outside and above every party, is the representative of the interests of the nation as a whole.

The history of the foreign policy of Germany shows us the efforts she made to raise herself to the highest pinnacle of power in Europe and the world. Her internal history shows us the gradual rise of the middle classes and the proletariat to power, the conflict of German democracy with the ruler by divine right and the governing class, which alone possessed any real authority in the eighteenth century, and the evolution which little by little transformed political institutions and substituted for the benevolent despotism of the era of enlightenment a system which, though strictly monarchical, was also constitutional.

In politics too, therefore, the growth of the spirit of enterprise had the result of letting loose the will to power both among peoples and parties. It created a sort of potential state of war among rival nations and rival parties. But in the domain of politics, as well as in the sphere of economics, modern Germany hopes for a modification in this respect. Side by side with the realistic struggle for power and material wealth she sees the development of a new idealistic spirit striving for education and high culture and an equitable solution of the social problem. And she does not despair, after having passed through the storms of the nineteenth century, of attaining a more stable equilibrium, founded upon the consciousness of solidarity and resulting in a happy compromise between the principle of authority and that of freedom, between monarchy and democracy.

.  .  .  .  .

If we cast a glance at the political condition of Germany about 1815, just after the Treaties of Vienna, we shall find that at that time she possessed neither unity nor liberty.

Let us take the question of unity first. The Holy Roman Empire had already for a long time dragged out a purely nominal existence, and when in 1806 it fell to bits beneath the blows of Napoleon, when the Emperor Francis voluntarily abdicated an absolutely illusory sovereignty and declared the imperial office extinct and obsolete, public opinion accepted without much concern the final fall of the glorious Empire of the Ottos and the Hohenstaufen. The "Mainz Gazette" restricted itself to observing, without any particular display of emotion, "that Germany was no more." And, indeed, why should it have been upset ? For a very long time "Germany" had ceased to exist in fact, and the feudal tie which bound the princes to the Emperor had lost all meaning. The imperial authority no longer exercised any appreciable influence on the internal life of the various states, which were governed and administered by sovereign princes and their tools—officials of every rank. It also showed itself incapable of securing the safety of Germany against outside aggression, or of creating and maintaining an army able to protect the frontiers of the Empire efficiently. And at the utmost it was regarded as a protector which was at the same time a source of danger for the small states who were not able to defend themselves. It sheltered them against the lusts of their neighbours, and restricted, to a certain extent at least in their favour, the struggle for existence which could not fail to make itself felt among the German princes. In short, the Empire had long lost all organic unity, and the life had gone out of the central body. Germany was broken up into a number of independent states, jealous of their own sovereignty, devoid of all feeling of national unity, and each one animated by the most cynical and ferocious spirit of selfish particularism. The official fall of the Empire in 1806 only gave a public sanction to a state of things which had long been in existence.

The War of Independence, which put an end to the Napoleonic rule in Germany, did not revive either in name or in essence that Empire whose restoration patriots and romanticists so passionately desired. It is true that the Act of Federation, dated June 8, 1815, and added to the final Act of the Congress of Vienna, founded a German Confederation. The thirty-seven sovereign states and free towns of Germany were united in order to secure the internal and external safety of the country as well as the independence and inviolability of the signatory states. But no one exactly knew what was meant by " Germany." Was it a political, a geographical, or an ethnical body ? It was impossible to say. Klüber, the great authority on federation, maintained that, properly speaking, the German Confederation possessed no territory at all. At all events, it had no Emperor or even a recognised head. All the efforts made by diplomacy to group the small states round the two great German powers—Austria and Prussia— had failed. The princes kept their full sovereign powers. They undertook, it is true, not to make war among themselves and to bring their disputes before the Diet, and they promised, in the case of a federal war, not to enter into any negotiations with the enemy without the consent of their brother princes. But, on the other hand, they reserved to themselves the right of concluding private treaties with princes outside the Confederation. Germany, without a sovereign, without a parliament, without any supreme tribunal, possessed only one central body in the shape of a diet, which met at Frankfort under the auspices of Austria, and enjoyed, in theory, fairly extensive political powers, but was in practice condemned to the most complete impotence. A mere congress of ambassadors, without any real authority, and completely out of touch with the nation, this diet was bound to inaction, because every important decision had to be passed by a majority of two-thirds, or even unanimously, and also because it possessed no efficient means for securing the execution of its decrees or of forcing the compliance of a rebellious member of the Confederation.

And just as Germany possessed no real unity, so also was she deprived of liberal institutions of any kind. All effective control was concentrated entirely in the hands of the princes and the officials who acted as the instruments of their power. As for the nation itself, it was kept entirely isolated from politics and had to obey the laws passed by the rulers without having any recognised means for making its wishes known or respected. The " patriots," who ever since the negotiations at the Congress of Vienna, had endeavoured without success to create in Germany a strong and respected central power, had also tried to secure the participation of the people in the affairs of their country. Baron von Stein had proposed the institution, in addition to the central executive body, of a Reichstag, which would have enjoyed fairly extensive legislative powers and would have served as a Court of Arbitration between the various states of the Confederation or between the princes and their diets. But all the measures which aimed at limiting the absolute power of the princes were rejected. The declaration of the rights of German citizenship which Stein would have liked to introduce into the Federal Constitution was finally reduced to a few very general stipulations regarding the civil rights which the members of any one state in the Confederation should enjoy in the others. No political rights were secured for the German citizen ; article 13 only contained the assurance that " diets should be held in the various federal

states." With the exception of this exceedingly
vague and ill-defined promise, there was nothing to
show that the princes felt disposed to grant their
subjects any greater share of self-government than
they had done in the past.

## II

If the Act of Federation, therefore, disappointed
the hopes of the patriots who dreamt of a free united
Germany, this was due to the circumstance that such
dreams were for the moment impossible to realise.
The failure of the schemes for unification in 1815 can
be imputed neither to the ill-will nor the incapacity
of the negotiators at the Congress of Vienna. It was
the inevitable result of a state of things against which
the desires of the patriots could avail nothing. Germany remained, in fact, essentially particularistic
at heart. The princes did not want a unity which
might possibly compromise their own sovereign
power, and as Prussia and Austria continued to
balance each other, neither country was strong
enough to impose her hegemony upon the rest of
Germany. Let us examine this situation a little
more closely.

In the first place, Austria was just as resolutely
opposed to the nationalist as she was to the democratic movement. The Emperor Francis and his
Chancellor, Metternich, regarded all aspirations for
unity and liberty as legacies from the French Revolution, and opposed them might and main. Upheld
by an aristocracy who saw in an unlimited monarchy
the surest guarantee of social order, and seconded
by an aristocratic bureaucracy which confined itself

to preparing and carrying into execution the decrees of the sovereign without displaying any will or free activity of its own, the Emperor enjoyed absolute power, which he exercised through the agency of the favourite councillors by whom he was surrounded and the heads of the various departments of the Civil Service. And he utilised this power to fight the " revolutionary " spirit in every shape and form. He himself declared that his Empire was an old house which would crumble to bits if people tried to repair it. He knew that Austria already possessed all she was able to hold, that any change would only be for the worse, and that her power was more apparent than real ; and he considered that under these circumstances the system best calculated to ensure her existence was absolute immobility. He consequently carried out with unflagging pertinacity " the policy of stability " of which Metternich had made himself the recognised champion in Europe.

Thus the policy of Austria always aimed at suppressing everywhere any attempt made to modify the existing state of affairs in Europe, created by treaties, and towards maintaining the *status quo.* In France she backed the Bourbons both against Bonapartist intrigues and democratic agitation. In Italy she endeavoured to perpetuate her own supremacy, and with this object in view she encouraged the state of strife and servitude which was such a heavy weight round the neck of that unfortunate country, and even countenanced despots as contemptible as the scandalous but " legitimate " Kings of Naples. In Spain she opposed the efforts of the Liberals to re-establish the constitutional government which had been abolished by a brutal *coup d'état.* And in the East she defended the integrity of the

Ottoman Empire both against Russian lust of conquest and against Greek revolt.

Similarly in Germany she looked with the most
profound suspicion upon all aspirations for unity.
The Austrian Empire is a heterogeneous aggregate of
incongruous elements—Germans, Czechs, Magyars,
Croats, Serbs, Ruthenians, Roumanians, and Italians
—who are only bound together by a common bond of
loyalty to the Crown. Her sovereign, consequently,
can have no *national* policy—he can only have a
*dynastic* policy. He does not feel that he is the
representative of one nation or of one race; his
only object is to enlarge his domain in every direction—in Germany, in Poland, in the Valley of the
Danube, and in Italy. He was, therefore, of necessity hostile to any exaltation of national feeling,
which, in his territory, could only prove a source of
conflict and a menace of dissolution. He did not
trouble his head about a German Imperial Crown
which might, on occasion, become an inconvenient
burden. And, under these circumstances, he had
no wish, either, to see the formation, between the
various German states, of any efficient and genuine
federal bond. He was suspicious of Prussia and
afraid of the ambition and patriotic enthusiasm
which she displayed so brilliantly in 1813. He had
a presentiment that this alert and essentially German
power would have an ever-growing influence in the
bosom of a strongly organised German confederation, and he consequently also refrained from seeking too great an intimacy with this disquieting rival,
but tried to isolate her from the rest of Germany
by carefully nursing the distrust which prevailed in
the petty states with regard to the House of Hohenzollern. And, moreover, he tried to drag her into

the wake of Austrian policy. In short, his whole scheme was systematically aimed at encouraging all the centrifugal forces in Germany. At the Congress of Vienna, Austria came to the assistance of the particularistic selfishness of the princes, which resulted in the failure of the projects for unity propounded by Prussian patriots and statesmen. Once peace was concluded, she raised obstacles in the way of every effort at drawing the federal bonds more closely together, she paralysed the action of the Diet of Frankfort, she encouraged particularism everywhere, and did all in her power to thwart the efforts of Prussia to form the centre of a group of petty states.

And just as the Austrian Government looked with no friendly eye upon any manifestation of national feeling in Germany, so also it showed itself intractably hostile to all liberal aspirations. It gave to Article 13 of the Act of Federation an interpretation which deprived it of all meaning. Instead of regarding it as a promise to establish constitutional government and a system of national representation, it read it as signifying that the princes would have carried out the requirements of the article, if they preserved or restored in their respective states the diets of the old system. This was the interpretation of the article which prevailed in the various states of Austria, in which it consequently remained a dead letter and the old absolutism flourished in all its integrity. And just as Austria eluded the establishment of constitutional government in her own domains, she also endeavoured to prevent its installation elsewhere. In Prussia Metternich by his diplomacy opposed the liberal tendencies which made their appearance among the King's councillors ;

he did everything in his power to dissuade the King from granting his subjects the Constitution he had promised, and thus contributed largely towards postponing, until the eve of the Revolution of 1848, the establishment of constitutional government in Prussia.   In the same   way   he   encouraged the constitutional princes of Southern Germany in their various plots for carrying out a *coup d'état*, and, moreover, extended the protection of Austria to the worst despots of Germany—the Princes of Hesse,   the   Elector   of   Brunswick,   and   the King of Hanover.   In short, the Austrian Government instituted itself the spiritual gaoler of Germany. It stifled in Austria itself all desire for free thought by organising in intellectual matters an oppressive and officious police system which prevented any criticism of the acts of the Government, superintended all meetings, eavesdropped at every conversation, carried on a rigorous censorship of all books and papers, and paralysed all higher culture for years.   And it tried to extend this system of repression and forced silence to Germany, and thus appeared in the guise of the instigator of every severe measure directed against university students or " demagogues " and of every reactionary attempt to gag the press and limit free thought.

## III

Prussia, although she too was a particularistic state and subjected to an absolute monarchy, presents in many respects a very distinct contrast to Austria.

Compared with Austria—a country that had grown senile, and whose real strength by no means corresponded with her external authority—Prussia stands

out as an organised and disciplined force of the foremost rank, with a " will to power " of remarkable
energy and exceptional vitality. She was guided to
her destiny by a dynasty of monarchs inspired by
a high sense of duty, solicitous, above all, for the
good of the State, living for their sovereign mission
alone and for the greatness of their kingdom. Her
nobility, bound to the monarch by ties of the most
ardent loyalty, formed a military caste, in which the
virtues of the warrior were transmitted from father
to son. She possessed an honest and well-informed,
though occasionally rough and pedantic, Civil Service,
strictly disciplined, but at the same time capable
of initiative, heartily devoted to the King, but free
from all servility and capable of defending, even
against the monarch himself, what it considered to
be the interests of the State. Her national army, in
a high state of efficiency, full of confidence and enthusiasm, had proved its mettle during the War of
Independence, and her hardworking and thrifty
population, filled with an instinct for obedience, was
sincerely attached to its princes and respectful of the
established order. Such were the chief elements
which constituted the power of Prussia. By the side
of an effete and sensual Austria, mad on pleasure and
demoralised by a degrading despotism, by the side
of the petty German states, in which a high scientific
and literary culture sometimes flourished, but where
the more manly virtues which go to making a useful
citizen had small scope for development, Prussia,
robust and pugnacious, seemed like a rough and
stern school of discipline and self-sacrifice and of
patient and determined energy.

It is true that the policy of Prussia was founded
upon a vigorous national egoism. Prussian particu-

larism, which was extraordinarily well developed
and full of vitality, had not the smallest intention
of sacrificing or subordinating the private interests
of her own kingdom to those of Germany as a
whole. But as, in addition to this, the Hohenzollern dynasty was an exclusively German power,
there were no essential differences between the interests of Prussia and those of Germany, and the
former was consequently, in distinction to Austria,
favourably disposed to the development of national
unity. Of course she would not have pushed her
disinterestedness to such lengths as to risk compromising her independence as a great sovereign
power. As an open rival of the Hapsburgs, she
would never have consented to abdicate in favour
of Austrian hegemony, nor did she wish to have laws
dictated to her by a confederation dominated by
Austria. But on condition of being given her
legitimate share of influence in any such confederation, she was ready to support the formation of an
effective central power, and was anxious that German unity should not remain an empty phrase.

The patriots who strove for unity founded their
strongest hopes, during the War of Independence,
upon Prussia. And the Prussian Government on its
side felt a certain sympathy for the Pan-German
aspirations of the patriots. Not that it ever dreamt,
at the time of the Congress of Vienna, of putting
into practice any drastic policy of unification.
Leading statesmen like Hardenberg and Humboldt
sincerely believed, on the contrary, that the partition
into independent states which counterbalanced one
another was not in itself an evil, and made Germany
more capable of becoming the central nation of a
Europe founded upon the principle of the balance

of power.  But at the same time they admitted the
necessity for a certain unity.  They disapproved of
the shameless particularism of the princes, and when
the negotiations on the German Constitution were
being carried on at Vienna they pronounced themselves in favour of Baron von Stein's schemes of
unification.  They publicly declared that " the King
considered it his duty as a sovereign to make his
subjects join a federation by means of which they
would form part of one German nation."  They did
all they could to consolidate the power of the new
confederation and to set up a constitution which
should exercise an effective control over the separatist
tendencies and the scandalous selfishness of the petty
princes.  And even if their efforts came to nothing
before the open opposition of the princes and the
covert antagonism of Austria, they at least, by their
attitude, conveyed the impression that Prussia understood the German patriots' ambition for unity and
sincerely desired to bring about their triumph in a
more or less near future.

Similarly, Prussia also showed herself, at least in
a certain sense and to some degree, favourable to
the liberal aspirations which began to make their
appearance about the same time.

We know the general conception which German
historians have of the evolution of their country in
the direction of political freedom.  They describe
the Germans as a people who, ever since the time of
Tacitus, had been essentially military and at every
moment in their history had felt the need of having
a chief or king.  But monarchy as they understood
it was very far removed from despotism.  The
sovereign, it is true, was heard and respected, as was
only right in the case of a leader in war, but he

possessed no arbitrary power. His position was only upheld and ratified by the tacit or open consent of the nation in arms. The German, therefore, had an instinctive tendency to reconcile the principle of authority with that of the free initiative of the subject. He was full of respect for the social order established by tradition, and animated by the sincerest feeling of loyalty to the Crown. Till the very height of the nineteenth century he preserved his traditional devotion to the nobility. He remained attached to the past, felt no desire to free himself from the established order of things or to break with the traditions in which he saw a guarantee for the safety of the State and for the orderly progress of civilisation. But he also wished to safeguard his own individual liberty. He wanted every man, in his own limited sphere, to have the right and to feel it his duty to make a free use of his own spontaneous activity. He thus aimed at reconciling obedience with independence, discipline with free initiative. He did not claim equality for all, as he was quite ready to admit that the sphere of autonomy should not be the same for every citizen. But neither did he admit the principle of despotism, as each individual was encouraged to give free exercise to his power in the realm assigned to him, and public opinion did not willingly tolerate any interference on the part of an outside authority in this specially reserved domain.

From the political point of view, therefore, the natural inclination of the German was not for the republican form of government, which suppressed the personality of the king and thus decapitated the national army by depriving it of its head. Neither did he demand a parliamentary system and the rule by charter and law, under which all real power is placed in the hands of deputies elected by the nation, and the king finds his authority either altogether destroyed or else irreparably reduced. The system to which he gave his entire sympathies was a constitutional monarchy under which authority is wielded by virtue of the *agreement* between the will of the king and the will of the people.

Now the transformation of the old absolute monarchy into constitutional government was carried out " organically " in Prussia, and was accomplished side by side with the development of the political education of the people. In proportion as individuals or social groups felt the need of self-government awake in their breasts and the ability to guide their own destinies, they were called upon to play an increasingly active part in the life of the nation. Immediately after the defeat at Jena, Prussian statesmen had the insight to perceive the fundamental reason for the disaster which had overtaken their country. They realised that Prussia had come to grief under her old system, because the enlightened despotism of the eighteenth century had ended by stifling all spontaneity, because the serf bound to the soil, the merchant tied to his trade and shut up in his own town, and the noble concerned only with the interests of his order, had lost all idea of national unity and had dissociated themselves entirely from the commonwealth. They grasped the necessity of liberating the nation, step by step, from this bureaucratic system, which, in the words of Humboldt, " made a machine of man," stifled in the people the capacity of acting on their own initiative, and caused the physical and intellectual downfall of the State. They saw that the regeneration of the country de-

6

manded, as an essential condition, the reorganisation of society, and that it was necessary to substitute for the old Prussia conquered at Jena a new Prussia upheld, as revolutionary France had been upheld, by the free, self-conscious will of every citizen; and that, in order to regain her rank among the nations of Europe, Prussia was bound to undergo, without violence, without bloodshed, or any brutal rupture with the past, a transformation similar to that which France had accomplished during the storms of the Revolution.

The reforms of Stein and Hardenberg began this great work of social education. By freeing the rural population from serfdom and paving the way for the institution of a class of independent peasant proprietors, by suppressing the guilds and inaugurating the era of the complete freedom of industry, the Prussian ministers emancipated the country from the tutelage to which she had been subjected. And at the same time as Stein led the people to freedom of labour he also aimed at making them accustomed to self-government. He considered that the time was ripe for the nation to be entrusted with parochial and local administration. With this object in view, he gave the towns a fair share of municipal self-government and endeavoured to free the rural communities from the exclusive rule of the aristocracy. From the top to the bottom of the social ladder it was his object to organise a system of co-operation between the Government and the people. In the district, the province, and the kingdom, he proposed to establish, in addition to the representatives of royal authority, a number of elective diets in which the aspirations of the people would find free expression, and by means of which they could discuss all matters of local, provincial, or national interest.

It is possible to have some doubts about the actual result of Stein's work, and to ask to what extent he really succeeded in liberating the people and in putting an end to the omnipotence of the aristocracy and the officious interference of the bureaucrats. It is possible to cast aspersions upon the efficiency of this sytsem of *self-government* which he tried to introduce into Prussia, and to maintain that it proved incapable of shattering the aristocratic oligarchy, whose rule still really kept the majority of the nation in a state of servitude. At all events, it is certain that this great minister, who was at once a feudalist and a democrat, filled with a profound respect for the royal authority and the traditional order of society, hostile to the constitutional government and the centralised administration of revolutionary or imperial France, but convinced of the necessity of supplanting enlightened despotism and feudal tyranny by an ever more comprehensive system of popular self-government, was a true representative of that conservative but not reactionary spirit which inspired a large number of Prussian statesmen during the nineteenth century. German public opinion is inspired by a feeling of gratitude to Stein and Hardenberg for having put the feudalistic past into liquidation and for having laid the foundations of a new society built on a basis of a wide parochial and urban self-government, ruled from above by the firm and undisputed authority of the sovereign and defended against all aggression by a national army recruited on the principle of compulsory military service for all.

·     ·     ·     ·

Thus at the beginning of the nineteenth century Germany was still hopelessly divided.  On the one side Austria was trying to preserve her traditional hegemony and to draw the German princes into the orbit of her own policy.  Prussia, on the other hand, without yet aiming at supplanting Austria, was, nevertheless, filled with the ambition to increase her sphere of influence as much as possible.  Between the rival aspirations of these two great powers, the German princes manœuvred to the best of their ability to safeguard their own independence.  Their sovereignty was, as a rule, purely illusory, owing to the fact that it was based upon no real power and was quite unable to make itself respected outside its own borders.  Nevertheless the princes exercised a more or less unlimited authority over their own subjects.  Some used their power well and for the benefit of their country.  Some even showed themselves disposed to grant their subjects a more or less liberal constitution and parliamentary institutions.  Others, on the contrary, were merely arrogant and hated despots— malignant tyrants who squeezed their subjects shamelessly and ruined the country by crippling it beneath a crushing system of taxation, ridiculous puppets foolishly infatuated by their fictitious majesty and giving themselves airs utterly out of keeping with their real power.

But they were one and all filled with the desire of carrying out a strictly particularistic policy.  They all knew, in fact, that national unity could only be established at their expense, and that the creation of a strong central power in Germany must necessarily level a blow at their precarious sovereignty.  They accordingly opposed the movement towards unification with might and main.  They were instinctively suspicious of Prussia, whose strength they feared and whose ambitions they guessed. They aimed, therefore, at balancing the two great powers who were fighting for the hegemony of Germany against each other, and thus hoped to stop all innovations which might strike at their own precious independence.

How, under these unfavourable conditions, was the national organisation of Germany, which had only been sketched in rough outline by the diplomatists at the Congress of Vienna, to be carried out ?

# CHAPTER II

## THE IDEALISTIC STRUGGLE FOR LIBERTY AND UNITY

### I

DURING the first half of the nineteenth century the struggle for German unity formed part of the fight for political liberty, and was of a highly idealistic nature. The parties which came into being at that time fought less for the conquest of power or for the realisation of practical reforms of a definite character than for the triumph of a moral doctrine—a sort of political religion. The apostles of liberty and unity seem generally to have been idealists who, in the presence of the worn-out powers of absolute monarchy and of feudal or clerical reaction, put forward the fundamental claims of modern subjectivism—the right of the nation to self-government and her demand to be consulted upon public matters. They were not so much party men with a definite programme in their hands aiming at securing certain practical reforms, as men of thought who brought forward a certain ideal, and relied, for the triumph of their cause, upon that irresistible power of persuasion which a truth once proclaimed has upon the minds of men. And they dreamt of founding the liberty and unity of Germany upon the omnipotence of the idea.

When about the beginning of the nineteenth century, soon after the disaster at Jena, aspirations for unity began to make their appearance in Germany, they showed themselves first among the intellectual minority of the nation, and were closely associated with literary and philosophical considerations.

Fichte was the characteristic representative of the first believers in unity. The German nationality, according to him, consisted of all who used the German language and shared in the philosophic, literary, and religious culture belonging to the German-speaking countries. And to this linguistic and literary test he added a metaphysical and moral criterion, and defined the Germans as the " primitive people," who believed in the liberty, the indefinite improvement, and the eternal progress of the human race, in distinction to " foreign nations," who imagine themselves subjected, and who really are subjected, to universal determinism, who regard liberty as an illusion, and see everywhere nothing but an inexorable and unchanging necessity. In Fichte's eyes, therefore, German unity was essentially a moral unity. Mere political unity seemed to him useless, and he regarded the division of Germany into independent states as a guarantee of liberty, and would have considered the absorption of the various states by any one of them and the establishment of a German monarchy as a calamity. German unity, he thought, could only be secured by the growth of freedom. Only when the dream of liberty had been gradually realised in the breasts of the various German states, could a German commonwealth come spontaneously into being, unshackled by any hereditary ruler or sovereign dynasty; and this was the living embodiment of the rationalistic State such as Fichte conceived of it, forming in the very centre of Europe a formidable but peaceful power, able not only to make itself respected by its neighbours, but also capable of imposing peace upon the rest of the world.

We thus see how Utopian and how far removed from hard historical reality were the political convictions of the author of the *Discourses to the German People*. And the most different minds shared with him this enthusiasm for the great German nation and divine liberty. Among them were men of action like Blücher and Gneisenau, Stein and Scharnhorst, who fought above all to deliver Germany from the yoke of France, but also believed, with Gneisenau, that " the triple supremacy of the army, the *constitution*, and science " was the country's best defence. Others, like Görres, were romanticists, who wedded in their minds dreams of the future of Germany with memories of the past of the Teutonic peoples and longed for the advent of a new Germany which should be a restoration of the glorious Empire of the Ottos. In the *Rhein Mercury* they preached the adoption of compulsory service for all and the abolition of all internal customs, or revived Dante's *Monarchia*, believing that they could reform the institutions of the nineteenth by the help of those of the thirteenth century. Then came the political dilettantes, the crowd of publicists, who enlarged upon the restoration of the German Empire and tried to discover a practical means of reconciling the ambitions of Prussia and Austria, or proposed, like Professor Lips, to allow the various German princes in succession to occupy the imperial throne for a period of five years ! The believers in unity and liberty did not yet form a regular party. The cultured middle classes of that period, inexperienced as they were in politics, saw no difficulty in reconciling their old particularistic customs with vague dreams of the restoration of the Empire or political emancipation. And they piled up, in newspapers and pamphlets, the most fantastic arguments about the measures which should be taken, without having the faintest notion of how difficult it was to put into practice the ideal of a free united Germany, which it was so easy to imagine in the abstract.

Just after 1815, during the first days of the German Confederation, democratic tendencies and ideas of unity began to shape and assert themselves with greater clearness and persistence. The aspirations of the " patriots " spread more and more among university students belonging to the *Allgemeine Deutsche Burschenschaft*, among the middle classes and the labouring population of the west and south, and the intellectual *élite* of the whole country. The reconstruction of Germany at the Congress of Vienna had profoundly disillusioned the whole nation, and public opinion naturally placed the responsi-bility for the bankruptcy of all the hopes aroused by the War of Independence upon the shoulders of the rulers. From that moment the Liberals fell gradu-ally into the habit of contrasting the people with the Governments in order to exalt the one and decry the other. The people had taken up arms to deliver Germany trampled underfoot by the foreign tyrant. The armies of Napoleon had been put to flight by the whole nation in arms—the line regiments, the *Landwehr*, and above all the volunteers—who rose up as one man to free the country from oppression. And behold ! as soon as the victory was won, Courts and Cabinets prevented the nation from enjoying the fruits of its labours. The diplomatists had failed to bring the work of freedom to a satisfactory conclusion. They had left Alsace in the hands of France, who in the past had torn it away from the German Empire, to whose security it was indispensable ; and they had shown themselves incapable of organising the material and moral unity which the nation demanded. The princes had selfishly prevented the formation of a powerful German confederation, and one and all had thus given proof of inefficiency and ill-will.

The Liberals did not realise that their reasoning rested in the last instance upon an illusion.

In the first place, they never imagined that in giving to the " people " the credit for the victories of 1813 they were the dupes of a romantic mirage. The War of Independence had not in any respect been a spontaneous popular outburst. On the contrary, it had been prepared with consummate care a long time beforehand by excellent organisers, and the victories had been won, not by the volunteers, who always played an insignificant part, but by the regular troops levied and drilled by Scharnhorst and his colleagues. As Treitschke points out, it was an error and an injustice to glorify the work of the people exclusively and pretend to despise the direct agents of freedom—the generals, diplomatists, statesmen, administrators, and nobles who had made the preparations for the war and directed its course. It was also a mistake to make the governments alone responsible for the check given to the hopes for unification. The spirit of particularism, local selfishness, the hatred between neighbours, were not invented by the Cabinets. It was untrue to say that there was a conflict at this time between the will of the people demanding unity and the will of the princes, who thrust it from them out of a selfish desire to preserve their own sovereignty. As a matter of fact, it was the soul of Germany itself which was divided between the desire for unity and the accustomed practice of particularism. A national parliament would in all probability have proved just as incapable of bringing about the unification of Germany as the Congress of diplomatists had been.

But public opinion did not give this verdict. It found it more convenient to cast the blame upon the various governments instead of saying *meâ culpâ* on its own part as well. And thus there grew up an antagonism which was destined to last for a long time between the adherents of Liberalism and unity and the governments. The Liberals grew more and more inclined to regard the heads of the states as selfish tyrants, who were both inefficient and ill-disposed. They longed for the moment when, in the words of Dahlmann, " the lamp of good constitutions should be lighted, before which the smoky torches of Cabinets would grow pale." They gave vent to their discontent and made professions of their democratic creed in bombastic and barren manifestations like the Wartburg and Hambach Festivals. The governments, on their side, haunted by the spectre of revolution, grew frightened without reason ; they took inoffensive idealists for dangerous agitators, and tried to dam the democratic flood which was hurrying along the whole of the modern world in its eddies. They imagined they were preserving the public peace by muzzling the press, gagging the universities, persecuting students and thinkers, and pursuing the " demagogues " with a brutality as hateful as it was foolish.

The conflict between Liberalism and absolutism

presents rather different features in Prussia on the one hand and the South German states on the other.

Prussia was, and has remained, essentially an absolute monarchy. Her kings, Frederick William III. and Frederick William IV. possessed the most lofty idea of their sovereign rights, and were resolutely decided not to relinquish any tittle of them. Frederick William IV. especially was *par excellence* the monarch by divine right. He really believed himself the medium through which God made known his wishes to the people, and he therefore listened to the voice of divine inspiration in his own heart, and would have thought himself lacking in his first duty if he had given way before the advice of his councillors, or above all had hearkened to the wish of the people when any great decision had to be made. Abdication on his part would have been treason against the nation, as it would have deprived it of the divine help it required. It was not only the right, but the duty of the king to exercise the sovereign powers which had been placed in his hands. And, consequently, Frederick William IV. ruled his councillors and ministers with a high hand. He regarded them as subalterns, who have no business to possess a will of their own or to carry out their own designs, but are merely the weapons for the accomplishment of the royal desires. He treated them as servants, whom he employed as long as he pleased, and could dismiss without the smallest scruple when they no longer served his purpose, as they were merely human instruments and adjuncts of the one, indivisible, everlasting, and divine will of the sovereign.

And the people of every rank and station were still profoundly impregnated with the belief in monarchy. This faith existed in the breasts of the princes of the blood—as for instance in Prince William, who expressed his opinions with the greatest freedom even when they conflicted with those of the Emperor, but gave way without a murmur as soon as the monarch had spoken. It existed among the officials, who felt they were simply the instruments of the royal will; they stated their opinions in all sincerity without fear of displeasing the King, although they felt bound to serve their master in all circumstances, even if he decided against their convictions and obliged them to act in a manner of which they did not approve. They did not think they had the right of leaving the service of the King without his consent; they did not even allow themselves to bring pressure to bear upon his decisions by threatening to resign; as loyalty demanded of them, even if they were beaten, to retain office if the King desired it. Like the ministers, the nobility had preserved its loyalty to the Crown intact, it remained faithful to the House of Hohenzollern, and served it faithfully either with the sword or in the royal councils. Among the people, also, the attachment to the dynasty was full of vitality; they fulfilled their duties to the State not in any spirit of utilitarian selfishness or out of any respect for authority in the abstract, but by virtue of a profound instinct, which made them see in the King the incarnation of the national will.

It is clear that under these circumstances no one dreamt of introducing into Prussia the system of parliamentary government as we understand it. The King of Prussia was absolutely determined to keep *the whole* of his power intact without surrendering the minutest portion of it to the hands of a parliament: And the patriots, too, had not the smallest intention of weakening the monarchy. When Stein proposed the establishment of a State diet in addition to the central government, he had no idea of creating a new power in rivalry to the King; he merely wished that the nation should be associated with the free decisions of the central power. The King, in any case, remained as much the absolute master of the diet as he had been of his ministers. He continued with his sovereign powers unimpaired to have the last word on every important question; he confined himself to taking counsel with the diet, and remained free to follow the advice of his ministers or not. Regarded from this point of view, the establishment of a constitution and representative institutions did not appear to the King and his ministers in the light of a revolutionary measure. There was no question of limiting the authority of the King or of creating, as a counter-weight to the royal prerogative, the rival power of an elective assembly. It was not even a question of bringing into existence something entirely new. The future was to spring from the womb of the past. The provincial diets, which the Prussian Government proposed to convoke, were to be the lineal descendants of the old provincial assemblies, which had once been conquered by the King and reduced to impotence. And the general *Landtag* of Prussia was on its side to arise out of the provincial diets. The deputies were not to be " elected by the people," but were to be the delegates of their peers, of their " wards," of the nobility and landed proprietors, the townspeople and the peasantry.

But if the proposed Landtag in no way resembled the typical English or French parliament, the formulating of a constitution and the convoking of that Landtag were none the less a concession to Liberal opinion and to the political aspirations of the educated middle classes. The King and many of his councillors, moreover, were sincerely desirous of connecting the people with the deliberations which concerned the general interests of the whole nation. They felt that the people had attained its majority, and that it was not possible to keep it in leading-strings for ever. This sentiment was very clearly and precisely defined in the minds of statesmen, such as Hardenberg, Humboldt, and Schœn, and the King himself was not opposed to them. He was inspired by no feelings of systematic ill-will against the meeting of the Landtag, though the realisation of the scheme gave rise to very great difficulties. In the first place, it was no easy task to convoke the provincial diets, which were to serve as the basis of the future Landtag. And it was still more difficult to found a Landtag which would not prove a Prussian Parliament and a rival to royal authority, but would remain a purely advisory body, whose decisions the King was in no sense bound to ratify, and which he was not even expected to summon at any regular intervals.

Consequently delays arose in the organisation of representative institutions, which irritated and estranged public opinion. Ever since May 22, 1815, the King of Prussia had been making solemn promises to give a written constitution to his kingdom and to convoke the national diet. More than twenty years passed by before this promise was fulfilled. Frederick William III., after having summoned and dissolved one after the other four commissions, which had been charged with drawing up the plan of the constitution, gave up the idea of organising a national representative assembly and confined himself to creating provincial diets in each of the eight provinces of his kingdom. And matters did not advance more rapidly under his successor. Once again preliminaries dragged on for years without resulting in any solution. And when, in February 1847, the King suddenly decided to issue a patent grouping the provincial diets into one common diet or *Vereinigter Landtag*, the concession came too late. Liberal opinion was no longer content to have an assembly whose powers were purely advisory except on the question of loans, and which, on all save financial matters, was bound to hold its discussions in two separate wards, and had not even secured the promise of being periodically united in one body.

During the long period of fruitless waiting, the Prussian Liberals, especially before 1840, gave proofs of untiring patience. Out of loyalty to the dynasty, and also inspired by a very comprehensible prudence—as Prussian authorities had a heavy hand—they avoided all loud agitation and took care not to indulge in any manœuvre which could possibly be regarded as forcing the hand of the King. No struggle took place between absolutism and the democratic party. The royal authority was exercised without meeting with any organised opposition. Only in every direction, especially after 1840, signs were multiplied which showed that the cultured and industrial middle classes were aspiring more and more to have a say and to make their influence felt in public affairs.

The situation in Southern Germany was very different.

The middle states—Bavaria, Wurtemberg, and the Grand Duchy of Baden—had adopted constitutional government very early. There were various reasons which combined to make the governments of these countries favourable to the establishment of representative institutions. In the first place, the territory of these states had grown to such an extent during the Napoleonic era that the national diets necessarily seemed to present to the governments a convenient method for creating a bond of unity between the old parties and the lands recently annexed. Moreover, these three states, by the very fact of their sudden expansion, and also because they had been subjected more profoundly than other parts of Germany to French influence, had been led into making a sudden break with the feudalistic past. The Grand Duke Charles Frederick and his successor, the Grand Duke Charles of Baden, the Bavarian Minister, Montgelas, and King Frederick I. of Wurtemberg, had abolished, not without brutality in some cases, the majority of the privileges of the nobility and the clergy, and had aimed at making the principle of equal rights for all before the law, and the duty of every man to contribute to State expenses, supreme. And in this task of social transformation they felt themselves forced to rely upon public opinion. Lastly, diets and constitutional government appeared to the various sovereigns in the light of a possible prop to particularistic sentiments, as a means of distracting the public mind from the dangerous chimera of unity, and as a last defence against the desire for unification on the part of the Confederation. Under these circumstances, when in 1815 the princes found themselves menaced by the Confederation with the danger of being *forced* into convoking a diet and drawing up a constitution, they hastened to be the first in the field and to promise *on their own initiative*

7

to give their subjects free institutions. Thus constitutional government was established in the south of Germany much earlier than in Prussia. And from that moment Prussia was regarded by the Liberals as the home of reaction, as a country which was behind the times, and the classic territory of lordlings and dragooning.

German historians, as a rule, have a low opinion of these southern states, which boasted of having set an example of Liberalism to the rest of Germany. They consider that their political development, to use a hackneyed expression, was "inorganic." Their institutions were not, as in the case of Prussia, the natural, spontaneous, and necessary result of the national growth. In fact, all the middle states of the South had come under the influence of France, both during the Napoleonic era and later—more especially in 1830. Some, like Bavaria, had purely and simply aped the institutions and administration of France. Others—that is to say, nearly all the states which had a constitution and representative government before 1848—had felt the same influence more indirectly, but none the less surely. The characteristic they all had in common was the fact that they were governed not by their own native institutions, but by a system imported from abroad.

Now in states like England, whose growth has been " organic," public safety has as its basis and guarantee the regular working of the fundamental institutions of the nation, the administration by rural, urban, and provincial councils. The line of demarcation between the royal authority and that of the people, between the functions of the central Government and that of the autonomous local administrations, has been settled by practice and by virtue of the experience of long periods. In "inorganic" states, on the contrary, these relations, instead of being regulated by elastic living customs and by an unwritten law, come under the jurisdiction of a legal compact and a code of judicial obligations on the part of the monarch towards the State. The free sovereign will of the prince is obliged to bow before the decrees of strict rule and imperative law. A sheet of paper, to use the well-known words of Frederick William IV., is placed between the King and his people. Thus a system of mutual confidence between a prince and his subjects gives place to a dry and barren legal formality.

The principalities of Southern Germany are " inorganic " states of precisely this type. The middle class, which formed the Liberal or Radical parties in them, was not an active living body endowed with organising powers which it wished to make supreme. It merely saw salvation in some abstract theory of a constitutional state, and in a number of political formulæ borrowed from abroad, which did not adequately reflect a real condition of things. Its leaders were doctrinaires mounted on the hobby-horse of constitutional dogmatism, living in a very narrow sphere, and devoid of all experiences or breadth of view. Quite incapable of formulating a practical programme to serve as a basis for the public life of that " Great Germany " of which they dreamt, they drew up beautiful plans *in abstracto* for a future which could never be realised in practice, and showed themselves clumsy in carrying out reforms that were actually possible. And these idealists, wedded to their belief in abstract ideas, these theorists in love with barren legal formalities, made grave mistakes in their estimate of the forces which were making them-

selves felt in the political evolution of Germany. They
remained cosmopolitan until after 1830, whilst the
country was developing more and more in the direction of nationalism. They were hostile to standing
armies, which they regarded as the mainstays of
despotism and schools of servitude, whilst Prussia
was destined to found her greatness precisely on her
military prowess, and Germany was to grow more
and more accustomed to looking upon the national
army as the great training school of civic unity and
morality. They hated the hereditary nobility, whose
ruin and extinction they prayed for at a time when
the aristocracy had just played a leading and glorious
part in the War of Independence, and was to keep for
some time longer, especially in Prussia, a position
of the highest importance in the life of the nation.
They often professed a pedantically narrow rationalism
and despised " the barbarism of the Middle Ages "
at a moment when the romantic spirit had everywhere
awakened the love of the nation's past and a religious
revival was making itself felt in the breasts of Protestants and Catholics alike.

Nevertheless, we may perhaps be allowed not to
accept without some reservations the harsh judgment which the historical school usually passes upon
Liberalism. It is true that the Liberals did not foresee
the turn events were to take. With rare exceptions, they neither guessed, desired, nor prepared for
the conquest of Germany by Prussia and the rise of
German imperialism in the second half of the century.
As advocates of peace and cosmopolitans, as supporters
of friendship between France and Germany, and dis-
approving of the fratricidal struggle between nations
for political power, they misread the signs of the
times. They were wrong in saying with Heine that

" in Europe there were no longer any nations, but only parties " ; they were wrong in prophesying the advent of a great German revolution which should sweep away kings and aristocracies and in dreaming of securing for Germany a supremacy which should be chiefly spiritual. But their idealistic efforts in the cause of democracy, as we shall see later on, were not devoid of influence upon the course of events. And if a united empire is not the final goal of Germany's ambition, if it proves to have been only a transitory stage in her evolution, and if she ever revives her humanitarian dreams of the beginning of the nine- teenth century, it is not unlikely that the Liberals, in spite of their mistakes and their narrowness, will one day be recognised as the first champions in Ger- many of a better future, of an era of peace and good will, in which the bloody strife of nations shall give way to a universal desire for progress and happiness.

## II

Nevertheless, about 1840 a split took place in the ranks of the Liberal Party.

On the one side the section which believed in nationalism and unity, with which Liberalism had from the first been associated, forced itself to the front for various reasons. This was due in the first place to the accession of Frederick William IV., who by his grandiloquent rhetoric fanned into a blaze the flame of national sentiment and the romantic cult of the past of the Teutons. At the same time, the war- like ambitions which showed themselves in France in 1840, when she found herself, by the London Con- vention, excluded from the concert of Europe and rudely checkmated in her designs on Egypt, provoked an extraordinary outburst of patriotism throughout the whole of Germany. In the first moment of anger and vexation France had rashly declared herself ready to resume the struggle against the Holy Alliance. French publicists denounced the treaties of 1815, demanded the left bank of the Rhine, and threatened Europe in arms to play " the terrible game of revolution " against her. Germany, who was living in the most profound peace, and had no idea of picking a quarrel with France, suddenly saw rising before her eyes the menace of a war which she had done nothing to provoke. She was angry at the idea that France should put forward the pretension of finding compensation on the Rhine for her disappointment over her Egyptian policy. The passions of 1813 blazed forth more fiercely than before. Journalists and poets, writers and soldiers, fulminated against the immorality of France, preached a war without quarter against the sinning nation, and demanded the restoration of Alsace-Lorraine. Convinced that the hereditary foe was preparing to reopen the everlasting conflict for the possession of the Rhine, the Germans were fired afresh with aspirations for unity. They felt the necessity for combining to resist aggression and to win back the imperial lands which still remained in the hands of France.

Liberalism, which had before been cosmopolitan and sincerely sympathetic with France, became from that moment strictly nationalistic. In vain did Heine protest against the outburst of Chauvinism, which he regarded as a foolish return to the spirit of the past. He grew angry with the " phrase-mongering patriotism " of poets, who enlisted their Muse in the service of the good cause and degraded her into a *cantinière* of liberty or the washerwoman of Christian

Teutonism. In the figure of Atta Troll, the dancing bear, he caricatured the new type of the convinced democratic patriot, the nationalistic and religious acrobat. He asserted his inviolable attachment to France and combated with all his passionate ardour the spirit of imperialism, greedy for war and conquest, which he saw appearing among his countrymen. It was of no use. He remained an isolated figure. On the whole, Liberalism developed along the lines of a decided imperialism, which longed ever more passionately for the unity and strength of Germany. The " Liberal " became the " National Liberal."

At the same time, the advanced wing of the party progressed to a more absolute form of Radicalism. During the 'thirties democratic aspirations demanded little more than the establishment of a constitutional monarchy. After 1840 they more frequently aimed at uncompromising republicanism. In Prussia the policy of drastic repression and clumsy reaction inaugurated by Frederick William IV., after a short period of liberal ambitions, profoundly irritated public opinion. The strict measures taken against the press and against political poets, the pedantic despotism with which the Minister Eichhorn weighed down the universities and scholastic establishments, the merciless severity with which every democratic manifestation was suppressed, made the Government more and more unpopular. Liberal opinion showed itself particularly hostile even to the person of the King, whom it regarded, not without reason, as responsible for the absolutist, feudalistic, and revivalist reaction which was again let loose in Prussia. Anti-religious and anti-monarchical Radicalism, as it was preached by Strauss, the Bauer brothers, Arnold Ruge, Karl Marx, and Feuerbach, gained ground every day. At the same time, a band of political poets like Hoffmann von Fallersleben, Dingelstedt, Freiligrath, Meissner, Karl Beck, Gottfried Kinkel, and others passionately espoused the cause of the people and of liberty and hurled inflammatory appeals across Germany. The hostility against the King rose to such a pitch that when Tschech attempted to assassinate Frederick William IV. public opinion was inclined to excuse the murderer, whilst some even went so far as to write lofty apologies for regicide.

Whilst in Prussia the opposition to the King increased in violence every day, in the constitutional states of the South also the conflict between the democratic chambers and the reactionary ministers grew ever more acute. In the province of Baden especially the struggle against the Government became resolute. In addition to the constitutional Liberals like Welcker, Bassermann, and Karl Mathy, there rose up a Radical Party under the leadership of Hecker, Struve, and Itzstein, who preached the establishment of a pure democracy, for which the country was far from ripe. This party tried to make the electors suspicious of the moderation of the constitutionalists, and by an inflammatory propaganda kept alive a dangerous spirit of discontent among the masses. When the February Revolution broke out in Paris, Germany also was in a state of seething ferment. Liberals of all shades, believers in unity or constitutionalists, Radicals or Socialists, were all agreed that the existing state of things in Germany could not continue, and that profound reforms were necessary in order to give the country the unity and liberty of which it stood so sorely in need.

### III

The Revolution of 1848 in France was immediately
followed in Germany by a general conflagration.   In
the space of a few weeks a good third of the country
was plunged into a sort of anarchy, which was, however, of a fairly pacific nature, as, in view of the
unanimity of the movement, the authorities scarcely
made any attempt at resistance.

The princes got frightened and gave way.   The
King of Wurtemberg, the Grand Dukes of Baden and
Hesse, and the Senate of Frankfort hastened to decree
the liberty of the press.   The Diet of Frankfort lost
its head, decided upon a revision of the Act of Federation " on really national lines," and invited the governments to send delegates to discuss this revision.   Disorders broke out in Munich, resulting on March 20 in
the abdication of King Ludwig I. and the accession
to power of Maximilian II. and a Liberal Cabinet.
In Vienna the Revolution broke out on May 13, and
swept away the system of Metternich ; Hungary and
Italy rose at the same moment.   In Berlin the rum-
blings of insurrection were heard in the streets on
March 18, and on the 19th the retreat of the troops
put the King and the capital in the hands of the
insurgents.   Everywhere absolutism was foundering.
At the head of the movement marched the educated
middle classes—professors, writers, lawyers, doctors,
merchants, and industrialists—demanding unity and
liberty.   Their fundamental claims were the convocation of a national parliament, the liberty of the
press, the institution of trial by jury, and the substitution of the nation in arms for a standing army.
In the very ranks of this great Liberal Party there
were, moreover, sections which were more or less

advanced, the more moderate ones counting on the help of the established authorities—the kings and princes—to bring the reforms to a satisfactory conclusion ; others, more radical, insisting upon the establishment of a republic and the abolition of rank and royalty.  Behind the middle classes the masses of the people rose up, demanding, in addition to political reforms, social changes, which were to bring universal happiness ; equality for all, the abolition of the privileges of the large landed proprietors in the country districts, the reform of the industrial system in the towns, the protection of the artisan against the competition of the factory owner, and of the factory hand against the exploitation of his employer.

All this revolutionary movement resulted in the meeting of the Parliament of Frankfort, whose convocation was demanded and its organisation prepared by the people themselves and the men in whom they trusted.  The governments, reduced to impotence, did not direct the movement ; but they countenanced the meeting of the Parliament, sanctioned the elections, and allowed representatives chosen by universal suffrage to come together in order to discuss the general interests of the country and offer their assistance to the princes who had been swamped in the floods of revolution.  In a moment German Liberalism had become a power, and found itself in a position to carry its programme into practice.  The result of the attempt is well known.  It ended in the complete confusion of the Liberals.  On May 18, 1848, the Parliament met at Frankfort.  At the beginning of June 1849 the remnants of the *Rumpfparlament* of Stuttgart melted away after having at their last meeting at the Marquardt Hotel launched forth a call to insur-

rection.   And as soon as the autumn came the forces
of reaction once more triumphed throughout Germany.   What were the meaning and scope of this
crisis ?

In the first place, what did the Liberal middle
classes want ?

Firstly, it is clear that they did *not* want to take
the government of the country directly into their
own hands.   The extreme Radicals had understood
perfectly well that if the people wanted to secure
power, it was necessary for them to lay hands on
the instruments of authority—the Civil Service and
the army.   Consequently, after the preliminary
meeting at Heidelberg, the Radicals of Baden demanded the proclamation of a republic.   And at the
preliminary meeting of the *Vorparlament* at Frankfort, Struve proposed the abolition of monarchy in
all the German states and the substitution of freely
elected parliaments, each of which should nominate
its own president.   Germany was to become a
federation modelled on the United States.   In the
meantime, whilst the transformation was being prepared, the national Parliament was to declare itself
permanent and take the executive power into its
own hands.   But the Radicals were in a minority,
both in the Parliament and in the country.   Parliament defeated their revolutionary proposals by overwhelming majorities.   And when they wanted to
make an appeal to arms, it soon became apparent
that they were few in numbers and that their ill-
disciplined bands, badly organised and still more
badly conducted, were no match for the regular
forces.   The democratic revolution was vanquished
by force of arms in Berlin, Vienna, Hungary, the
province of Baden, and Dresden.   The little group of

German republicans, unable to draw into their ranks the bulk of the moderate Liberal Party, and ill-supported, on the other hand, by the mass of the people, who had no discipline and no cohesion, finally proved too weak to seize power and create a new political and social organisation in Germany.

Consequently the Liberal majority, both in Parliament and in the country, remained royalist. It did not wish to strip the sovereigns of their power, and had no intention of taking their place, but aimed simply at putting them under the control of a constitutional and parliamentary system. Now the princes represented the only effective and organised force remaining in Germany. It is true their power had been weakened and shaken by the disturbances of March 1848. But it still existed. And it rested upon a double foundation, one which was both moral and material. On the one hand, in spite of everything the sentiment of loyalty to the Crown still remained alive in the hearts of a considerable fraction of the people, and German public opinion would have been loth to see the old reigning houses swept away by the revolutionary whirlwind. On the other hand, the princes still had in their own hands the instruments of power, which formed the chief advantage they possessed ; the army and the Civil Service almost everywhere remained resolutely loyal. Thus they had at their command, in order to make themselves obeyed, the civil and military machinery of the State, which they could set in motion whenever they pleased.

But the Parliament, which had been born from the will of the people, had, for its part, a purely moral influence. Its strength consisted in the weakness of the governments. The more the authority of the

princes was lessened by the disorders, the more did
the machinery of the State become useless owing to
the confusion in the streets, and the more also did
the power of Parliament seem something positive
and real. But apart from its moral credit, Parliament had no weapon at its disposal to secure the
execution of its wishes. It was free to decree its
own sovereignty, to appoint a Chancellor of the
Empire, to form its ministries, to pass laws, and to
promulgate a constitution. But for its decisions to
be carried into effect, it was necessary for them to be
accepted by the governments, failing which they
remained a dead-letter and purely Platonic manifestations. The sovereign Parliament could, to give
a concrete example, decree that the federal troops
should wear a red, black, and gold cockade; its
Minister of War could give an order that on August 6,
1848, there should be a grand parade of all the imperial forces, who were to give three cheers for the
Chancellor of the Empire—the supreme head of the
whole imperial army. But it had no means of
forcing the obedience of the Emperor of Austria, the
King of Prussia, the King of Bavaria, and the Elector
of Hanover ; and these princes, for their part, paid
no heed to its decisions, and thus publicly proved
the weakness of that central authority, which had
not the power necessary to make itself respected.

Under these circumstances, only one alternative
remained open to Parliament, if it wished to attain
any practical results ; and this was to come to an
understanding with the governments.

Parliament made an attempt to do this. Guided
by a sure political instinct, it knew that German
unity was the one goal to be attained, and that the
process of unification could be carried out only by

means of Prussia.  It therefore decided to offer most
solemnly, in the name of the whole German people,
the Imperial Crown to Frederick William IV.  We
know the ill-success with which this attempt was
met.  For a variety of reasons—dislike of accepting
from plebeian hands a " Crown of the stones of
barricades," antipathy for the democratic constitution, which would have to be accepted at the same
time as the imperial sceptre, scruples about profiting
by the embarrassment of Austria to turn her out of
Germany, fear of the war into which the acceptance
of empire might lead Prussia—Frederick William
refused the Crown which was offered to him.  The
verdict of history upon the act is faltering.  Some
see in his refusal an inevitable necessity.  They admit
that the King of Prussia could not have held his
throne as a gift from an assembly which had no
regular mandate, and that if he had accepted it he
would have been involved in an adventure in which
he might have risked his crown  and perhaps the
future of Germany.  Others, on the contrary, are of
the opinion that owing to absolutist prejudices he
prevented German unity, created by the free vote
of a national parliament, from becoming a reality.
They maintain that if the King had taken into his
hands the sceptre held out to him, German unity
would have come peacefully into existence on a
grander and more magnificent scale than ever before.
But, whether we put the blame on the shoulders of
the Parliament or of the King, the fact remains that
the co-operation required between the National
Assembly and the Prussian Crown could not be
secured, and this meant the inevitable failure of the
whole policy of the Parliament.
It must be added that if this check was perhaps

largely due to the mistakes of individuals, it also arose to a great extent out of far more general causes.

The Parliament failed, in the first instance, because it was intrinsically impossible to find a solution which could reconcile the conflicting interests involved. On nearly every fundamental question German public opinion was, as a matter of fact, hopelessly divided. What with believers in unity and particularists, Conservatives, Liberals, and Radicals, the partisans of a " Great Germany," including Austria, and the upholders of a " Little Germany," excluding her from the Empire, it was extremely difficult to come to any understanding. The result was that precisely the most important decrees of the Parliament were passed by bare majorities. When, for example, Parliament, after having previously come to a contrary decision, decided at the third reading on March 27, 1849, by a majority of *four* votes, that there should be an hereditary Emperor of Germany, and on March 28 nominated the King of Prussia to this dignity by 290 votes to 248, it is clear that the moral weight of such a decree was very small, and that there was little chance of its imposing itself finally upon German public opinion.

But the most fundamental reason for the failure of the Parliament, and the one which German historians are generally agreed in advancing, must be looked for in the character of the men who found themselves at the head of the movement. Many of the leaders of German Liberalism were apparently men of thought, who aimed with ardent enthusiasm at the realisation of a theoretical ideal, rather than political minds endeavouring to reach the practical attainment of a definite object. And this fact is easily explained if we examine the general evolution

of the middle classes in Germany. During the first
half of the century it was the intellectual minds, the
men of high culture, and especially the university
professors, who held the most important position
and played the chief part. The middle class was
still essentially a cultured *élite*. The capitalist
middle class and the aristocracy of enterprise were
only in the course of formation and still took but a
small share in public life. Now the German thinker
of that period was fundamentally an idealist. He
believed in the omnipotence of the idea, which, once
it had been grasped, is bound to be realised by virtue
of the irresistible immanent power of expansion
possessed by truth. He consequently regarded the
foundation of German unity as a theoretical problem,
the solution of which was to be found in beautiful
academic discussions. He did not clearly realise that
this question was above all made up of a conflict of
forces, and could only be solved by an appeal to force
—" by fire and steel," to use Bismarck's expression.
This idealistic temperament, prevalent among a large
number of the members, provides an explanation of
some of the mistakes with which the Parliament has
often been reproached, such as the abstract and
doctrinaire character of its debates, the facility with
which it believed that a division was quite capable
of solving every difficulty and settling all disputes,
the rashness with which it passed measures on
principle, without thinking whether their practical
realisation was possible. The Parliament of Frankfort sought with a touching sincerity and ardour,
with a profoundly impressive good faith, for a
scheme of German unity, and it believed that the
moment it had hit upon a plan, unity would at once
be realised. This was a dangerous illusion. The

historians of to-day try to render justice to the generous effort—which was perhaps less barren than it was long thought to be—of these idealists. They allow that they too helped in the building of the edifice of German unity, and give them a share in the homage they pay to the real architects of that unity. But they confess that these idealists must inevitably have succumbed to circumstances. It required men of exceedingly strong wills to bring to a successful issue the arduous task of calling the German Empire back to life.

# CHAPTER III

## THE FOUNDATION OF GERMAN UNITY

### I

THE Revolution of 1848–49 marks a decisive crisis in the evolution of Germany. It would be correct to define its essential character by saying that Germany from that moment passed from an idealistic to an ever more definitely realistic and practical conception of political problems.

This transition becomes quite clear if we examine the evolution of the middle classes. And, indeed, towards the middle of the century there was a rapid development in its ranks of the instinct of capitalistic enterprise, of the desire for wealth and for power in general. We have already discussed the material manifestations which bear witness to this rise of capitalism during the 'fifties. But this change in the general direction of men's minds is not to be discerned only in the economic life of the nation—it also made itself felt in the domain of political events. The most vital element in the middle classes was, at the beginning of the century, the intellectual *élite*, who aspired, not to material power, but to scientific and artistic culture, and who consequently had aims which were above all spiritual. This cultured middle

114

class now began to be ousted and gradually degraded to the second rank by the new aristocracy of enterprise. The representatives of capitalism—the large manufacturers and merchants—began to play an increasingly important part in public life. Their social influence began to predominate, and they rejoiced in an ever higher consideration. And from that moment their mental outlook also began to take the lead. Now this aristocracy of enterprise was very clearly differentiated from the old intellectual *élite*. It did not aim at culture, or, to be more exact, it did not regard scientific culture as an end in itself, but simply as an instrument of power. It aspired, on the contrary, to wealth and authority. It had no desire for spiritual, disinterested, or general aims, but only followed positive, concrete, and tangible interests. It no longer allowed itself to be guided in its actions by general theories or abstract principles, but aimed at bounding its ambitions by its power, and making an exact calculation of the forces it had at its disposal and the opposition it was likely to encounter, so as to adjust the means to the ends it had in view. From that time forward business men were destined to rise to an ever higher position among the middle classes of Germany. Their realistic ambitions and concrete desires gradually took the place of the idealism of the men of thought, who, until the meeting of the Frankfort Parliament, had guided the destinies of the Liberal Party.

But it is not only in the middle classes that we find this change from idealism to realism, which was the natural result of the spread of the spirit of enterprise. It was also to be discovered among the nobility and the leading statesmen. Here

it is true, the sense of reality had never lost
ground, for it existed, without doubt, among the
country squires, in whose ranks, as we have already
seen, the first representatives of the spirit of capitalistic enterprise in Germany were to be found ; and
it also existed in the minds of the statesmen who
paved the way for the War of Independence, and
among the administrators who, when peace was
established, gradually raised the edifice of Prussian
greatness, reorganised the finances and the army,
and brought the work of the *Zollverein* to a satisfactory conclusion.  But there were also indications
of a certain liberal idealism among men like Stein
and Humboldt.  And in others, more particularly in
the case of the advisers of Frederick William IV., this
was allied to a more or less strong dose of romantic
conviction.  And the Conservatives of this type—the
champions of the divine right of kings and dynasties,
who abhorred the Revolution with all their might,
dreamt of restoring the Christian State and the
hierarchy of the Middle Ages, were filled with a pious
reverence for the Holy Alliance, and could conceive
of no German Empire of which the House of Austria
was not the head—were idealists quite as doctrinaire
as the enthusiasts of constitutional Liberalism, or of
the republican ideal, could be.

It is possible to measure the progress made in the
direction of realism if we contrast with these romanticists the statesman whose giant figure dominates
the whole of the second half of the century, and whose
entrance into public life dates precisely from the days
of the Revolution of 1848—I mean Prince Bismarck.

Bismarck was, it is true, the highest product of
feudalism.  Uniting in his single personality the
proud and pugnacious arrogance of the Brandenburg

squire with the commercial spirit and business experience of the Pomeranian noble, imbued with the
doctrines of the historical school and with romanticism, fashioned in the school of Hugo and of Heeren,
Savigny, and Hoffmann, he shared from the bottom
of his soul in the great prejudices of his caste.  He
was a fervent upholder of monarchy by right divine,
a mystic whose piety was deeply sincere, and a
hearty convert, after a youth of infidelity, to the
religion of the Gospels.  Like a good romanticist, he
was in love with the " real people ! "—that intangible
multitude of souls that " draws from the sense of
tradition the power which leads it to its predestined
goal " ; while he also believed that the sovereign
alone, by means of the grace vouchsafed him from
on high, was able to read the soul of the nation, to
decipher its will, and guide it to the destiny appointed
by Providence.  He hated and despised revolutionary
forces—the undisciplined mob which rose against
legitimate authority, and the workman who indulged in the desire to think and to reason.  He
hurled his thunderbolts against the spirit of impiety
and demoralisation, which had sprung up throughout
the urban civilisation of the modern world.  But,
above all, he could not find any sarcasm sufficiently
strong for the middle-class man and the thinker who
made clumsy attempts to gain power, for members
of Parliament who aspired to regulate the sovereignty
of the people, for the constitutionalists who granted
to incompetent deliberative assemblies—those grotesque caricatures of the national will—the sacred and
divine right of legislation.  He detested from the
bottom of his heart those arrogant idealists who
placed their foolish overweening faith in abstract
reason and its artificial creations.

But this feudalist, this romanticist, this " red reactionary," who bewitched and at the same time disturbed Frederick William IV., possessed to a supreme
degree the essential characteristics of the modern
mind : the will to power, intellectual lucidity, and
intensity of nervous energy.

He desired with an incredibly violent passion
power for himself, for his party, for his country, and
for his race. And this without any shadow of
sentimentality, but by virtue of the most elementary
of instincts, which was the mainspring of his whole
being—an instinct which proclaimed itself openly and
was not ashamed. He possessed to a most extraordinary degree the love of power, and revelled in
exercising and spreading his own influence and that
of his country. And he was constantly putting into
practice this " combative " idea of existence, without remorse and without scruple, without pity for
the feeble or generosity for the vanquished, an indefatigable fighter, ever ready to guide his people in
their hard ascent to power. He has been accused
of cynicism, he has been reproached with putting
into practice the principle that " might is right."
It would be more just to say that in the case of
Bismarck—as indeed is true, more generally speaking, of the conscience of the whole of Germany—it is
a mistake to try to establish between might and right
the antagonism which the judicial mind of France is
quite ready to admit.   In his eyes there was no right
without might or might without right. He saw in
the insatiable thirst for power no cynical usurpation
of the seat of justice by brute force, but the primordial
duty and the sacred mission of strong men and
healthy nations.

This will of iron was backed by a marvellous

ability for summing up reality with absolute exactitude, for understanding men and things, and unravelling the mesh of events. It has been truly
remarked of Bismarck that his peculiar genius did
not consist so much in the capacity for conceiving
vast designs and preparing for some distant future,
as in the marvellous dexterity with which he was
able at any given moment to extract the best possible results from the present. He is said to have
had no greater joy than in visualising every day and
every hour, as news poured in, the ever-changing
image of the state of the world at the time, and in
constantly discovering by an infallible instinct the
action that was required and the attitude which it
was necessary to assume in order to advance his
designs. Thus he lived always in the present, which
by a genial effort of the imagination he embraced
whole ; he gave himself up to the task of the
day without bothering overmuch about distant con-
tingencies. And to this rare gift of being able to
reflect with clearness and fidelity the multitudinous
and diverse changes of everyday actual reality, he
added the subtle power of divining the current of public
opinion, the meaning of *imponderabilia*, in such a
way that almost up to the last he was able to guess
the essential tendencies of contemporary evolution
and adapt his policy to the profoundest needs of his
time.

A realist by the possession of a will directed towards the conquest of material power, wealth, and
supremacy, as also by the clear lucidity of his intelligence and the infinite resources of his co-ordinating
faculties, Bismarck, on account of the complexity
of his psychic organism and the exceptional intensity
of his nervous energy, was also the legitimate son

of the new age which was being inaugurated. One has only an incomplete idea of Bismarck if one imagines that he was a sort of robust and healthy giant, a soldier of genius, a voracious eater and drinker, mad on hunting and violent riding, open air and country life, and finding in the primeval vigour of his constitution the strength to bear the crushing burden of public life. One must also take into account that an existence so active and full as his presupposed the possession of a nervous system which was both marvellously sensitive and marvellously hard. And, as a matter of fact, Bismarck had a highly nervous temperament, which sometimes vibrated to distraction, and was subject to strange disorders, which seemed to be the physical manifestation of psychic upheavals and disturbances. But in spite of everything he was strong enough to keep his balance and to endure without irreparable damage the incredible expenditure of nervous energy in which he indulged. But the sort of internal vibration which constantly animated him betrayed the accelerated speed and the terrible tension under which his sensitive, and at the same time powerful, organism worked.

With the rise of the realistic spirit in politics, a new phase in the evolution of Germany began.

## II

In the first act of the political drama, the great struggle for German unity, with all its various vicissitudes, takes place. And since the beginning of the century this struggle had changed very much in character.

The aspirations for unity arose, at first, out of the

feeling of solidarity between the Teutonic nations who spoke the same language and had the same culture, as distinguished from the foreigner, and tended to create between these nations a moral rather than a material tie. Those who believed in unity thought that the federation of the German states would be the result of the reasoning will of the whole nation, which would gradually triumph over the particularist egoism of the princes. Without sacrificing the autonomy of the various divisions of Germany, it would secure the realisation of a union which was not only demanded by the national conscience, but was also as necessary for the external safety as for the economic development of the country. We have already seen how this desire for unity almost attained its object on the day on which the Parliament of Frankfort offered the imperial crown, in the name of the German people, to the King of Prussia, and how the refusal of Frederick William IV. caused the miscarriage of this brilliant hope.

From that time forward the problem of unity gradually assumed a different aspect. Instead of being an idealistic impulse towards national solidarity, it became above all a question of dynamics.

The system of German states contained in Prussia and Austria two rival centres of attraction, which mutually neutralised and cancelled each other. This rivalry, whether it was open or covert, paralysed the powers of the Teutonic body politic and encouraged the centrifugal and particularist tendencies of the minor states. For unity to be established it was necessary for this dualism to be stopped and for Prussia, the most vigorous state of Germany, gradually to increase her power, affirm her superiority, drive her irreconcilable rival, Austria, out of the Empire,

and group all the other German states around her,
either by force or by the prestige of victory.  The
history of this slow conquest by Prussia is sufficiently
well known for me to confine myself to giving a rough
sketch of its most important phases.

The first step towards the practical realisation of
unity was the establishment of the *Zollverein*.  Prussian statesmen deserve credit for having understood
the vital necessity for modern industry to have a
wide market at its disposal, and this at a time when
Austria had not yet realised that fact.  Moreover,
they were clear-sighted enough to see the political
advantage Prussia would derive from drawing closer
the economic ties with the other German states, even
at the price of certain material sacrifices.  And in the
end they succeeded in this difficult enterprise, in spite
of the obstacles which stood in their path.  They baffled
the hostility of Austria, who scented in this movement towards unity a revolutionary manifestation,
and a dangerous manœuvre on the part of Prussia
for extending her sphere of influence.  They succeeded in calming the particularist suspicions of the
minor states, who saw a slight to their sovereignty
in the interference of Prussia in their administration
and finance.  They resisted the blundering impatience
of certain over-hasty partisans of unity, like List,
who would have liked to see the economic unification
of Germany proclaimed at one stroke by a decree of
the diet, instead of proceeding gradually by successive stages.  They triumphed over all these difficulties by the firmness of a persevering and loyal policy,
pursued methodically, without haste, brutality, or
weakness.

Their action was, moreover, seconded by the
natural play of economic laws.  Prussia, which was

the only large state in Germany, was the one power
in a position to secure the prosperity of industry on
a large scale, which must of necessity have been
confined and hampered in the minor states. Consequently, a customs union with Prussia was so
clearly to the advantage of the latter, that in the
long run there was no alternative but to resign themselves to it. The customs duties, moreover, constituted a financial resource of the first importance ;
so much so that for the states whose finances were in
low water, the prospect of an immediate and certain
increase of revenue was one of the most enticing
baits. Lastly, tariff walls and rights of transit might
prove exceedingly efficacious weapons against obstinate hostility, and Prussia did not hesitate to use
them on occasion to bring some recalcitrant neighbour to repentance. During the 'thirties a customs
union including the greater part of Germany—only
Hanover and a few petty North German states remained outside the *Zollverein*—was definitely established under the hegemony of Prussia. The economic
results of this arrangement were immediately noticeable everywhere. And soon the *Zollverein,* founded
on the solid basis of material interests, became a
definite institution, capable of defying all assaults
and of victoriously weathering the storms of the
revolutionary period of 1848–1849.

As soon as she had been placed at the head of
the German Customs Union, Prussia immediately endeavoured, in the spring of 1849, after the refusal of
King Frederick William IV. to accept the Imperial
Crown offered him by the Parliament of Frankfort,
to realise the political unity of Germany by means
of diplomacy.

On the advice of his friend General von Radowitz,

the King of Prussia tried to create within the Confederation, and with the consent of Austria, a smaller
" union " which was to come into being through the
voluntary adherence of the petty states.  This was
a strangely complicated scheme, in which there was a
curious admixture of the enthusiasm for unity of
1848, Prussian aspirations to the hegemony of Germany, and fidelity to the traditional policy of friendship with Austria.  It was foredoomed to failure
—in the first place because the desire for unity,
weakened by the check with which the Frankfort
Parliament had met, had not sufficient strength to
demand the sacrifices required from the particularist
egoism of the minor states ;  secondly and chiefly
because Austria, in proportion as she regained the
power which had been shattered by the revolutionary
crisis, showed herself more clearly hostile to a programme which would destroy her influence in Germany.  The weakness and indecision of Frederick
William IV. in this difficult position almost brought
about a catastrophe.  After having in the first place
grouped around him a certain number of petty states,
he did not know how to anticipate defection on the
part of his allies by the use of force, he could not make
up his mind to beat a retreat in time, nor had he the
courage to accept an open conflict with Austria under
the disadvantageous circumstances in which he was
placed.  This diplomatic campaign, foolishly undertaken, and then conducted without spirit and energy,
finally ended in the disastrous reverse of Olmütz.
Prussia, isolated and ill-prepared for war, found herself
constrained to give way all along the line and to submit to the humiliating terms which victorious Austria
imposed upon her.

During the years that followed Prussia retired into

herself, and gathered together her forces for the great struggle which had become inevitable, and which was to decide to whom the hegemony of Germany was to belong.

First, the Prussian Government re-established its authority at home by means of the reaction, which immediately after the crisis of 1848 began to set in throughout Germany and the whole of Europe. And it regained its position all the more surely inasmuch as it used its victory with comparative moderation. In Austria, Schwarzenberg and his successors returned to the most superannuated forms of absolutism. They cancelled all constitutional guarantees and established a centralised bureaucratic and clerical system which ruffled the most elementary instincts of the modern conscience. And they thus condemned themselves to a reign of systematic suppression, levelling despotism and brutal violence. In the minor German states the princes, who had recovered from the revolutionary scare, wreaked their vengeance on their foes at home by a series of petty persecutions, without seeing that they were thereby destroying in the hearts of their subjects the last vestiges of that devotion to the dynasties which had hitherto been their chief instrument of power. It is true that in Prussia also the forces of reaction triumphed. The officials of all kinds were subjected to a stricter discipline, and found themselves reduced to the alternative either of resigning or of becoming the docile weapons of the central power. The right of forming societies was practically restricted to those who were friendly to the Government. The press was sedulously gagged and reduced to impotence. The all-powerful police force made its heavy fist felt everywhere, and all too complacent tribunals sanctioned, by audacious interpretations of the law, the most arbitrary actions on the part of the central power.   But the feudalistic and revivalist Right, nevertheless, did not succeed in destroying the parliamentary institutions which had been accepted by the Government, nor in restoring the edifice of social privilege, nor in founding that Christian state of which romanticists dreamt.

On the day following that on which the King of Prussia, thanks to the support of the army, dissolved the National Assembly elected after the March Revolution, and thus re-established by force of arms the sovereign authority which he had at one moment seemed on the point of abdicating, he promulgated a written constitution almost identical with the one he had presented only a short time previously to the National Assembly, and containing the fundamental clauses of the Belgian Constitution.   This constitution satisfied, at least in theory, the chief demands of the Liberal Party ;  it officially proclaimed the liberty of the subject and civil equality, and instituted a representative system in addition to the royal authority.   In short, to the great disgust of the extreme feudalists, it put an end, once for all, to the reign of autocracy, and organised the co-operation of the Crown and the people on a definite system.

It is true that the concessions made by the King were more apparent than real.   The monarch preserved his sovereignty and his entire independence of the Chambers.   The Lower House, held in check by the House of Lords, had no real influence over the Government.   The method of election to the Lower House was such as to secure the preponderating voice to the most highly taxed electors.   Prussia, therefore, did not suddenly become a parliamentary state—she remained an absolute monarchy, on to which had been

more or less badly grafted the chief characteristics
of a constitutional system.  But at least the Crown
had had the wisdom not to profit by its victory in
order completely to overwhelm its foes.  It had had
the good sense to assimilate a large part of the Liberal
programme and institute of its own free will a system
which was on the whole acceptable to the more moderate among the middle classes of Germany.  By these
clever concessions, which did not weaken its influence
or compromise its authority, it succeeded in con-
ciliating the sympathies of an important section of
public opinion, and thus consolidated its power on
a broader and more secure foundation.

With the accession of William to power, first as
Prince Regent and then as King, and, above all, with
the appointment of Bismarck to the post of Prime
Minister, the attitude of the Prussian Throne towards the various political parties became still more
clearly defined.

It proclaimed itself more loftily than ever a monarchy by right divine.  The king possessed, by virtue
of a special grace, the instinct for supreme decisions
which would realise the will of God upon earth.  In
his hands were placed the right and the duty of disposing, in accordance with the dictates of his inspiration, of all the vital forces which together
constituted the strength of the nation.  In Prussia,
the king, according to Bismarck, was not a mere
ornamental accessory of the constitutional edifice ;
he did not only reign—he governed.  After having
been illuminated by the advice of his councillors, he
gave his orders in the plenitude of his sovereignty.
He was free to choose the ministers in whom he
reposed confidence, without Parliament having any
right to impose upon him the councillors whom they

wanted. Upon him, in the last resort, rested the
right of deciding the great questions of armaments,
diplomacy, peace and war, and the ratification of
treaties ; the House had no business to interfere in
these matters over which it possessed no jurisdiction.
And lastly he had the right of supplying all " de-
ficiencies " in the constitution and of ensuring, if
the need arose, the normal working of the State on
his own responsibility alone, and of acting on his own
initiative without the consent of Parliament, in any
case in which the usually necessary agreement
between the will of the king and the House had
failed to be secured.

But the royal will did not draw its inspiration
only from the feudalists of the Right. It acted in
accordance with the sum-total of *all* the national
forces. It was the necessary arbitrator between the
parties who struggled for power, but was the prisoner
of none of them. And Bismarck excelled in discovering this aggregate of the national will.

About 1860 he gauged with marvellous accuracy
the power which the love of monarchy had among
the mass of the people in Prussia. He realised that
the immense majority of the nation, sick of political
agitation and little desirous of renewing the attempt
which had failed in 1848, would gladly range itself
behind a master who was capable of satisfying the
fundamental aspirations of the new realistic and
positivist generation and its will to economic and
political power. And thus with admirable certainty
of instinct he determined the bold outlines of his
policy. An imperialist with regard to foreign affairs,
he led Prussia with indefatigable zeal and energy to
the conquest of Germany, and thus succeeded in
contenting both the champions of Prussian expan-

sion and the believers in German unity, as the victory
of Prussia seemed definitely to promise the practical
realisation of the dream of unification.   An upholder
of absolutism at home, he satisfied the loyalty of
the country to the Crown by maintaining the royal
authority intact.   But he also reconciled the capitalist middle class by giving his support to the new
movement towards a system of enterprise, and he
remained sufficiently free from all class prejudice
and from any taint of Conservative doctrinairism to
be able, when the decisive crisis arrived, to appeal
in all sincerity to the support of democratic public
opinion.   In 1866 he brought against the reactionary
federalism of Austria the identical Liberal programme
of 1848, including the convocation of a German
parliament elected by the universal suffrage of the
whole nation, from which Austria was to be excluded.

And whilst the policy of Bismarck was grouping
all the forces of the nation around the Prussian
Throne, it was working at the same time to raise the
might of Prussia to its highest power in every domain.   The *Zollverein*, extended to Hanover and her
*Steuerverein*, was renewed in spite of the intrigues of
Austrian diplomacy, which attempted, after 1850, to
introduce Austria into the Customs Union, and
thereby to snatch away from Prussia the direction
of the economic development of Germany.   The army,
whose inefficiency had been revealed by the crisis
of 1850, was reorganised by the efforts of the Prince
Regent and Roon.   In spite of the violent opposition of Parliament, which was afraid of seeing the
national army, as it had been organised by the
patriots of the War of Independence, transformed
into a body of Prætorian Guards, and which stiffened
its back for foolish and barren resistance, the military

9

forces of Prussia, largely increased and modernised, became an excellently drilled and disciplined weapon of war, kept well in hand by the King, and ready to act at the first signal against any adversary that might be pointed out.  Moreover, the diplomacy of Bismarck was constantly engaged in placing every possible contingency in his favour for the decisive struggle with Austria, which he foresaw long before it actually took place.  He secured for Prussia the sympathies of the Muscovite Empire by remaining neutral during the Crimean War, and by consenting in 1863, to help the Tsar in his bloody suppression of the Polish insurrection.  He broke with the traditions of the Holy Alliance and with Legitimist prejudices by trying to put himself on good terms with Napoleon III. through negotiating an alliance with revolutionary Italy.  In short, he managed with marvellous dexterity to plot the necessary war with Austria, to ensure its birth at a propitious time, and at the psychological moment to force the hands both of Austrian statesmen, who could not be ignorant of the perils of the venture, and of King William, who was reluctant to engage in a fratricidal struggle.

Nevertheless, it was on the field of Königgrätz that Prussia for the first time proved in the most brilliant manner the superiority of her power.  The decisive step towards unity was taken there.  The old dualism was abolished by the defeat of Austria, who was wiped out of Germany, and thenceforward ceased to hold the influence of Prussia in check. Prussia, reinforced by the accession of Hanover, Nassau, Hesse-Cassel, Frankfort, and the Duchies of the Elbe, definitely grouped the minor states north of the Main around her, under the title of the Northern

Confederation.  A constitution, which ingeniously reconciled the claims of unity and particularism, which
preserved the independence of the princes whilst it
secured the undeniable supremacy of the King of
Prussia and the close cohesion of the whole country
in the face of the foreigner, bound the states together
by a solid tie without suppressing their individuality
or enslaving them, at all events openly, to Prussia.
And the latter, owing to her size, and thanks to the
glory of victory, found herself in the first place in
the position to dominate the Confederation of the
North.  Moreover, she exercised an irresistible power
of attraction over the states situated south of the
Main, who were destined to form the Confederation
of the South, and who already found themselves
bound to the Confederation of the North by the
material tie of the *Zollverein*.  The Customs Union
between these two groups in Germany prepared the
way for their political unity.  It only required the
princes of the Southern Confederation to be represented in the *Bundesrat* and for the Customs Parliament, which every year united the delegates of the
South with those of the North for the discussion of
indirect taxation, to extend its functions to the
domain of politics and legislation, for the German
Empire to be realised.  As early as 1867 Bismarck
asserted in the Reichstag : " From the day that the
Confederation of the South becomes a reality and
only two national parliaments meet in Germany, no
human power will be able to prevent their joining
any more than the waters of the Red Sea could
have remained divided after the crossing of the
hosts of Israel."

.     .     .     .     .

The war of 1870, by uniting the whole of Germany

in a paroxysm of hatred against the hereditary foe, put the finishing touches to the work of unification, which had remained incomplete in 1866, and gave birth to the German Empire.

The causes of this war are still very obscure. It is impossible, even to-day, to tell with absolute certainty the exact intentions of the leading statesmen either on the French or the German side.

At all events it is in the first place certain that France, generally speaking, did not want war. The myth, upheld by Bismarck and afterwards repeated *ad nauseam* by official historians, of a bellicose and vindictive France who had long been brooding an invasion, and who, in the belief that her forces were superior, would suddenly have attacked peace-loving and unsuspecting Germany under the most frivolous of pretexts, cannot hold water.

As a matter of fact, the soul of France was torn in two by conflicting sentiments. At heart no one *wanted* war. The Emperor, who was a phlegmatic fatalist, had faith in the wisdom of the nations, and believed in the gradual pacification of all men's minds. His advisers—the most clear-sighted at least—could not shut their eyes to the possibility of a struggle with the victors of Sadowa. The middle classes, unaccustomed to warlike virtues and the spirit of sacrifice, dominated by the love of comfort and luxury, in their positivist materialism hated the barbarism of bloody conflicts between one nation and another, and gladly plumed themselves on possessing a generous though vague humanitarian idealism. And lastly the great majority of the people was as peaceably inclined as the middle classes, and nourished no violent animosity against neighbours of whom it knew next to nothing. But, on the other

hand, France could not disguise the fact that after
Sadowa all national security was at an end, and that
the birth of a bold and ambitious military power
upon her eastern frontier was a serious menace to
her tranquillity and to her position in Europe. All
this produced a complex state of mind, made up of
surprise, irritation, and anxiety. The friends of the
Imperial Government passionately desired some
foreign victory, which would to a certain extent
counterbalance in the eyes of public opinion the
enormous advantages gained by Prussia. The representatives of the middle classes—men like Thiers—
pointed out, not without some anxiety, the danger
to France of the growth of Prussia, and bitterly
denounced the mistake made by French diplomacy
in allowing German unity to come into existence
without securing any compensation for its own
country. They were angry with Prussia and with
Bismarck for having " deceived " France, and they
contemplated the possibility of war without believing
in it. They even talked of military preparations.
But the middle classes, whilst they refused to accept
the situation and consent to the renunciations which
the position of affairs inevitably entailed upon Frenchmen, were also not willing to resign themselves to the
sacrifices which would have been required if France
had really meant to fight. And the Government,
who demanded a thorough reorganisation of the
army, did not, on the other hand, possess sufficient
energy to impose it forcibly upon a public opinion
that was against it. And thus a dangerous spirit of
vacillation sprang up in France, in which the desire
for peace was the chief factor, but in which there
was also a certain element of dull irritation, permeated by vague desires for war, which evaporated

in words and schemes without ever resulting in a practical act or a virile resolution.

The public opinion of Germany was infinitely simpler and more decided. Hatred for the frivolous, vain, and blustering *Welsche*,[1] resentment against the perfidious nation, which in 1815 had only escaped the extermination it deserved, thanks to the ill-timed and cowardly weakness of England and Russia, the desire to win back Alsace, which had been fraudulently snatched away from the German Empire by Louis XIV., were feelings very generally prevalent in Germany, especially in Prussia, and revived periodically, with an elemental force, during the nineteenth century, every time that Germany imagined herself menaced by the ambitions of France. These feelings had much greater consistency and real weight than the superficial Chauvinism, which before 1870 made itself conspicuous in France by its vain boasting and harmless chatter. Germany, moreover, had at her head a man who knew what he wanted, and realised all the advantage he could derive from this hatred of the hereditary foe in order to put the coping-stone to the edifice of German unity.

Did Bismarck in the bottom of his heart share the national prejudice against the hereditary enemy ? It may well be doubted ; and French historians have pointed out that he was at all events free from any taint of romantic Chauvinism, and perhaps better able than the majority of his fellow-countrymen to render justice to the sterling qualities of their race. It is suggested that he even believed in the inevitable necessity of a Franco-German war, and that he

---

[1] A term applied generally to the foreigner by the ancient Teutons, just as the Anglo-Saxons used the word Welsh.—Tr.

worked systematically to hasten its outbreak. The
question as to the exact date on which the necessity
for war became clear in his mind has often been
discussed. Did this happen in 1866, when the indiscreet attempt of France to act as mediator, and
the blustering of the imperial press, unloosed a
unanimous paroxysm of rage throughout the whole
of Germany ? Was the Luxemburg affair a trap
laid for the French Government to push France into
war ? Or did Bismarck only make his decision in
1869, when he realised that Bavaria would never join
the German Confederation peacefully of her own free
will, and that it was necessary to reduce her to
the dilemma of either marching with France against
Germany or with Germany against France ? No one
can tell for certain. But the fact which is beyond
dispute is that sooner or later the hour arrived when
Bismarck was convinced that war was inevitable, as
France would never resign herself to the formation
of a great military power on her frontier, and that
consequently she must not be allowed to choose her
own time, but must be forestalled. Nothing, moreover, would be a better seal for German unity than
blood spilt upon the common field of battle. German unity under the hegemony of Prussia had been
imposed upon Austria and Germany by the war of
1866 ; it only remained to impose it upon the rest
of the world by a national war against France, which
would convince Europe of the power of united
Germany.

From the day that Bismarck realised this necessity he decided upon his plan of action. It was
necessary to hasten the outbreak of war. But it
was also essential to make France the aggressor.
We all know the consummate art with which he

made capital out of the state of exasperation and irritation existing in French public opinion to precipitate France into a war which, in the bottom of her heart, she did not want, and which a little level-headedness might have been enough to ward off. We also know how he forced the Imperial Government into committing the irrevocable mistake of appearing to be the disturber of the public peace, and thus put every semblance of right on his side, while he persuaded his countrymen and the rest of Europe that Germany was the victim of an unjustifiable act of aggression. The war might perhaps have been avoided had the French Government known how to obtain a clear conviction that a pacific spirit was prevalent in the country, and had France remained calm in the presence of the cunning methods whereby her adversary tried to rouse her into action. From this point of view, certainly, the onus of the war rests upon the French nation. But the will that desired it most passionately, that plotted and planned it with a fully conscious cleverness, and which in the end made it inevitable by his " audacious emendations " of the Ems despatch, was without a shadow of doubt Bismarck. And this desire was not due to the arbitrary resolution of personal ambition. Bismarck had the firm conviction that in letting loose the dogs of war he was leading his country to the fulfilment of her divine mission ; he was the incarnation of the will to power of imperial Germany, which impelled her to regain her position in Europe and brought her, after centuries of eclipse and humiliation, to the threshold of a glorious and prosperous future.

When the verdict of war had been pronounced, when for the second time the boldness of the great minister had been crowned with success, and when on January 18, 1871, in the Galerie des Glaces at Versailles, King William had resumed " the throne of the German Empire, which had remained vacant for over sixty years," national unity was once for all secured. It is true that the treaties by which the southern states, like Bavaria, Wurtemberg, and Baden, were in their turn bound to the Confederation of the North proved at first a disappointment to the Liberal believers in unity. They would have liked a radical reconstruction of Germany, and dreamt of a great kingdom with a strong central government. But the " reserved rights " which Bismarck consented to recognise in the southern states were merely harmless, formal concessions made to particularist susceptibilities or prejudices, and were never a real menace to the unity of the nation. The German princes kept up the appearance of a fairly wide autonomy ; but in reality they had lost all effective power for ever. The rivalries which had before paralysed the strength of Germany could never again arise ; they were from that time forward reduced to the level of insignificant provincial bickerings, to which no serious importance could be attached. After the war of 1870 there were no longer any states in Germany, but only provinces. The authority of the Emperor grew stronger and stronger, and the institutions of the Empire were developed on lines favourable to unity. The new Germany founded by Bismarck was not merely a federation of independent states, but a really strong military monarchy hardly less centralised than the other states of Europe.

# CHAPTER IV

## THE GERMAN EMPIRE AND HER FOREIGN POLICY

### I

FORCE had accomplished the task in which free will had failed. Conquered by Prussian bayonets and then led forward to victory under the auspices of Prussia, Germany had succeeded in gaining unity, not by virtue of any spontaneous decision on the part of the nation, but through the indomitable will to power of the Prussian State. But none the less had she attained the goal towards which her hopes had soared for a whole century. The Empire was restored. And from that moment Germany became sincerely desirous of peace. Indeed, it is a remarkable fact, and one entirely to the credit of the nation, that her successes in war did not inspire her with a lust for battle or tempt her to continue the extension of her territory by force of arms. After 1870 neither the people nor their rulers desired fresh wars. They realised that Germany was " satiated," and that she required long years of peace in order to consolidate her conquests, organise her internal affairs, and develop her industry. All classes alike longed for peace.

But the position Germany had won by force of arms could not be maintained unless she commanded the respect of her adversaries by the superiority of her power.

Internal difficulties, it is true, were no longer to be feared. Germans quickly forgave Prussia for having handled them rather roughly in order to lead them to unity. Complaints were, indeed, occasionally heard of Prussian pride and arrogance. But the bitterness which existed here and there and the trifling differences which occasionally arose in no way compromised the feeling of national solidarity. Particularism had been conquered once for all, and was incapable of creating any serious difficulties for the new masters of Germany.

But the opposition on the part of the non-German nations which the victories of Prussia had incorporated in the Empire was more serious. On the east, the Poles continued to prove refractory against every attempt to Teutonise them, and obstinately maintained their nationality in the face of their German masters. In the north, Northern Schleswig remains to this day so irreconcilably Danish, that even after forty years of separation the people have not ceased to protest against an annexation about which, in spite of the stipulations made by the Treaty of Prague, they were never consulted, and which did violence to their national feelings. In the west, Alsace-Lorraine, after having for years asserted her loyalty to defeated France and her hatred for the victors, at last, it is true, ended by bowing to the inevitable. But although to-day she makes no difficulties for Germany from the national and political point of view, she none the less continues to oppose her in matters of culture, and openly proves her determination not to be stripped of her own individuality, but to remain a land of mixed culture—half-French and half-German. Thus, immediately after 1870, and even to-day, there are

a certain number of subjects of the Empire who
submit with more or less resignation to the established state of things, and have never given their
heartfelt adhesion to the verdict of battle which
made them Germans. But it must be remembered
that these cases of opposition, however legitimate
and imposing may have been the causes which
inspired them, remained as a rule fairly passive
and ineffectual. They were too isolated and too
obviously impotent for the nation to take offence
at them.

But if the material and moral unity of the Empire
was an accomplished fact, Germany had provoked
external enmities, which immediately after the war,
it is true, were not very formidable, but which might
become dangerous. The Treaty of Frankfort created
between France and Germany a condition of covert
hostility, which by being indefinitely prolonged, was
destined to inflict a reign of armed peace and mutual
mistrust upon them both.

Germany did not think it necessary to show France
any consideration after her defeat. Convinced that
a war of revenge was inevitable after a short interval,
and that France, as soon as she had renewed her
strength, would reopen the everlasting conflict
against Germany, Bismarck and the military party
had concerned themselves exclusively with the task
of making it impossible for her to do any harm
for a long time to come, and of securing for Germany,
in view of the future war, a favourable strategic
position. Under these circumstances, they did not
hesitate to demand the cession of Alsace-Lorraine,
which they regarded as a military bulwark, the
*glacis* which was indispensable to the security of
Germany, and also a gate of entry which gave them

the power of invading France at any moment. Little did they care for the heartbreaking protestations of public opinion against a stipulation which lacerated the profoundest depths of the French spirit. They placed the interests of their own country before every other consideration. That which force had created, force would surely know how to retain. And thus the worship of force became more deeply rooted than ever in the German mind. It was in this case not merely the expression of that feverish desire for material power in every shape and form, which we have seen was one of the fundamental psychological characteristics of the new era. It was also fortified by the feeling that the international compact which laid the foundations of the German Empire of to-day was never accepted by the enemy save as the expression of an established condition of things. The maintenance of that superior strength upon which her present greatness was based, therefore seemed to Germany a matter of life and death !

Thus the maintenance and development of her military power continued to hold the first place in the mind of Germany. She was persuaded—and carefully cultivated this conviction among the people —that France desired revenge, that she was preparing for it with determination, and that she would take it without a moment's hesitation the instant she felt herself the stronger power. It was therefore imperative for Germany to be, in Bismarck's words, " ever on the watch " and for her to keep " her powder dry and her sword sharp." The more formidable the German army was, the more crushing and indisputable would be her superiority, and the better would peace be assured. Immediately after the war, preparations began to be made for the con-

flict of the future.   A war fund was put in reserve in
the fortress of Spandau to meet the expenses of the
first days of mobilisation.   The principal fortresses
were restored and rebuilt and numberless strategic
fortifications constructed.   Then in 1874 the " sep-
tennarian " military law was passed by the Reichstag,
fixing for seven years the peace footing of the army
and the amount of the military budget.   In 1875
came the law about the *Landwehr*, and in 1887–88
fresh military grants were wrung from Parliament
by means of a dissolution, and by parading before
the country the spectre of an immediate war with
France and Russia.   In 1890 there was the reform
of the artillery, followed in 1892–93 by the successful
establishment of compulsory military service for all,
which increased the peace strength of the army by
over a hundred thousand men, and was made acceptable to the nation by the reduction of the period of
service to two years.   In 1899 a fresh increase in the
army estimates was obtained from the Reichstag by
the Government.   In short, there was an untiring
solicitude to keep alive the military spirit of the
whole nation, classes and masses alike, and to maintain the prestige of the army and of the career of the
soldier.

And these persevering and methodical efforts bore
their fruit.   Preached to the children in school, firmly
implanted in the breasts of the soldiers during their
service in the regiment, carefully fed by numberless
patriotic associations throughout the country, the
cult of the army has few infidels in Germany.   It is
true that the more disagreeable aspects of militarism
have begun to make themselves felt.   Opposition
papers, novels, and plays, to-day attack certain
abuses, denounce the bad treatment meted out to the

soldiers, criticise the aristocratic organisation of the staff of officers, and paint in the blackest colours the artificial and depressing life led by the soldier in time of peace. But these pessimistic opinions are certainly only current in a very restricted circle. The country as a whole remains profoundly attached to the army, and is imbued with the martial spirit which made the greatness of Prussia. It bears without a murmur the heavy weight of its formidable armaments. It regards the maintenance of great military power as an inevitable necessity, which is even beneficial and glorious, and considers all idea of wishing to alleviate this heavy burden as purely illusory.

At the same time as Germany brought all the weapons of pride and good management to bear in order to raise her armaments to the highest pitch of perfection, and ensure her position as the first military power in the world, she also aimed at making her situation in Europe impregnable by a system of alliances which were intended, in the case of war, to secure her a conspicuous superiority over any enemy.

It will be sufficient to recall in a few words the way in which the diplomatic genius of Bismarck succeeded in solving this problem, how he reassured Europe as to the pacific intentions of his country, how he prevented a coalition of the discontented and jealous elements which existed in nearly every nation owing to the sudden elevation of Germany, and how he negotiated first the Treaty of the Three Emperors and the organisation of the Austro-German Alliance (1879), then the Triple Alliance (1883), thus grouping round Germany against Russia on the one side, and France on the other, first Austria, who had been cleverly humoured after Sadowa, and then a little

later on Italy, who found her interests conflicting
with those of France on account of her Mediterranean
policy. And we all know the strong position which
this diplomatic combination won for Germany in
Europe. It can, of course, be pointed out that other
groups also came into being which combined forces
that were almost as strong. The Franco-Russian
Alliance and the more recent Anglo-French understanding were counterweights to the Triple Alliance.
It has even been open to question whether Italy had
not some idea of loosening a little the bonds which
united her to her Teutonic allies. At the Algeciras
Conference Austria alone upheld the pretensions of
Germany against all the Western Powers. And influential organs of the German press have had reason
to complain of the " isolation " of Germany in Europe
and to blame the policy which led to this result.
Nevertheless it must be confessed that the Austro-
German Alliance, even if it is reduced to these two
powers alone, forms an exceedingly impressive body,
and is sufficient to ensure for Germany, in the concert of Europe, an influence which no one will dream
of disputing.

Under these circumstances German public opinion
considers that France has ceased to be a formidable
rival to Germany. Germans regard her as definitely
out-distanced and incapable of ever again being in
a position to reopen the struggle for supremacy
with any chance of success. They consider it proved
that the superhuman effort made by France immediately after the war to create for herself a military
force as strong as that of Germany has failed. The
ever-increasing difference between the population of
France and that of Germany ensures the military
superiority of the latter with ever greater certainty.

Moreover the decrease in the number of marriages and in the birth-rate in France are symptoms of a deep-seated evil, of a dangerous exhaustion, which deprives her of all chance of regaining lost ground. And it is also admitted, on the other hand, that the Russian Alliance and the understanding with England have not modified the situation in her favour. These alliances, in which France is obliged to be satisfied with the minor rôle in relation to the more enterprising and "expansive" Powers with whom she has allied herself, have at present brought her no nearer to the goal at which she is aiming—that continental revenge for which we are assured she has never ceased to hope. Russia has gained considerable financial advantages from her alliance with France. But none the less has she continued to follow an entirely independent international policy, and has apparently put off to some dim future all idea of a Franco-Russian crusade against Germany. As for England, she would like nothing better than to set Germany and France by the ears as she did Japan and Russia, and the Anglo-French understanding almost involved France in a war in which, on the Continent, her armies would have found themselves alone in the field against the forces of Germany. This is a combination which has had but small advantages for France. And the Morocco business has just proved—in the eyes of certain German publicists—that if France was obliged some time ago to renounce all idea of acting as a counterweight to the military power of Germany, she must in the future also give up all hope of kindling a coalition war against Germany, and of destroying her legitimate power by the menace of a Franco-Russian or a Franco-Anglo-Russian Alliance.

10

We cannot hide from ourselves the fact that conservative Germany regards France with a suspicion
tinged with contempt.  She is looked upon as infected to the marrow with the poison of revolution,
given over to the hands of Jacobins and Socialists,
condemned to inefficient government and chaotic
administration, diseased even in her living institutions
and in her military power, to which the internationalist and anti-militaristic propaganda is such a grave
menace.  She is considered a nation undermined by
decadence, whose vitality is too low to allow of her
entering boldly into international politics, and who
is gradually falling to the position of a second-rate
Power.  Too vain to confess her weakness and too
impulsive to know how to consent to the necessary
renunciations, France remains in spite of everything
capable of sudden outbursts of violence, because at
heart she is uneasy and not quite mistress of herself.
People still believe that an ardent desire for revenge,
the aspiration to the hegemony of Europe, and lastly
the lust of conquest—the only one of the old traditions of French policy which has survived under the
Third Republic—still inspire her acts to-day.  And,
under these circumstances, the foreigner's attitude towards France is one of watchfulness.  German public
opinion is periodically filled with the suspicion that
she is nourishing designs of invasion, and is constantly
interpreting—or pretending to interpret—as warlike
designs or as calculated insults any efforts made by
her to free herself from the position of restraint and
dependence in which she was placed immediately
after the war, and to secure her own safety, as others
have done, by increased armaments and diplomatic
machinations.  And Germany on her side sometimes
arouses in the hearts of Frenchmen, by the stiff-

ness of her attitude and the ostentatious display
of her forces, the suspicion—unjustifiable perhaps—
that her intentions may possibly be less pacific than
she declares, and that she would not be sorry to repeat against France the manœuvre in which Bismarck
succeeded so well in 1870.

This is not the place in which to discuss this
" legend " about France which is current in an
important section of public opinion in Germany.   Is
France undergoing a process of social *decomposition*,
or is she simply in the midst of a *transformation* ?
Does the French democracy, which is so resolutely
pacifist, really dream of any act of *aggression* against
Germany, carried out with the object of winning back
her lost provinces by force ?   Or is it not rather
Germany who is haunted by the suspicion that
France is spending her whole time in planning a war
of revenge ?   These are questions which it seems to
me useless to discuss here.   I will confine myself to
pointing out that although intellectual and artistic
intercourse between the two nations is more active
than ever, though great progress has been made
towards a closer understanding, which all regard as
in the highest degree rational and desirable, and
though on both sides people are learning to know
and respect each other better, yet, ever since the
peace of Frankfort, there has existed between France
and Germany a certain mutual mistrust difficult to
eradicate, which is ever ready to spring once more
into existence.

Just as in the domain of economics the unchaining
of universal competition everywhere gave rise to a
vague feeling of discomfort, that profound sentiment
of insecurity which hovers over the whole of modern
existence, so too in the life of nations the intense

development of the will to power and of " nationalistic " or " imperialistic " policy has resulted in the
pessimistic conviction that brute force is the only
arbitrator between countries, and that the weak are
always exposed to the danger of being violated by
the strong.　Hence arose the passionate desire to be
strong at all costs, and to push to its most extreme
limits the offensive and defensive strength of the
nation.　It was, beyond a doubt, the experiences of
1870—corroborated and confirmed, moreover, by
many other episodes in contemporary history—
which inclined the mind of France, as well as that
of Germany, to this way of thinking.　To what
extent is this attitude justified by the nature of
things themselves ?　To what point is it necessary for an increasingly large proportion of national
energy to be expended with the sole object of
securing a country against the brutal aggression
of a powerful neighbour ?　Will the efforts of the
pacifists succeed in creating an international code of
morality which will make armed conflicts between
nations an impossibility ?　These are questions
which with painful insistency demand an answer from
the man of to-day.　German public opinion, by an
overwhelming majority, has decided that they are
still very far from being solved.　Germany remains,
as we have seen, faithful to the cult of the army,
proud of her power, and determined not to allow it
to decline.　Even among the mass of Socialists the
feeling of the international solidarity of the masses
has not seriously undermined the patriotic spirit.
More than ever does united Germany stand erect
upon the threshold of the new century as an admirably organised will to power, which is quite determined not to go in for disarmament.

## II

Nevertheless, the ambition of Germany no longer aims entirely at asserting her power, in the midst of Europe in arms, by the superiority of her military organisation and the solidity of her alliances. She has no longer an exclusively *European* policy—she has also a *universal* one. The idea of German imperialism underwent, during the last stage of the national evolution, a fresh extension, which we must now describe in all its bearings.

In the first place, the present German Empire does not consist of *Germany*. It is—and German historians are quite willing to acknowledge it—an incomplete and doubtless provisional solution of the German question. " Germany " extends to every region in which the German language is supreme and German culture flourishes. On every side she overflows the boundaries of the Empire. Cisleithanian Austria contained in 1900 a sum-total of 9,171,000 Germans—that is to say, 36 per cent. of the whole population—who energetically preserve their nationality, their language, their culture, and their dominating influence, and are engaged in a bitter struggle for territory—especially in Bohemia—with the Slav majority among whom they live, and endeavour by every possible means to establish their superiority. Trans-Leithanian Austria, in spite of the desperate struggle of the Magyars against the Teutonic element, still contains 2,135,000 Germans—that is to say, 33·3 per cent. of the whole population—who keep their footing with tenacity, or even gain ground, as in Croatia and Slavonia, where the German population has more than quadrupled during the last fifty years. To the east " Greater Germany " claims the 250,000

Germans who constitute the rich cultured minority
in the Baltic provinces of Russia. To the south she
embraces German Switzerland, though here apparently the Teutonic element has undergone a slight
decrease in comparison with the *Welsche* population.[1] On the west she includes Holland and
Flemish Belgium, with their large German colonies
(32,000 in Holland, 68,000 in Belgium and Luxemburg). In these two countries of Teutonic extraction,
whose commercial relations with Germany grow more
active every day, an independent culture has sprung
up in opposition to the French culture, which must
necessarily renew the traditional bonds which once
bound them to Teutonic civilisation.

Then, in addition to the countries in which the
Teutonic element has flourished for a long time, and
in more or less compact masses, ideal Germany also
contains all Germans who have left their native land
either with or without the intention of returning ;
soldiers who offered their services to foreign masters,
Catholic and Protestant missionaries, Asiatic and
African explorers, and above all emigrants who,
driven out by poverty or by a spirit of adventure,
go to seek their fortunes across the seas. All these
Germans, whom destiny has planted in every corner
of the globe, form also a very appreciable element in
the power of Germany.

The increase in emigration, especially since 1830,
is well known. It is estimated that at least 5
million Germans left the mother country during the
nineteenth century, and that chiefly during the ten
years from 1881 to 1890 (1·3 millions). Thus large
numbers of German colonies have come into existence,
the most important of which is that in the United

[1] See note on p. 134.

States.  According to statistics, there are 25 million Americans of German extraction, and 10 to 12 million whose German origin is more clearly marked, either by the fact that they have German parents or that they have preserved, in their customs and their culture, some tie with the mother country.  And this imposing colony—there are almost as many Germans in the United States as in Austria—would be an asset of the highest importance for Teutonic power were it not that the German element allows itself to be assimilated with such facility, and loses its racial characteristics in the second and third and sometimes even in the first generation.

In South America the emigrants, who are far less numerous than in the United States—their numbers have not quite reached half a million—have on the contrary preserved their national character better. Important establishments are to be found in Chili, in Bolivia, in Buenos Ayres, and above all in Brazil, where, in the state of Rio Grande do Sul especially, a flourishing colony of almost 200,000 people has sprung up—that is to say, about half the entire German population of Brazil.  In Australia the German colonies seem destined, as in the United States, to become rapidly absorbed by the Anglo-Saxon element.  On the other hand, the German colonies which have emigrated eastwards in the direction of Turkish and Russian possessions, or which have penetrated as far as the Caucasus, Turkestan, and Siberia on the one side, and Palestine on the other, seem to have preserved their racial characteristics better and are likely to develop and prosper.  The same may be said of the other German centres in Asia (especially in the Dutch colonies) and in Africa, where—above all in the Cape—the German

element is exceedingly strong, and may one day be
called upon to play a very important part in spite
of the recent defeat of the Boers. Lastly, in order
to complete this enumeration of the forces of
Teutonism, we must include the crowds of Germans
scattered throughout the countries of Europe, especially in France (87,000), in England (53,000), in Italy
(11,000), in Denmark (35,000), in Scandinavia,
Servia, Bulgaria, Roumania, Turkey, etc.

At the end of the nineteenth century the sum-total
of Germans resident in Europe was estimated at
76½ millions, to which must be added 12 million
Germans settled in other parts of the world—that is
to say, over 10 million in the United States, 400,000
in North America, 18,000 in Central America, a few
less than 500,000 in South America, 623,000 in Africa,
110,000 in Australasia, and 88,000 in Asia.

We have now completed the enumeration of the
living forces of Teutonism outside the Empire. But
Germany does not confine herself to sending forth
her people all over the world : her capital also seeks
for good investments abroad. In proportion as she
has become an exporting country and has increased
her industry and developed her maritime trade,[1] her
material interests abroad have grown to considerable
proportions.

In Central Europe Italy is the chief country to

[1] The German mercantile marine has, as we know, developed
since the foundation of the Empire to an extraordinary degree.
Statistics show that its transport capacity has trebled since 1871
and doubled since 1880. It does not only trade between German
ports or between German and foreign ports : it has been calculated that in 1901 out of 53·9 million tons of goods carried by
the German marine, 3·3 million tons went from one German port
to another, 12·4 million from a German to a foreign port or *vice
versâ*, 38·1 million from one foreign port to another.

see her industry being developed, thanks to German capital. In the East the influence of Germany makes itself felt principally in Turkey. The relations between these two countries, which have been very cordial ever since the Russo-Turkish War, were still more firmly cemented in 1882 when the military mission under Von der Golz and Rüstow-Pacha undertook the reform of the Ottoman army. Soon Turkey became a regular happy hunting-ground for German merchants, bankers, and engineers. German finance gradually became mistress of the chief railways of the Ottoman Empire. And by a bold policy of peaceful penetration, based upon the construction of great railways, German finance is endeavouring to open up Asia Minor and then Mesopotamia, and thus by a great trans-continental railway connect Constantinople with the Persian Gulf.[1] The commercial relations of Germany with the Far East have also become exceedingly active since the *Norddeutscher Lloyd* organised in 1886 a regular service between the German ports and the principal ports of Asia and Australia, and above all from the moment when Germany obtained in 1896 the concession of Tientsin and Han-kow, and in the following year occupied Kiao-chou. And if the influence of German capital is not felt so much in Australia or North America, and if it is not developing in Africa either as much as Pan-German " colonials " would like, it is on the other hand very powerful in South America, especially in Mexico,

[1] German capital built in Asia Minor the lines from Haïdar-Pacha to Eski-Cheïr and Angora, from Eski-Cheïr to Konia, and from Afiaun to Smyrna. Of the Mesopotamian Railway it has as yet only succeeded in building the portion from Konia to Boulgourlou, and is for the time being stopped by the expense incidental to the crossing of the Taurus range.

Guatemala, and Venezuela ; but above all in Southern Brazil, where, as we have already seen, there is a very flourishing German colony.

In 1899 statistics gave 7,000 or 7,500 millions of marks as the sum-total of German capital invested in concerns abroad, and 12,500 to 13,000 millions of marks as the aggregate of German capital invested in foreign securities.

The growth of German industry and the necessity of protecting her interests abroad was inevitably destined to lead the Empire to the gradual formation of a colonial territory.

Germany, it is true, only ventured upon this path very late in the day, and then with great prudence and almost against her will.  Public opinion showed but little enthusiasm for colonial expansion, and Bismarck was of the opinion that the Government could not successfully embark upon an active colonial policy unless it was forced into it by a strong current of national feeling.  Under these circumstances, next to nothing was done to acquire colonies during the ten years following the foundation of the Empire. The Government contented itself with protecting German subjects and German interests abroad.  This it believed it could do quite efficaciously, without proceeding to any annexations of large tracts of land, by confining itself to occupying at most a port or a coaling station, and by putting into practice in favour of its subjects the policy of the " open door."  Now this policy resulted in some disappointments.  Germany found herself involved on several occasions in disagreeable and by no means glorious conflicts with England, the United States, and Spain.  And in the end she was turned out from various places in which she had tried to secure a footing.  The Fiji Islands,

South Africa, and the coast of Somaliland slipped out of her hands altogether ; and her attempts on the north coast of Borneo, on the Sulu Isles, the Caroline Isles, the Pelew Isles, the Marianne Isles, Samoa, Formosa, and the Philippines, only ended in defeat or in moderate success.

About the end of the 'seventies a fresh feeling sprang up in Germany with regard to colonial policy.  A number of powerful societies—of which the principal one was the *Deutsche Kolonialgesellschaft*, whose president was first Prince Hohenlohe, and then the Duke of Mecklenburg—were formed with the object of obtaining colonies for Germany into which she could pour her surplus population and to which emigration would henceforward be directed.  The idea of colonisation and of national expansion was thus one of their principal ambitions.  As a minor object they also hoped—and this afterwards became the chief goal of German colonisation—to secure fresh outlets for German industry and to offer good investments for any available German capital.  During the 'eighties a distinct movement in public opinion could be discerned ; bold traders, courageous pioneers, and enterprising financiers, worked hard to gain and organise some colonies, and, thanks to the intelligent initiative and the persevering push of high finance and commerce, Germany laid the foundations of a colonial empire in Africa on the one side and in the Pacific on the other.

Bismarck, who, on principle, looked with mistrust on any colonial enterprise, and who was above all concerned with preserving the power of Germany intact, was dragged into this movement.  It was impossible for him to refuse his support to schemes which arose in this way, but he only pledged himself with extreme caution. His first idea was to allow the large companies themselves to organise and administer the conquered territories on their own responsibility. The only practical help he promised them was to subsidise the quick steamer service to East Africa and the Pacific. He thus counted on encouraging the commercial expansion of Germany in Africa, the Far East, and in the Australian Archipelago. Circumstances, however, forced him to make this protectorate much more active and effective than he had at first intended. He was driven not only to create a number of maritime mails, and to secure the existence of the young German colonies by means of laborious negotiations with England, but was also obliged to form a Colonial Office in Berlin, and administer the colonies in the name of the Empire, and give them military protection. The task of colonisation, begun without him and almost against his will by private enterprise, thus gradually became a national concern.

Public opinion in high places, moreover, still showed some hesitation with regard to colonial policy. If Bismarck had followed the development of the task of colonisation with growing sympathy, his successor, Chancellor Caprivi, on the contrary, showed himself decidedly hostile. Under the influence of the distaste, prevalent among an important section of the community, for distant enterprises, the Government for some time gave up any active colonial policy, and even showed signs of being inclined to proceed to a sort of liquidation of the past. The Anglo-German Treaty of 1890, which ceded the protectorate of Zanzibar and Pemba to England, in exchange for the little island of Heligoland, marks the profound change which had taken place in official circles with regard to colonial enterprises.

But this system only prevailed for a fairly short period. After the fall of Caprivi, the new Chancellor, Prince Hohenlohe, once more revived the traditions of Bismarck. And from that moment colonial questions have never ceased to grow in importance. They formed an essential part of the imperialistic policy into which Germany has thrown herself ever since the 'nineties, and which we shall describe in greater detail presently. Germany has experienced the difficulties which no colonising power is ever spared. The reclaiming of new countries from barbarism was not accomplished as quickly as hasty speculators hoped. Germany learnt to know what bloody revolutions, military expeditions, and " colonial scandals " meant. But apparently the country is not yet tired of the policy of expansion. The Colonial Minister, Herr Dernburg, said recently, in one of his propagandist speeches, that during twenty-two years Germany, with an average expenditure of 20 millions of marks a year, had increased the value of her colonial empire by 30,000 millions. These were certainly encouraging results full of promise. We do not know, of course, to what extent the future will confirm or disprove the optimistic prophecies of the Colonial Minister. The fact remains that for the time being he is gaining popularity in public opinion, and that, in spite of recent disappointments, Germany shows herself more determined than ever in her desire to maintain, exploit, and if possible extend, the colonial empire she has actually won, or over which her influence is growing.

### III

We are now in a position to give a more detailed description of the new path upon which the Germany of to-day has entered. For a long time her policy had been above all *national*. Taking as her basis the German *State*, she had had as her aim the power and prosperity of this state. She had therefore been above all a *European* nation, chiefly if not exclusively concerned with the European interests of Germany and her position in that continent. Then gradually her policy began to grow *universal* and *imperialistic*. She founded it no longer solely upon the real and concrete German Empire, but on Germans and German interests throughout the world. And she tended to favour German *expansion* in every shape and form in the four quarters of the globe. Imperialistic " Germany " is not confined within the limits of the Empire—she embraces the whole domain of Teutonic interests ; she can be extended to the same limits as those interests, and she is capable of a peaceful development in proportion as the rays of German activity spread not only in German territory, but also abroad. In her conception states are no longer territories with rigidly barricaded frontiers, but rather spheres of influence with ever-varying limits, which become every day more inextricably involved in each other, which penetrate each other mutually, and are constantly being modified according to the development of the activity and industry of a certain race. In other words, the struggle for power no longer takes place only between organised states, and is not only embodied in wars and the conquest of fresh territory. It is incessantly going on between German, American, English, and French " enterprises." It is a never-ending war—no longer a military contest, but an industrial, commercial, and scientific one, whose seat is the whole world, and every spot in which rival interests find themselves face to face.

German imperialism, therefore, does not stop at claiming a dominant position among the Powers of Europe.   It aims at developing German might everywhere and in every shape.   It works hard to tighten the bonds of solidarity between the Germans of the Empire and their brethren abroad, and to develop all the German communities and all the emigrant colonies in foreign lands.   It encourages the outside investment of German capital and takes an interest in the diffusion of German culture in the world by means of schools, science, and books.   Imperialism is, in short, the programme of the system of enterprise applied to politics.

The transition from a national to a universal policy has, however, not been carried out without opposition, and has not even yet been radically accomplished.

The history of the economic policy of Germany shows very distinctly how the change from nationalism to imperialism was brought about, the obstacles with which it met, and the extent to which imperialism in the end succeeded.   The crisis was reached in 1891— the year in which the commercial treaties which were to come into operation in the following year, and bind the contracting parties for twelve years, were negotiated and discussed by public opinion and in the Reichstag.   We all know the important alternative which was then placed before the country.   Did Germany wish to preserve her full autonomy in the matter of the Customs dues and involve herself more deeply in the system of industrial and agricultural protection, and thus progress towards the ideal of a close State which is sufficient unto herself and makes herself as independent as possible of the foreigner ?   Or, on the contrary, after her experience of the protectionist policy carried out since 1878, did she wish to return

to a more liberal standpoint, and, while still granting
to home industries the protection they required, yet
by means of commercial treaties favour the development of international intercourse and the growth of
the German export trade ?

The German Government decided in favour of the
Liberal solution, and that not only for economic
reasons, but also for political considerations—the
desire to cement the friendship between the Powers
forming the Triple Alliance and their satellites, by
means of economic bonds, and also the hope of
gradually opening up the path to a European Customs
Union. Under these circumstances the Government
was supported by the whole of Liberal public opinion,
including even the Socialists, who saw in the abandon-
ment of the Protectionist system an approach to the
ideal of Free Trade, but met with decided opposition on the part of the Conservatives, who imperatively
demanded an effective protection for agriculture,
and showed themselves hostile to the conclusion of
treaties of commerce with countries that exported
corn-stuffs. Thus Germany was divided into two
camps. On the one side were ranged the representatives of capitalistic enterprise, who called for
a policy which would facilitate the development of
international exchange, and thus favour the growth
of industry and commerce. On the other side were
the agrarian Conservatives—the large landed proprietors east of the Elbe—who protested against the
radical transformation of Germany into an industrial
country, as they considered the maintenance of German agriculture an essential condition of national
health and strength, and detested from the bottom
of their hearts the idea of entering upon the perils
of world politics.

As may be seen, it was the very destiny of Germany that was at stake. Was she to carry out to the bitter end the evolution she had already undergone under the influence of the system of enterprise ? Was she resolutely to turn her back upon agriculture in order to take up industry and transform herself into a huge factory, and sacrifice everything to the development of her export trade ? Or, on the contrary, should she have a reaction against the tide which was sweeping her on towards industrialism, subsidise her agriculture by means of protective tariffs, and thus preserve her economic independence and her national character more securely ? These were the vital questions which were fought out between the representatives of industrial capitalism on the one hand and the agricultural feudalists on the other, with the Government as arbitrator between them.

We know the spirit in which the German Government solved the problem. It was manifestly impossible for it to curb the great movement towards industrial expansion which was dragging the country in its wake, or to restore the patriarchal, agricultural, and individualistic Germany of the first half of the nineteenth century. It was at the same time not anxious to throw overboard the Conservatives, who had always furnished the kingdom with its highest civil and military officials, and who represented a social power with which it had no wish to dispense. It also considered that the hour for making a radical decision had not yet struck. Although there was no question of sacrificing German industry to agriculture, it was nevertheless premature to sacrifice agriculture to the development of the export trade. It was therefore necessary to find a

11

*via media* between an imperialistic and a nationalistic policy, which would allow industry and agriculture alike the opportunity of developing in accordance with their strength, and not to pledge the future irrevocably to either alternative. This is the policy which the Imperial Government attempted to put into effect. And in this task it relied chiefly upon the Catholic Centre, which, as we shall see later on, was itself a composite party embracing the representatives of the most diverse political and economic opinions. This party, which was obliged by its constitution to support moderate measures under pain of dissolution, was for this very reason peculiarly qualified to serve as the pivot for a policy of balance and conciliation.

I will confine myself to describing in a few words the most important contemporary events in which this policy of the Imperial Government was carried out.

In the first place, under the Chancellorship of Caprivi, the German Government concluded between 1891 and 1894 a series of commercial treaties with the various Powers of Europe, and thus definitely became involved in a universal policy in spite of the vigorous hostility on the part of the Conservatives. Then from 1894 onwards there were constant discussions about the opening up of a system of canals from the Trave to the Elbe, from Dortmund to the Rhine, and between the Rhine, the Weser, and the Elbe. Though these great schemes were violently opposed by the Conservative Agrarian Party, who saw that they were tantamount to a subsidy to industry, they were strongly supported by the Government in the Reichstag, which ended by giving way on nearly every point to the powerful will of the

Emperor. On the fall of Caprivi (1894), who had always shown himself hostile to the policy of colonisation—the Pan-Germanists have never forgiven him for having said that the greatest evil that could befall him would be the offer of the continent of Africa as a present—a new spirit began to animate German diplomacy. The imperialistic ambitions of Germany began to make themselves ever more distinctly and consciously felt. The extension of Germany as a colonial and worldwide Power in the Far East, in Africa, in Turkey, and in Morocco, took the first place in the mind of William II. In 1896 the Government, by submitting to the Reichstag a scheme for the increase of the navy, showed its desire to give Germany a fleet capable of providing a strong support for this new imperialistic policy. It is well known how public opinion, worked up to enthusiasm by an ardent propaganda in which the Emperor himself played an active part, ended in 1898 by imposing upon Parliament, in spite of its unwillingness in the first instance, the adoption of the schemes demanded by the ministry, and how, ever since, Germany has never ceased from methodically developing her navy, which is to-day one of the strongest in Europe.

Thus by its commercial policy, by its attitude towards the canal question, and the development of the navy, and by its new spirit of solicitude with regard to colonial questions, the Imperial Government has proved its determined desire to favour the universal expansion of Germany. But, on the other hand, it has quite recently, by the establishment of a general customs tariff in 1902, and the renewal of the treaties of commerce in 1904, also shown that it does not intend, on that account, to withdraw its protection from German agriculture. By an increase in the duty on agricultural products and by restrictions with regard to the cattle and meat trade, it has made great concessions to agrarian interests. The new treaties of commerce are, on the whole, a distinct victory for Protection. In a large number of cases the customs barriers separating the various countries of Europe have been materially raised, and in spite of a few slight improvements in the mechanism of commerical relations, the exchange of goods has by this means been made more difficult than it was in the past. At the same time the evolution of Germany towards industrialism, and of Europe towards economic unity and the rational organisation of trade, have been thrown back.

To what extent has the German Government succeeded in its mission of arbitrator ? It is clearly impossible for the historian to give an answer to this question yet. The imperial policy has been the object of violent attacks both by the Agrarian Party and by the representatives of industry, as well as the Liberals. The latter have recently shown themselves exceedingly discontented. Without disputing the economic development of modern Germany, without even denying that the year 1906 was particularly prosperous, and that the national industry was continuing to increase in the most brilliant manner, they yet refuse to admit that the Government has had anything to do with this progress. It was to be laid entirely at the door of the felicitous initiative on the part of capitalists and business men. The Government, according to them, has done nothing to facilitate their task. On the contrary, it has handicapped them by a commercial policy which sacrifices the interests of German labour to those of the agricultural party, and by a too personal foreign policy, which through its ambitious designs and its capricious and blustering behaviour has sown unrest and suspicion everywhere, and has ended by isolating Germany in Europe.

But if the parties of the Left have clearly but little sympathy for a Government which " combines a universal and imperialistic policy with that of the Prussian country squire," their discontent is apparently not shared by the mass of the people. Universal suffrage has just given its verdict in favour of the policy of national expansion favoured by the Government, and has thus proved the Emperor right, in distinction to the " pessimists " (*Schwartzseher*), who decry the " new system." Under these circumstances one is tempted to admit that the imperial will has hitherto succeeded fairly well in unravelling the multifarious tendencies which have come to light in the country, and that the imperialism of contemporary Germany has its roots not only in the ambitious dreams of a single monarch, but in the soaring will to power of the nation itself.

# CHAPTER V

## THE GERMAN EMPIRE AND HER HOME POLICY

### I

IF after the foreign policy of Germany we turn to the consideration of her internal evolution, we find in the first place that the new Empire, from a confederation of nominally autonomous and independent states, is steadily progressing towards unity. It shows itself a vigorous monarchy, in which the real power is placed in the organs of the Central Government —the Emperor, the Chancellor and his Secretaries of State, and the Reichstag. The central power has the supreme control of the army and the navy. It directs foreign policy without the individual states having ever attempted to make use of the legal rights, conferred upon them by the treaties, to exercise any control over the actions of the imperial diplomacy. It has its own revenues, derived from the customs and from certain indirect taxes and monopolies ; and in this way it is no longer obliged to have constant recourse, for the balancing of its budget, to the matricular [1] contributions of the states of the Empire. It has not succeeded in putting its hand upon the railways, which have definitely remained the property of the various individual states. But as Prussia, by

[1] This refers to the " Matricula," which is the list of the con- tributions in men and money, which the several states are bound to furnish to the Empire.—TR.

166

reason of the importance of her own railway system, has gradually acquired an ever-increasing influence, first over the systems of Northern Germany and subsequently over those of the centre and south as well, the Central Government finds itself in a position to exercise considerable control over the administration of the railways and the whole transport policy. It has, moreover, the chief voice in the postal and telegraphic services. The currency and the issue of bank-notes have been made uniform throughout the Empire. Legislation also tends more definitely every day towards being carried out for the Empire as a whole. In short, in all the chief departments of public life, the central power exercises the preponderating influence.

" Germany," says a recent historian of the Empire, " remains a relatively decentralised country, but she has no longer any states—she has only parties." We shall not, therefore, have to occupy our minds in the future as we did in the past with the rivalries between the various sovereigns of Germany. They form a chapter in German history which we may regard as closed. In the foreground of the political life of the nation we now see the conflict between political parties fighting for power. What are these parties ? What do they want ? What influence have they over the existence of the nation ? How and under what conditions does the Emperor exercise his functions of arbitrator between the rival pretensions of these parties ? These are the questions which immediately spring to the mind, and with which I propose to deal in this chapter.

Let me first point out one general characteristic, which stands out clearly when one examines political life in the new Empire : and that is that even the idea of a *party* has undergone, during the last stage in the evolution of Germany, a most remarkable transformation. We have already seen how, towards the middle of the century, political struggles assumed a more and more realistic complexion, and how conflicts of ideas and principles gradually gave place to conflicts of forces. We also saw how, in consequence of the development of capitalistic enterprise, the will to power and the lust for wealth everywhere increased in intensity. Now these tendencies were only accentuated during the last thirty years of the century, and their influence can be traced very clearly in the internal evolution of political parties. In this case also the original idealism gave way to an ever stronger realism.

In the early stages the bond which united the members of a party was above all one of ideas; men fought for the triumph of a principle. The Liberals struggled, in the name of liberty, for the establishment of a constitutional or a republican system, the Socialists for the realisation of the communist or collectivist ideal. The Conservatives defended, under the banner of the principle of authority, the power of the King and the prerogatives of the nobility. But, little by little, parties "socialised" themselves in some way, and became social groups which no longer struggled for some abstract general principle, but for class interests. From the very beginning the Socialist Party had stood for the "Fourth Estate," the proletariat, whose cause it espoused. The Liberal Party gradually became the party of the middle classes, especially of the middle-class capitalists, and supported the interests of German industry and commerce. The Conservative Party included the landed

nobility and the large landed proprietors, and constituted itself the champion of agricultural interests.
In short, one gradually sees the conflict of ideas
giving way to class antagonism. The party tends
to become a syndicate of vested interests. Let us
examine this transformation a little more closely.

## II

The Socialist Party, as is well known, sprang from
the welding of two distinct elements—the intellectual and the popular.

On the one side we see the proletariat rising up
against the conditions of existence imposed upon
it by capitalism, and against the exploitation to
which it was subjected and the hardships which resulted therefrom. From this arose the spontaneous
sporadic revolts, which had no plan or organisation,
in which bands of working men, driven on by hunger
and despair, entered into violent rebellion against
the power which oppressed them, broke machines,
burnt factories, and rifled the houses of the detested
manufacturers. A typical example was the revolt
of the Silesian weavers, immortalised by Hauptmann
in his famous drama, *The Weavers*. On the other
hand, there took place in the educated classes an
intellectual and sentimental revolt against the abuses
of capitalism. Philosophers undertook the task of
criticising modern society, and elaborated systems
destined to make the whole community profit by
the discoveries of science and the improvements in
technical processes. And they saw in communism,
and in a more equitable redistribution of wealth, the
only remedy for the evils of the working classes and
for the colossal injustice which is at the basis of the

social life of to-day. Out of the blending of these two currents Socialism was born. It was necessary for the instinctive and brutal revolt of the masses to become calculated, disciplined, and organised. And it was necessary for the philosophical " Utopia," germinated in the brain of a few idealists and writers, to be spread among the populace. Thus Socialism became the rational organisation of the proletarian forces with the object of a conflict against capitalism.

By very reason of its ancestry, Socialism was from the beginning a Utopian idea. The problem which it faced with the greatest eagerness at this period of its evolution was that of the redistribution of property. And it solved it by the simple process of transferring to the economic and social sphere the political ideal of liberty, equality, and fraternity. Thus Heine, for instance, changed from an ardent political Liberal to a Socialist with views strongly tinged by the doctrines of Saint-Simon, and proclaimed the advent of a " democracy of terrestrial divinities, who would all be equal in their blessedness and sanctity."

But in proportion as Socialism became organised as a doctrine and as a party, it also became more and more practical and positive. It turned from wild speculations upon the ideal " State " to investigate in the first place the problem of production. Its object was from that time forward to organise and regulate the production of wealth in such a way as to secure to the working classes the highest possible amount of security and well-being. With Marx, Socialism turned resolutely and consciously in this direction. It remained " revolutionary " in the sense that it proclaimed the necessity of a radical social upheaval and incited the masses to unite for the conquest of political power. It foresaw, as a result of this conquest, the general expropriation of the capitalists and the centralisation in the hands of the State of all the means of production, which would bring about the advent of a new society " in which the free development of each individual was the necessary condition of the free development of all." But on the other hand, it discouraged any vague dreams about the social organisation of the future, it definitely condemned all recourse to violence, and repudiated Blanqui's doctrine of forcible measures on the part of minorities. It confined itself more and more to the perfectly practical task of the organisation of the masses with the object of a class conflict, and the peaceful conquest of power by means of the verdict of the ballot-box and the propagation of ideas.

And the recent development of Socialism shows us the constant increase in the practical activity of the party. Its attitude was at the beginning purely negative, and the " revolutionary " spirit was everywhere uppermost among its adherents. But in the course of its evolution, it occupied itself more and more with positive reforms, and it may be said that the " opportunist " frame of mind made constant progress in its ranks. The party thus finds itself as a rule balanced between radical and reforming tendencies, without, however, either of them succeeding in stifling the other. The " red " revolutionaries, with their Blanquian and anarchist aims, the anti-parliamentarians, such as Most and Hasselmann, at the beginning of the era of repression, and men like Wildberger, Werner, and Auerbach, after the Socialists had been given back their civic rights, never succeeded in dragging the majority of the party in

their wake. And in the same way the party refused
to give an unqualified submission to " moderates "
like Bernstein, who regarded the hypothesis of a
great social cataclysm as an illusion, cast doubt upon
the theory of revolutionary expropriation, and from
his colossally creative mind advocated the organisation and systematisation of labour from *inside* the
capitalistic form of society, and pointed out how
by schemes of nationalisation, by the progress of
Syndicalism and co-operation, and by improvements
in legislation, the new society is gradually developing
out of the world of to-day.

Thus the Socialist Party is at once a revolutionary
and a reforming body—reforming because it has
always definitely repudiated violence and forcible
measures, and advocated a peaceful and positive
policy ; revolutionary because, in spite of all, it has
kept its faith in a radical transformation of society,
because it has remained hostile to " a state containing
orders of rank " of middle classes and capitalists, such
as it exists to-day, and because it intends to go on
defending the interests of the working classes against
all others. But the sum-total of these two tendencies
shows without a doubt a marked progress in the
direction of reform. Socialism has made its way
into the Reichstag, into several Landtags, and many
municipal bodies. It has entered into alliance with
the middle-class parties in order to secure the triumph
of its candidates. It tends more and more to repudiate all extreme solutions of questions, such as
internationalism, anti-militarism, and general strikes.
It exercises a vigilant control over the application of
the laws for protecting and insuring labour, and
demands the organisation of a scheme of state
insurance against unemployment. If Socialism is

still hesitating between the creed of reform and that
of revolution, if, as Milhaud asserts, " the ideas and
the way of regarding and feeling things tend to group
themselves, as though they were attracted to two
opposite poles, around the conception of organic and
continuous development and that of revolution," it
is none the less clear that the side of reform is gaining
ground every day, and that the activities of the party
are now tending far less towards the planning of a
radical upheaval than towards hastening the gradual
*socialisation* of capitalistic society.

What is the strength of the Socialist Party in Germany ?  It is without doubt considerable.  Bismarck
felt some anxiety about its increase as early as the
'seventies.  He tried to stop it by passing special
laws against Socialists in 1878, by destroying their
organisations, and by hindering their propaganda in
every possible way.  The futility of all these coercive
measures is well known.  The masses continued to
organise in spite of the interference of the police.
And if the Socialist Party lost votes in the elections of
1878 and 1881, it let no time slip by to make itself
more powerful than before.  Ever since the elections
of 1884, when its candidates obtained about 550,000
votes, it found its strength steadily increasing.  In
1902 it secured over 3,000,000 votes, and sent a body
of 79 members to take their seats in the Reichstag.

Nevertheless this triumphal march could not
continue indefinitely.  It is certain, in the first place,
that the electoral successes were not entirely to be
accounted for by the diffusion of the ideas of Marx.
There are not 3,000,000 militant collectivists in the
whole of Germany.  The Socialist Party, as the most
advanced portion of the Opposition, benefited by all
the discontent aroused by the Imperial Government.

It rallied around it not only active Socialists, but the
majority of those who wished to show their hostility
to the " new system " in as forcible a way as possible.
Then, if for a long time the labour movement in Germany confined itself chiefly to the realm of politics,
the proletariat ended by forming a solid organisation in the domain of economics also. In addition
to the political Social Democratic Party powerful
syndicalist organisations have lately come into being.
And these, without doubt, in many respects combine
in action with the political party, though they none
the less constitute to some degree a power which is
up to a certain point a rival. Between syndicalist
and political Socialism controversies have occurred
which, especially recently, have assumed an extremely
acrimonious tone, and have given the impression that
a considerable portion of the proletariat shows a
tendency towards losing interest in political activity
and is inclined to concentrate its efforts upon Syndicalism.

These circumstances explain the defeat of Socialism
in the elections of 1907. This defeat was certainly
a warning to the *party*. The Socialists are paying for
the bitterness of their internal discord, the violence of
their attacks against individuals and of their press
campaigns, and perhaps also for the arrogance they
display towards their opponents of the " reactionary
section " and the contempt which they heap at every
opportunity upon middle-class Liberalism. Their
prestige in the eyes of the country, and above all in
the eyes of the younger members of society, has been
more or less gravely compromised. But if the verdict
of the last elections proved once more that nationalist
and imperialist feeling has preserved its strength in
Germany, it is nevertheless doubtful whether this

implies a reaction against socialistic *ideas* in the country. The nation has shown its disapproval of certain methods and proceedings on the part of the Socialists, but there is nothing to show that the knell has sounded in Germany for the downfall of collectivist doctrines. With the votes of 3,259,000 electors in its favour, Socialism, although it has lost thirty-six seats, remains the most important party numerically —if not in Parliament, at all events in the country.[1]

## III

The Liberal Party, unlike the Socialists, was not at first founded upon a definite class of society. Although it drew its recruits chiefly from the educated and industrial middle classes, and from the working men bordering upon the lower middle class, it also included a fairly large number of nobles. As Liberalism was above all a political *doctrine* it welcomed indiscriminately, regardless of their origin, all those who subscribed to its essential principles. It was only during the period of reaction which followed the Revolution of 1848, from 1850 to 1870, that the antagonism between the Conservative Party, in which the nobility and clergy were grouped, and the Liberal Party became accentuated. The latter from this time forward became exclusively middle-class, and shared the destinies of that section of the community.

Now the middle classes, as we have already seen, underwent, in consequence of the development of

[1] The Centre and the Opposition members received 2,904,000 votes ; the Liberals and Democrats 2,052,000 ; the Conservatives of all shades 1,802,000. Since the redistribution of seats, which was extremely unfavourable for the Socialists, the latter have had on the average one member to every 72,000 electors, whilst the Centre, the Liberals, and the Conservatives have one member to every 22,000, 18,000, and 17,000 voters respectively.

capitalism, an exceedingly grave crisis at the end of
the century. The artisans who clung to the skirts
of the lower middle class sank in the social scale. The
educated middle class also found its influence de-
clining. On the other hand, the representatives of
capitalistic enterprise acquired an ever larger share
of power. The evolution of Liberalism shows us the
reflection of this internal crisis. The artisans, menaced
by the development of capitalism, became more and
more hostile to the principle of unrestricted competition, and ended by swelling the ranks of the Conservative or the Catholic Centre Party. The idealistic and
purely political element in Liberalism began to grow
weaker, and dropped to a subordinate position. It
only maintained its power among a small section of the
middle class who formed the left, progressive, and
democratic wing of the party, both in the north and
south of Germany. This section was opposed both to
Conservatism and to Socialism, and seemed condemned for the moment, in spite of some temporary
successes, to a chiefly negative attitude and a somewhat barren and futile opposition. The bulk of the
party, however, was formed of the representatives of
the system of enterprise, who, after having fought
in the front rank of the cause of German liberty and
unity, are struggling to-day, not so much for any
abstract principles, as for the defence of their economic
interests.

The evolution of this section of the party—the
National Liberal group—is peculiarly instructive and
deserves our attention for a moment. It shows in
a significant way how the party tended to become
the political organ of a social group.

Just after 1848 the representatives of the middle
classes, especially in the Prussian Landtag, were at

once believers in unity, and Liberals, as much from the political as from the economic point of view. The doctrines of Free Trade and unrestricted competition seemed to them merely an extension into the domain of economics, of the great principle of liberty which inspired the whole of their political action. Moreover, until 1866 the political struggle against reaction and against the arbitrary exercise of the royal prerogative occupied the first place in their minds.

In 1867, after the battle of Sadowa, the elections made a clean sweep of the democratic and progressive opposition, and in the place of these advanced elements we find a new party come into being—the National Liberal group, containing renegade progressives, the friends of the Crown Prince, and the representatives of the newly annexed provinces or of the small duchies. The motive power of this section was patriotic faith and enthusiasm for unity. They became the firm supporters of the policy of Bismarck. Their Liberalism, which had gained curiously in wisdom and was ready for every compromise, had become with regard to politics more theoretical than real. On the other hand, it faithfully reflected at this moment the tendencies of the business world, which was in favour of Free Trade, and passed a series of Liberal measures in the domain of economics. During the 'seventies this was the strongest party in the Reichstag.

But in 1878 a decisive crisis occurred in their history. Bismarck, moved by a very sound presentiment with regard to the industrial and agrarian interests of the country, abandoned Free Trade for Protection. And from that moment the National Liberals found themselves face to face with a formidable dilemma. They

12

had to choose the alternative of either remaining
faithful to their principles, and consequently breaking
both with the Government and the business world,
which was being dragged in the wake of the Protectionist reaction, or else denying their faith of economic
Liberalism as they had denied—or almost denied—
their political Liberalism, and thus throwing overboard
the fundamental principle in the name of which they
had in the beginning formed themselves into a group.
Under these circumstances a split took place in the
party. The minority remained faithful to their
principles, and in 1880 organised a movement towards
the Left, and held out their hands to the Progressives,
whose importance was thus once more increased.
The majority, on the contrary, followed the evolution
which was dragging the business world in its wake,
and from that moment fell into an ever more complete
dependence upon the representatives of the system
of enterprise. The latter had, since the middle of the
century, and more especially since 1870, gradually
formed innumerable local or professional societies,
and had ended by constituting enormous associations
like the *Zentralverband Deutscher Industrielle* (founded
in 1876), which included about three-quarters of the
industrial workers of Germany, or the *Bund der
Industrielle* (founded in 1900), to which a certain
number of industries belonged which did not consider
themselves adequately represented in the *Zentralverband*. These colossal organisations and the great
employers' syndicates, which possessed very considerable power, naturally aimed at defending the
interests of German industry in official and parliamentary circles. And their influence among the
various parties of the Reichstag, and especially among
the National Liberals, is such that the latter party

has come to be regarded, probably justly, as a sort of political instrument in the hands of the great German industries.

On the whole, therefore, the *political* power of middle-class Liberalism does not seem for the moment to be very great in Germany.    The progressive section has remained faithful to the Liberal *idea*, but inasmuch as it is a party of democratic reform, it is menaced by the rivalry of the Socialistic reformers, who are attracting an ever-increasing following among the working classes.    And it may well be doubted whether Liberalism possesses a sufficiently comprehensive and vital basis in the heart of the nation to enable it to increase or even maintain its power. As for the National Liberals, they have sacrificed their political and economic principles in order to follow the capitalistic middle class they represent. But their future is far from secure.    Whilst the rural populations vote, as a rule, with the large landed proprietors, the working classes, won over by the Socialist propaganda, have emancipated themselves politically from the tutelage of their employers. Consequently the industrial middle class finds its parliamentary power more and more seriously menaced every day.    Moreover, the aristocracy of wealth has for some time past been striving to give to its position in the State some stronger basis than that constituted by a political party.    It aims at exercising a direct influence over the Government, and even over the Emperor himself, and has thus entered into rivalry with the old Conservative and agrarian nobility.

### IV

The Conservative Party was, like the Liberal Party, founded upon an ideal.    In opposition to the principle

of liberty, they upheld that of authority. Against
the doctrine of the sovereignty of the people they
maintained the legitimacy of the royal power and
the sacredness of historical tradition. The political
ideas of Conservatism found expression in the theories
of romanticism, of the historical school, of Savigny
or of Eichhorn, and above all during the reactionary
period in the doctrine of Stahl, who exercised a very
considerable influence over the young Conservatives
of the day. Against the Liberals and Democrats the
Conservatives defended the prerogatives of the King
and the privileges of the nobility. In the face of
rationalistic scepticism they gladly avowed themselves
the champions of religion, whether Catholic or Protestant, and advocated an alliance between the Throne
and the Church. In opposition to the believers in
unity they upheld the cause of particularism, and
showed themselves, especially in Prussia, very hostile
to the absorption of the small states by that great
German nation which roused the enthusiasm of the
National Liberals.

But, from a very early period, the Conservatives
sheltered behind these principles exceedingly positive
ambitions and exceedingly realistic desires. In their
capacity as large landed proprietors, more especially
in Eastern Prussia, they aimed at preserving their
supremacy in the rural districts, at consolidating
their economic power, and consequently at taking in
hand the interests of agriculture. As the accredited
supporters of the monarchy, the feudalists occupied
a very important position in the army, in the higher
Civil Service posts, at Court, and in the immediate
circle of the sovereign. This position they had every
intention of maintaining, and thus preserving for
themselves a practical influence in the State, by which

they set great store.  Regarded from this realistic
point of view, the Conservatives were an aristocratic
body, whose power depended upon a fairly large
following in the country, consisting of peasants,
members of the lower middle class, and artisans.  They
form " a small but powerful party," which stoutly
defends its own economic and social interests, and
even to-day possesses an authority, perhaps justified
if one is to believe certain historians, by its experience
of affairs and its political knowledge, but which at
all events seems out of proportion with its numerical
importance, if not with its wealth and talents.

Forced into opposition for some time by the policy
of Bismarck, who had ceased to share the prejudices
of his feudal friends and did not hesitate, in the
interests of German unity, to put a great strain upon
the dynastic principle, the Conservative Party was
at first hostile to the new order of things.  Bismarck,
in the pursuit of his Liberal German policy, and supported by the National Liberals, was opposed by the
Conservatives in Parliament, in the country, and at
Court, with incredible determination.

Gradually, however, their sound common sense
won the day.  They silenced their dynastic and
particularist prejudices, frankly accepted the accomplished fact, and reconciled themselves to the idea
of national unity.  At the same time the agrarian
crisis, which was beginning to make its power felt,
and directly attacked their interests, induced them
to seek help from the State, and to demand that
agriculture should be protected by a tariff.  Bismarck, on his side, was beginning to grow tired of his
alliance with the Liberals, and considered that by
founding and organising the new German Empire
he had realised the greater part of their programme,

and that, consequently, he had less need of their
support. He became convinced of the economic
and financial necessity for the Empire to abandon
Free Trade and defend by a protective tariff her
agriculture, which was menaced by the competition
of new countries, and her industry, which was in the
process of development.

Under these circumstances a reconciliation was
cemented between the Conservatives and the Chancellor about the end of the 'seventies. The Government engineered a change of front, and looked for its
majority no longer among the Liberals, but in the
Centre Party and the feudalists. The "Black
Syndicate" of the Conservative Parties, backed as a
rule by National Liberals, who had gained in wisdom
and become a little more domesticated, formed the
parliamentary basis of the imperial policy. But
these defenders of the Throne preserved a very independent attitude with regard to the sovereign, and
did not hesitate, when their own interests were at
stake, to oppose him, on occasion, in a very lively
fashion. The obstinate struggles of the Agrarian
Party against the commercial policy of the Chancellor
Caprivi, and against the canal schemes advocated
by the Emperor, are well known. Nevertheless, the
Conservatives, as a rule, in spite of some outbursts
of discontent and temporary estrangements, rallied
wholeheartedly round the new Empire, and became
one of the constant elements in the Government
majorities.

At the same time as the Conservative Party
abandoned its particularist opposition, it also underwent an exceedingly curious modification in a democratic direction. Under the system of universal
suffrage it was clearly impossible for it to dispense

with seeking the favour of the masses without seeing its own power rapidly decline.

Now it attempted to win the masses by various devices. It endeavoured to exploit the hatred against the Jews, which is always smouldering somewhere in the country districts of Germany, and held out its hand to the anti-Semites. It also tried its luck with Christian Socialism, first under Stöcker and Wagner, and afterwards in a more radical form under Naumann. And lastly it above all took under its protection the cause of German agriculture. In 1893 the *Bund der Landwirte* was founded for the defence of the agrarian interests menaced by Caprivi's commercial policy, and this society at the end of the century had 250,000 subscribers, 3,000 delegates, a well-organised press, and a whole army of agitators and speakers at its disposal. This powerful and active association lost no time in securing an altogether preponderating influence in the Conservative Party. It rapidly became an agrarian party, with Christian and anti-Semitic tendencies, and a strongly demagogic bias, little hindered by any scruples of loyalty to the Crown, but ready, on the contrary, to carry on the most violent opposition against the Government if the latter showed the slightest signs of refusing the claims it imperatively demanded.

Thus the Conservative Party developed into the agricultural party, just as the National Liberals had become the industrial party. It tried, more or less successfully, to reconcile its old traditions with the new developments it had undergone. It endeavoured to be at once the aristocratic Court Party and a popular league of agriculturists—out of 250,000 members there are 177,000 small proprietors in the *Bund der Landwirte!* It sometimes pushed its opposition to the imperial policy to such lengths, and especially over the canal question, that the Emperor was obliged to warn it, in a speech he made in September 1894, that if it persisted in such demagogic courses a complete rupture would be the inevitable result.  But on the other hand the right wing of the party reacted vigorously against the Socialistic tendencies which had come to light in certain quarters, and which it considered incompatible with the traditional Conservative position at Court.  Thus the party oscillated between the attitude of docility becoming to loyal defenders of the Throne, and the rebellious behaviour demanded on behalf of agrarian interests.  And the Conservatives—up to the present at all events—have apparently found this double policy a fairly paying one, as it allows them on the one hand to keep their influence at Court and in the army and the higher Civil Service, and at the same time secures their power over the rural populations, whose interests they defend, and whose claims they support.

## V

When we come to the study of religious thought in Germany, we shall examine in greater detail the tendencies of the fourth great political party—the Catholic Centre.  For the moment it is sufficient to point out that this party has not been " socialised " to the same extent as the others.  The tie which binds its members together is not one of common interests, but has remained an ideal principle.  While Socialism forms the party of the people, Liberalism that of the middle classes and of industry, and Conservativism that of the nobility and of agriculture, the Centre is the party of Catholicism. It has, properly speaking, no political and social programme, as it includes members belonging to the most varied social positions—from the great Catholic nobles of Silesia to the industrial population in the Valley of the Rhine. It is therefore obliged by the very force of circumstances, and in order to preserve its unity, to find such lines of policy as shall more or less combine the various class interests of its members.

Perhaps it would be right to agree with Lamprecht in saying that the Centre Party includes all those who, in the various different layers of society, disapprove of the system of capitalistic enterprise and aim at restricting free competition and at substituting a united system based upon Christian principles for the unlimited development of subjectivist individualism characteristic of the new era. This would explain, for instance, the great solicitude which Catholicism has for centuries shown for the Fourth Estate, and its persistent and time-established efforts to solve the social problem in a Christian way. But one is also forced to acknowledge that although the Catholic Centre condemns in general terms the spirit of free enterprise, it is yet difficult to find among its representatives any clear idea as to what that Christian society should be which would cure the evils caused by the inordinate growth of subjectivism. It appears to-day much more in the light of a group of clever opportunists, who show a rare genius for defending the temporal interests of Catholicism, rather than a really idealistic party which is systematically endeavouring to find a Christian solution of the great international, political, and social problems of the moment.

## VI

We are now in a position to sum up the internal evolution of the various parties in Germany. They were, in the beginning, international groups founded upon abstract principles, such as equality, liberty, or authority. Then they became " socialised," each party including a certain class of society to the exclusion of the others—the masses, the middle class, the nobility, and the peasantry. Lastly, they developed into mere syndicates based upon economic interests—the interests of the workers, of industry, and of agriculture. Of course this evolution did not take place in any regular or uniform way. Socialism, for instance, was from the very beginning founded upon a certain social stratum. The Centre, on the other hand, has hardly been " socialised " at all. And none of the parties has altogether renounced the idealistic basis upon which it was first built. But, generally speaking, this evolution of parties in the direction of economic realism is most distinctly undeniable.

And the results of this are not always good. German historians do not hesitate to confess that the intellectual level in the deliberative assemblies was far higher in 1848, or during the period of reaction, than it is in our days. They remark that the debates have become less interesting and less profound, and that the democratic " grand style " of modern assemblies has yet to be discovered. They all agree that the output from the legislative machine is mediocre, and they believe that decadence is to be found throughout the whole of political life. Members attend the meetings of Parliament less and less, and the intellectual worth of the delegates of

universal suffrage grows constantly lower. The
political influence of the representative body of the
nation is consequently on the decline.

" It is almost impossible to believe," writes Sombart, " that the country where a hundred years ago
men like Stein, Hardenberg, Schön, and Thaer made
laws; where during the 'twenties and 'thirties a
Nebenius, a Humboldt, and a List set the tone;
where fifty years ago an assembly like that which
met in St. Paul's Church deliberated over the destinies of the nation; where, only a generation ago,
a Treitschke and a Lassalle hurled their thunderbolts on the political horizon; where scarcely ten
years ago men like Bennigsen, Lasker, Bamberger,
Windhorst, and Reichensberger crossed swords in
Parliament with a Bismarck—it is I repeat, almost
impossible to believe that such a nation could have
fallen into the political decay in which we find ourselves at the end of the century."

What is the reason for this decline in public life ?
The first and foremost is apparently the evolution
made during the nineteenth century towards economic
materialism. " The great ideals," Sombart continues, " which still inspired our fathers and grand-
fathers, have lost their lustre ; the ideal of nationality
ceased to be current coin as soon as the new Empire
had been founded in a powerful access of enthusiasm.
That which we are offered to-day under the name
of nationalism is a feeble copy for which no one can
get up any lasting warmth of feeling. The hollow
phrase but poorly conceals the emptiness within.
And it is the same with the other great political
ideals for which our fathers faced death. Some have
been realised, and the vanity of others has been
recognised. The rising generation only gives a

superior smile when the struggles for political liberty
are mentioned, and the festivals in honour of times
of great enthusiasm are grotesque farces. But the
new political ideal has not yet come into being.
The incredible poverty of our times in the domain
of idealism is revealed by the remarkable fact that
the so-called revolutionary party of the present—the
Social Democratic Party—gets all the equipment of
political formulæ it requires from the arsenal of the
old Liberal Parties. To this day nothing better, in
fact, nothing else, has been offered to the people
than the battle-cry which was re-echoed on the day
the Bastille was taken by assault : ' Liberty, Equality,
Fraternity ! ' "

Discussions on questions of interest have taken the
place of political debates ; and an opportunist indifference to all principle has become prevalent in
Parliament. Men of ideas, who are not so well
endowed for economic and political bargaining, have
been gradually ousted from the assemblies. Legislation and administration have been handed over to
specialists, who fulfil these difficult duties like expert
operators, with as much skill and as little trouble
as possible. Hence that decadence in political life
which numbers of German historians deplore so much
at the present moment.

In the presence of the decline in the influence of
Parliament, it is natural that the power of the Crown
should have preserved a considerable prestige in the
Germany of to-day. This is due in the first place to
the fact that loyalty to the dynasty and respect for
authority are sentiments which are deeply engraved
upon the German mind, and have preserved their
strength even in our democratic age ; and secondly
because Germany has hitherto had at her head

princes who were in some way or other remarkable,
who were filled with a lofty consciousness of their
mission, and derived from a deep and sincere belief
in monarchy the energy and authority necessary to
impose their sovereign will ; and lastly and chiefly
because the Emperor, who is the heir of the " tribu-
nician mission " of the Hohenzollerns, is still the
arbitrator between the parties and the classes who
struggle for power.  It is before the Emperor that,
in the last resort, the interests of the various great
powers that come into conflict in modern Germany
are fought out—from the feudal nobility and the
capitalist middle classes to the lowest strata of the
working proletariat.  It is the person of the Emperor
that the two aristocracies who are struggling for
supremacy—the aristocracy of birth and landed property, and the aristocracy of industry and finance—
are trying to win over to their cause.  And it is the
rivalry between these two parties which has to a
large extent contributed towards consolidating the
power of the Emperor and maintaining the authority
he enjoys to-day.

Will the Emperor be able to play this part much
longer ?  Will he be capable of remaining the
sovereign of the *whole nation*, and escape becoming
the prisoner of one party or one privileged group ?
There is no doubt that a fairly large section of public
opinion in Germany is beginning to show signs of
growing tired of it, and is raising ever louder protestations against the system of personal government, the instability of the " new system," and the
abuses which spring from it.  But it is difficult to
say how much weight these complaints will have, and
to what extent they are indications that Germany
is progressing towards a more democratic system.

It is sufficient at present to say that the royal power does not yet seem to be seriously menaced. It can rely absolutely upon its two chief weapons—the Civil Service and the Army. And the last elections have once again proved the popularity it enjoys among the masses. The defeat of the Socialists, who represented the decided opposition to the system of personal rule, the success of all the parties of the Right, from the Conservatives and the National Liberals to the anti-Semites, and the victory gained by the Government, which from that moment ceased to be at the mercy of a coalition between the Socialists and the Centre, and found its national and universal policy highly approved by the voice of general suffrage, are so many signs that the country, as a whole, is not seriously discontented with the actual state of affairs, and that no radical change in the direction of the internal policy of Germany is to be expected for the time being. The Emperor has been justified in showing his satisfaction at seeing the great majority of the country giving its entire adhesion to his imperialistic policy. And the people loudly applauded the speech in which he borrowed a metaphor from Bismarck, and compared Germany to a good rider who could not only sit firm in his saddle, but was able by the fury of his gallop to " sweep aside " all the adversaries who tried to bar his path.

# CHAPTER VI

## MODERN POLITICAL IDEALISM

### I

IT only remains for us to end our study of political Germany by pointing out certain symptoms which various observers interpret as indications of a profound change which is being prepared in the very depths of the nation's soul.

I have hitherto described the evolution of Germany as essentially a struggle for material power in every shape and form, and as a triumph of the principle of imperialism. But it also seems to have been a struggle for a higher and more complete national *culture*. In fact, it is clear that if in the eighteenth century the State considered its chief task was to organise its offensive and defensive forces, to insure an increase in its population and its wealth, and to guard the security and material well-being of its subjects, the idea of the functions of the State was widened during the nineteenth century. From the beginning of that century German idealism, under the influence of Fichte and Hegel, saw in it " the realisation of the moral idea in an institution," and the organism by means of which a nation raised itself to its highest attainments. And this belief has never ceased since that time to develop and grow stronger.

This has brought two great results in its train.
On the one hand the State has gradually usurped
the place of the Church in the task of organising
and controlling instruction, and it has at the same
time developed educational facilities of all kinds to
enormous proportions.  And on the other hand the
nation thus organised has become more and more
conscious of its responsibility towards all its members.
It has learnt to feel that it is its duty to preserve its
human capital, and especially to protect the humble
and the weak, to defend them against a demoralising
and depressing exploitation, to sustain them in
times of crisis, and to ensure them against the danger
of invalidity.  Thus the progress of public education
and the organisation of social insurance take the first
place among the functions of the State in Germany.

In the first place, the State has been gradually
secularising education.  It has destroyed in this
department the supremacy of the Church, which in
the Middle Ages was the only channel of culture.
From the end of the Middle Ages the universities
began to fall under State control.  Then after the
Reformation a similar fate befell the institutions for
secondary education.  Lastly, in the eighteenth and
nineteenth centuries came the turn of the elementary
schools.  And at the same time as the State took in
hand the organisation of education, it also changed the
very nature of the instruction given.

Formerly the principal mission of the universities
and the Latin schools had been the training of priests
and theologians, and the task of the elementary
schools had been to spread among the people the
elements of religious faith and prepare the children
to follow the Sunday sermon later on.  Now these
educational establishments were gradually stripped of

their ecclesiastical character. The universities became scientific institutions, and the chief place in them to-day is no longer occupied as it once was by theologians, or even, as was the case at the beginning of the nineteenth century, by philosophers or philologists, but by men of science and doctors of medicine. The German public school, a type of institution which came into being at the beginning of the nineteenth century, has no longer anything ecclesiastical about it either. It is entirely impregnated by that classical and neo-Hellenic spirit which spread about that time throughout Germany, and it dispenses an enclyclopædic instruction, including philology and history, mathematics and natural science. And lastly the schools in their turn have detached themselves from the Church, and under the impulse given by Pestalozzi, consciously strive to stimulate their pupils to spontaneity and activity, and to develop in them, in accordance with the ethical doctrines of Kant, the belief in free autonomous personality. And if, even as late as about the middle of the eighteenth century, popular instruction maintained a strictly denominational character, especially in Catholic districts, the elementary schools of the nineteenth century tended more and more, owing to the importance ascribed to the teaching of the German language and German history, to become national schools, in which the cult of the Fatherland was inculcated upon the minds of the children like a second religion.

Nevertheless, the Church still possesses, even to-day, a fairly important influence in Germany, especially in the domain of elementary education. The schools have as a rule remained denominational, and continue to give dogmatic instruction—although it is

13

somewhat paradoxical to see Catholic, Lutheran, and dissenting establishments teaching, *under the patronage of the State*, absolutely contradictory religious truths. They are even subjected, in many cases, to ecclesiastical inspection. It is, indeed, asserted that more and more numerous protestations are being raised against this condition of things. Those who object complain of being forced to see their children taught doctrines which are contrary to their own faith or to their scientific beliefs. In the teaching body, above all, many masters protest against being obliged to give religious instruction in accordance with the tenets of a creed which is at variance with their own deepest convictions. An important section of public opinion demands the immediate institution of *Simultanschulen* which shall include pupils of every denomination. Nevertheless, Germany does not for the moment seem disposed to " dechristianise " the schools. Even free-thinkers, who are not subject to any denominational narrowness, regard the radical secularisation of education in Germany as neither possible nor even desirable. They are convinced that if ever the schools become " atheistic," a large part of the population of the Empire, among the Catholics especially, will leave the State schools and organise private schools in which the children will receive the religious instruction their parents regard as indispensable. And, moreover, many Germans do not consider the " neutral " school of the French type as by any means a model to be copied. Paulsen, one of the most influential and highly esteemed historians of education in Germany, is of the opinion that although Catholic France was obliged to institute a secular and neutral school system for education to be made *national*, this necessity fortunately does not exist in the case of Germans. The very circumstances of their religious history have made them accustomed to reconcile science and religion, knowledge and faith; they have in the Bible a peerless instrument of moral culture, which the finest " chosen extracts from the literature of the world " could not replace. There is consequently nothing to prevent the teachers " from keeping religious instruction and the Bible in their hands," and from moulding the minds of German children by teaching them the elements of a *historic* and *interdenominational* Christianity, shorn of its dogmatic character, and reduced to its moral principles. And I should not be surprised if these conciliatory views of Paulsen were more in harmony with the general opinion of the country than the more radical doctrine which would banish all religious instruction from the schools.

At the same time as public instruction emancipated itself from the Church, it also became more democratic.

Education had from the beginning been the privilege of a caste. There had first of all existed in Germany in the Middle Ages a *clerical* culture; this was followed by a worldly and *aristocratic* culture, from the Renaissance to the eighteenth century, and lastly by a *middle-class* culture, when, with the diffusion of rationalism and neo-Hellenism, the middle classes of Germany took the lead in the intellectual movement. During the nineteenth century a gradual approach was made to the *national* culture preached by Fichte in his *Discourses to the German Nation.*

The barriers between the various kinds of instruction were gradually lowered. Latin ceased to be the language necessary for all high culture, and the grammar school lost more and more of its character

as a " Latin school " of the old order. On the other
hand, the progress made by the elementary schools
brought them constantly nearer to the level of the
secondary schools, and the distinction between the
masters who had been trained in the seminaries
(*Seminarisch gebildet*) and those who had received a
university education (*Akademisch gebildet*) gradually
grew less and less. But above all education in every
rank assumed an ever more realistic and practical
character. The culture of the higher classes of society
was at the end of the eighteenth century chiefly
æsthetic and literary, and the classical education of
the public school at the beginning of the nineteenth
century was of a similar nature. But we have already
seen the evolution towards realism, which took place
among the educated classes in consequence of the
development of the system of enterprise. This evolution was very naturally reflected in the domain of
learning. Instruction in all ranks became less
exclusively literary or philosophical, less confined to
books. In addition to the classical public school,
there came into being the more modern type of
polytechnic and of technical and commercial schools
(*Realgymnasium, Oberrealschule, Realschule, Reform-
gymnasium*), which, by increasing the attention paid
to the teaching of science and living languages, corresponded better with the needs of the middle classes
engaged in trade and commerce. Side by side
with the universities, technical institutes (*Technische
Hochschulen*) everywhere sprang up and grew more
flourishing, and were held in higher esteem every day.
And thus the old distinction which separated the
classical and philological " man of letters " of the past
from the " unlettered " man who had no knowledge
of the classical languages, tended gradually to dis-

appear. Thus the idea of a specifically æsthetic and
philological culture reserved for the intellectual
*élite* alone, little by little gave way to the more
democratic conception of a universal culture, an
infinitely complex and differentiated one it is true,
which nobody was expected to assimilate in its
entirety, and which was not the same for all, but of
which each individual was at liberty to appropriate
whatever he could, according to the measure of his
intellectual or physical abilities.

In short, Germany, during the course of the last
century, worked with untiring energy to dispense
instruction with an ever more liberal hand to all her
children. It is true that her enthusiasm for the task
of education had many ups and downs. It was
exceedingly intense during the first thirty years of the
century, when the foundations for the reorganisation
of public instruction from the elementary schools to
the universities were laid. It cooled down in an
extraordinary way in the course of the second forty
years of the century, when, during the revolutionary
and reactionary era between 1830 and 1870, the
various governments showed themselves suspicious
even to the point of hostility with regard to the task
of public education. But it was rekindled once more
after the great military triumphs of Prussia and the
restoration of the Empire. It is regarded as an
axiom that it was the German teacher who really won
Sadowa and Sedan, and that the victories of Germany
are essentially due to the superiority of her culture.

But it cannot be denied that doubts are again beginning to be felt to-day with regard to the efficacious
virtue of education. In university circles it is possible
to discover symptoms of fatigue here and there, and
a state of mind similar to that which drove certain

thinkers in France to proclaim " the bankruptcy of
science." The melancholy observation is made that
science, from which some complete conception of the
universe was expected, and a general guidance to direct
the will of man, never results in any definite or
absolute truths, but only gives partial and provisional solutions, which are always open to revision
and correction. Many a man feels himself weighed
down by the enormous mass of knowledge which must
be assimilated by any one who wants to be " up to
date " in any particular branch of science, and is
also not a little discouraged by the state of perpetual
*development* and by the endless evolution into which
science is always plunged.

In the ruling class and in certain middle-class
circles also, the pessimistic tendencies which were
prevalent about the middle of the century occasionally
reappear to-day. Men are beginning to wonder
whether the task of popular instruction has not
been carried to inordinate lengths—whether, for
the greater part of the nation, education is not
more a source of danger than of benefit, and whether
people are not infinitely more difficult to govern
when they are half-educated. The anxiety caused
by the recent progress of Socialism may have helped
to spread these doubts in circles which, only a short
time ago, would never for a moment have enter-
tained them, but really believed that the State had
no more pressing duty than to give education on a
liberal scale to all its subjects.

Nevertheless, generally speaking, the average
opinion is, in the words of Paulsen, that "in the
universal struggle for power and pre-eminence,
the superiority will rest with those nations who
have succeeded best in securing for their children

a solid education and culture by means of well-
equipped schools, and by the formation of economi-
cally prosperous and morally healthy families."
The successes attained by Germany are attributed
to the fact that she forestalled other countries by
starting compulsory education early in the day,
and by applying her mind to training excellent
teachers for every branch of instruction. And
the conclusion is drawn that the ignorance of the
masses can never be a guarantee of order and
stability in the State, that the obvious interests
of the monarchy demand an ever wider diffusion
of knowledge, and that the future belongs to those
nations who have solved the problem of national
education most successfully.

## II

At the same time as it pursues an ideal of national
culture, the German State also forms a clearer
conception of the social mission it is called upon
to fulfil.

And, indeed, the development of the system of
free enterprise puts the social question into an
absolutely new form. All the relationships of
personal dependence which formerly existed between
the employer and his men, between the lord and
his peasants, the master and his journeymen and
apprentices, disappeared during the nineteenth century. The labourer no longer *owes* his time, or part
of his time, as he once did, to a master to whom
he is personally subjected. In this respect he is freed
from any sort of obligation. He is at liberty to
*sell* his labour under the best possible conditions,
and no one can force him to accept a contract for

work which he considers unfair or merely disadvantageous. But the worker, in breaking the personal bonds which united him to his master, also at the same time lost the right of being *protected* by him. The modern capitalist who purchases labour has the right to secure this commodity on the conditions most advantageous to himself, and without having to worry his head about ensuring a competency for those he employs when he does not need their services any longer.

Theoretically, the " liberty " of the worker and that of the employer are supposed to balance each other. The one is free not to sell his labour under unfavourable conditions ; the other, on his side, is free not to buy the labour for which too high a price is asked. Thus by the normal interplay of supply and demand the just price of labour should be established in a natural way.

But as a matter of fact the extreme precariousness of labour under the system of free enterprise is well known. It is in the first place exposed without any protection to all kinds of risks—illness, accident, old age, and unemployment—which are constantly weighing down the life of the working man. And, moreover, it is clear that he is very far from being in a position, as a rule, to contest the conditions of his contract with his employer " freely." He is, in the last resort, *obliged* to sell his labour under pain of dying of hunger. And he therefore constantly runs the risk of having disastrous terms dictated to him by an unscrupulous employer who is ready to speculate on his need. A great problem is thus presented to modern society. It has become imperative to organise upon a new basis the protection afforded to workers, which under the patriarchal system, was provided by the lord or the employer. It was necessary to find a remedy for the condition of the labourer by the development of workmen's insurance schemes, and by instituting normal relationships between an employer and his men. The maintenance of public health and national strength and the preservation of social peace depended upon the solution found for this problem.

German public opinion soon recognised the evils produced by the system of free enterprise, and realised the necessity of fighting them. As early as the 'forties there was founded in Berlin an *Association for the Improvement of the Condition of Labourers and Artisans*, which was recruited chiefly from the ranks of those engaged in enterprise, and received a large donation from the King of Prussia, Frederick William IV., himself. About the same time the first signs of Christian Socialism began to appear. Men like Wichern, the founder of the *Home Mission*, on the Protestant side, and the priest Kettler on the Catholic side, drove the Church to descend into the region of practical acts, and preached the fundamental application of Christian morality to social life. Then the political economists in their turn came upon the scene, and in the name of science rose up against the gospel of unrestricted competition and the doctrines of Adam Smith and the Manchester School. During the 'forties the trend of thought afterwards known as " Pulpit Socialism " came into being, and resulted in 1872 in the foundation of the *Social Policy Association*, whose principal members were scientific men like Brentano and Nasse, Schmoller and Schœnberg.

Thus, whilst the Socialists looked for the cure of all the evils from which the masses were suffering to the conquest of power by the democracy and a radical upheaval of the social order, a constantly growing group, consisting of members of the capitalist middle classes, Protestant and Catholic Christians, and political economists, supported, on their side, a gradual reform of the obvious and undeniable abuses of the capitalistic system. Among these reformers some saw in the Church and Christian principles the chief power capable of regenerating modern society. Others preferred to pin their faith upon the State to put an end to the oppression and degradation of the lower classes. The part the latter played in the evolution of Germany is very important. The Prussian State, and afterwards the German Empire, as we shall see, has to a large extent adopted their programme and gone far enough along the path of State Socialism.

But it must also be admitted that, although the Government has given at least partial satisfaction to certain Socialist demands, it remains invariably hostile to the tendencies of the Democratic Socialist Party. It is true that it is perfectly conscious of the duties it owes to the working classes. Bismarck, for instance, declared in the Reichstag that he accepted, without hesitation, the Socialistic doctrine of the *right to work*. He found this idea in embryo in the federal legislation. One of the principles of the Prussian *Landrecht* was that it was unlawful for any one in the kingdom to be reduced to death by starvation. There was, consequently, no reason why the modern German Empire should refuse workers the protection which had been afforded them by the old Prussian monarchy. On the contrary, stern duty called it to take an interest in their fate and to bind them to it by material benefits. On the other hand, however, the Government would not on any account tolerate the social upheaval of which the followers of Marx dreamt. It opposed every effort on the part of the democracy and its adherents to take in hand the direction of public affairs, and defended the prerogatives of the Crown against them with the greatest energy. It vigorously opposed all revolutionary or even merely republican tendencies. In short, the German State was by no means in subjection to the capitalist middle classes, but meant to play the part of a loyal arbitrator between employers and employed. But if it was determined to put a curb upon the absolute power of the masters, it did not, on the other hand, tolerate any attempts on the part of the workers to bring pressure to bear upon it or to dictate their own terms.

The workers, on their side, had but a very limited confidence in the feudalistic, capitalist, and middle-class State, and they were impatient of being held in tutelage by it. They suspected it of partiality and weakness towards employers, and regarded it less as a just arbitrator than as an ally of their adversaries. Just as there existed in the heart of the Government a mixture of sympathy and suspicion with regard to the working classes, there was noticeable among the workers a deep-seated mistrust of the capitalistic State. And it was not astonishing if, under these circumstances, the work of social reform advanced with a somewhat uneven and capricious pace.

Until the end of the 'seventies, and as long as Bismarck relied chiefly upon the National Liberals for support, his economic policy was, very naturally, also " Liberal." The State did not, so to speak, intervene in order to restrict free competition. The Chancellor, it is true, felt " that there was much to be done for the working man," and he endeavoured to get enlightenment with regard to the social question from all quarters, and drew his information as much from Wagener, the sociologist of the parties of the Right, as from Lassalle, Rodbertus, and Dühring, or the Pulpit Socialists. But for the time being he limited all positive action to a few discreet attempts to organise co-operative schemes of production, and to a few measures for the protection of the working man, which were of no great significance or any real effective power.

But in 1878, after the attempts made by Hœdel and Nobiling upon the life of the Emperor William, Bismarck took in hand the task of fighting the dangerous progress of the Socialist Party by means of drastic measures, and applied his mind to the severe repression of the impetus towards emancipation which was beginning to manifest itself among the masses. And, moreover, he also inaugurated at precisely the same moment a social policy of a perfectly fresh kind. In short, he completely realised that the solution of the social question required something more than coercion, and that positive benefits were needed. And it was for this reason that at the same time as he suppressed " Socialist excesses " with the severity which is familiar to all, he also endeavoured to " improve the condition of the working man by substantial concessions." He perceived quite clearly the grave evils which unrestricted competition entailed for the masses, and he considered that the State ought to give such help and protection to the workers as it could safely do without injuring the great industries

or placing too heavy a burden upon them. " We
wish to create the greatest possible contentment,"
said the Chancellor. And to this he added, with
an eye to the eventuality which might necessitate
a bloody suppression of revolutionary intrigues :
" I say this in case we have to come to blows."

From this moment an era of social reform was inaugurated for Germany. Bismarck now relied chiefly
upon the Conservatives, who for a long time past
had shown a disposition to criticise the industrialism
of the towns, and were quite ready to support a
policy which set itself the task of destroying the
abuses of the capitalistic system. He was, moreover, supported in this object by the Catholic Party,
who, ever since the middle of the century, had felt
the necessity of reforming society in accordance
with the principles of Christian morality. With the
help of this majority, which was increased by the
adherence of a few powerful industrialists, like Baron
von Stumm, who wished for the re-establishment of
patriarchal relations between masters and men, the
Chancellor undertook the task of laying the foundations of the great scheme of workmen's protection
with which he desired to endow the country. And
after years of struggle he succeeded at last in securing
the triumph of his ideas. Under his initiative, and
thanks to his tenacious will, the great laws of social
insurance of which Germany is justly proud to-day
—insurance against sickness and against accident,
invalidity and old age pensions—were drawn up and
forced upon the acceptance of the Emperor, the
Federal Council, and Parliament. It is true that
from the lack of sufficient resources he was not able
to carry out the work on as ample a scale as he had
intended. He was refused a monopoly in tobacco,

which would have formed the "patrimony of the
disinherited," and would have allowed him to dispense succour and pensions to the masses of Germany
with a less niggardly hand.  But even as it is, and
in spite of its imperfections, the system of workmen's
insurance in Germany is an exceedingly impressive
monument, and forms one of the most lasting titles
to glory of the great Chancellor.

Thus the German workman found himself insured
against some of the greatest risks which the development of the system of capitalistic enterprise brought
in its train.  On the other hand, hardly anything
had been accomplished in the direction of protecting
labour.  The right of forming societies and the right
to go out on strike were badly secured.  Women and
children, in the absence of sufficient regulations for
work, were exposed to the most ruthless exploitation.  Arbitration was not regularly organised.  The
inspection of work remained almost an illusion, owing
to the limited number of inspectors and the inefficacy
of the control they were allowed to exercise.  Nothing
was done to improve this state of things.  Every
scheme of reform came up against the passive resistance of Bismarck.  In fact, the Chancellor did not
wish to enter upon this path systematically.  He
admitted that the insurance laws, by bringing into
being a host of people with small independent means,
put the working classes under the protection and
in the power of the State.  He hoped, on the other
hand, to attach the class of contractors to his cause
by refraining from passing too rigorous measures for
the protection of labour, and by thus leaving the
former free to organise industrial work to the best
advantage for themselves.  Thus the employers and
the men alike found themselves in a position of

dependence upon the State. But Bismarck regarded this as a good thing. In case the working classes ever showed any indiscreet desire to free themselves from this control, there always remained the possibility of having recourse to military measures of repression to keep them in the path of duty.

The check which this over-clever policy of balance received is well known. The working classes never for a single moment felt inspired by any affection for the State. They accepted as their due the pensions and compensations which the insurance laws gave them. But they did not feel the smallest gratitude towards the statesman who presumed to keep the masses under control because he had conferred material benefits upon them, denied them the right of organising, and persecuted the trade unions. Bismarck's calculations accordingly did not work out as he had expected. Arrested for a moment in its ascent by the police regulations made after the assassination attempts of 1878, Socialism, during the course of the 'eighties, once more resumed its upward march.

In 1890 a new era of social reform was inaugurated. The repeal of the law against Socialists, the appointment of Herr von Berlepsch to the Board of Trade, the famous rescripts of William II., the convocation at Berlin of an international commission to prepare the ground for a European understanding on matters connected with the protection of labour, and the resignation of Bismarck, marked the beginning of it. The organisation of arbitration tribunals for the settlement of disputes between employers and their men, and the law securing a holiday once a week, were the principal results of this movement. But, in spite of opening well, it did not take long to grow slack. It soon became evident that the representatives of capitalistic enterprise were strong enough to make most of the proposed reforms miscarry. The Conservatives, who were for the moment thrown into opposition under the government of the Chancellor Caprivi, showed themselves just as hostile to the schemes for protecting labour as the Liberals and Progressives who defended the interests of capitalism. Reactionary influence gained the upper hand more and more in the immediate circle of the sovereign. The war against Socialistic tendencies was renewed. A law proposed against revolutionary intrigues (*Umsturzvorlage*) aroused the greatest anxiety in Liberal circles. The attacks against the Pulpit Socialists were redoubled in intensity. The social agitation in the ranks of Protestantism was stopped by a rescript of the Supreme Evangelical Council (December 16, 1895). A sensational telegram from the Emperor declared that the " Christian Social " movement was nonsense, and that the clergy should cultivate charity and abstain from politics, of which they understood nothing. And at last, in June 1896, the reform minister, Herr von Berlepsch, sent in his resignation.

Yet the movement in favour of social reform was not dead in the country. In spite of the disapproval of the Emperor, Christian Socialism, in the first place, spread further and further. On the Protestant side it detached itself from the Conservative Party and assumed a complexion more nearly approaching to Socialism, especially in the case of the pastor Naumann and the group of thinking men who followed him. On the Catholic side, also, social propaganda became more active and more practical, in spite of the occasionally sharp dissensions which took place among the promoters of the movement. Statistics show that in 1906 evangelical workmen's associations contained about 80,000 members, the specifically Catholic associations about 81,000, and the inter-denominational Christian workmen's syndicates, whose membership increased with marvellous rapidity, numbered altogether at least 250,000 adherents.

And this current of social idealism was not only found in religious circles. It seems to have gained ground in all directions. It spread more and more among the representatives of enterprise, whose solicitude for the welfare and protection of the working man grew ever more active. In scientific and artistic circles questions of social hygiene, the problem of cheap housing, and that of popular education and democratic art, were studied and discussed with renewed ardour. The municipal councils of the large towns gave particular attention to any measures which might better the condition of workers, from the construction of workmen's dwellings to the building of public libraries and the laying out of public gardens. In Parliament, also, a few new measures for the protection and insurance of labour have been discussed or passed during the last few years. And there are also signs that in Government circles the possibility is being broached of once more carrying out a social policy in the spirit of the rescripts of 1890. The check given to the Socialists by the result of the elections has only strengthened this inclination. Everything points to the assumption that the task of protecting labour, which was interrupted or abandoned in 1896, is about to be resumed with renewed activity.

This renewal of social idealism may well be regarded as an interesting symptom in the general evolution

14

which is taking place in Germany at the present
moment.  We have already seen how in the domain
of economics ever more significant signs are appearing of a reaction against the system of free enterprise and the principle of unrestricted competition.
In politics similar tendencies are making themselves
felt among the enlightened members of the Conservative Party, among the Christians, whether Protestant
or Catholic, and in highly cultured scientific and
artistic circles.  In addition to the realistic struggle
for national and universal power, there has also come
into being a distinct movement towards national
culture and social peace.  It seems certain that an
important section of German public opinion is tending to-day towards a system of restricted competition
resting upon an idealism founded upon religion, and
is endeavouring to solve the social problem by the
help of modern Christianity and the practice of
Christian ethics.  To what extent will these tendencies prevail over the more definite solutions
advocated by the Right or the Left, absolute authority
on the one hand, or democratic Socialism on the
other ?  The future alone can decide to what degree
a compromise of this nature between imperialistic
rationalism and the religious instinct that believes in
tradition is either possible or practicable.

# BOOK III

## THE EVOLUTION OF RELIGIOUS AND PHILOSOPHICAL THOUGHT

# CHAPTER I

## THE RENAISSANCE OF CATHOLICISM IN GERMANY AT THE BEGINNING OF THE NINETEENTH CENTURY

### I

I SHOWED at the beginning of this study how the development of science and the scientific organisation of life are the principal facts which differentiate the modern era from the Middle Ages. Now this profound modification of man's attitude of mind brought in its train a radical transformation of all the traditional ideas about human destiny. The modern mind no longer regards the universe in the same way as the Christian of the Middle Ages; it no longer feels the same religious emotions or sets itself the same problems. It may, perhaps, be correct to say that a " scientific " conception of the world is tending to take the place of a " religious " interpretation. I should prefer to express the same idea by saying that the rise of theoretical and practical rationalism has renewed the " religion " of the modern European.

In fact, I do not believe that any diminution of the religious spirit has taken place, especially in Germany of the nineteenth century. Men perceive more and more clearly, it is true, the fundamental differences that exist between the religion of to-day and that of the past, but they do not, as a rule, willingly resign themselves to admit that they necessarily represent

two irreconcilable principles.  It is, of course, impossible for me to say whether this belief is right or
wrong, whether the future evolution of rationalism
will prove fatal to Christianity or not, whether we
shall see a definite and irrevocable rupture between
the old religion and modern thought effected, and
whether man in the future will be content with science
and take refuge in absolute agnosticism with regard
to everything else.  But this is a question we may
well set aside in a work like the present.  The fact,
however, which to my mind seems absolutely certain,
is that modern Germany does *not*, as a rule, maintain
the necessity of antagonism between Religion and
Science, but, on the contrary, endeavours passionately
to reconcile the two.  She does not desire in the domain of the spirit that violent rupture with tradition
for which she strove in the political sphere.  She
believes that a continuity exists between the Christianity of the past and the " religion " of the present
day, and she is convinced that Christianity is capable
of development, and will prove able to assimilate to
some extent the successive conquests of the human
mind.

Let us, then, turn to the examination of the evolution of religious thought in Germany during the
nineteenth century, and begin our study of it with
the history of Catholicism.


## II

Catholicism, relying as it does more upon tradition
and authority than Protestantism, which we shall
discuss later on, seemed at first to be most seriously
menaced, by the development of the rationalistic
spirit, with regard to its time-established pretensions

to rule the souls of men.   And it is true that in Germany, both at the beginning and towards the end of the nineteenth century, it passed through some grave crises.   Yet, at the same time, it must be pointed out that they do not seem to have weakened Catholicism to any appreciable extent, but that its practical and visible power is apparently more secure at the present moment than it was a century ago.

Towards the end of the eighteenth century it was open to question whether Catholicism, with its authoritative and absolutist doctrines, would not be obliged to make the most serious concessions to the modern spirit, and whether it was not even marching towards disasters which might perhaps prove irreparable.   The rationalist spirit, which until about that time had allied itself to the Protestant spirit and had determined the course of the " era of enlightenment," did, as a matter of fact, also invade Catholicism. A reforming party came into existence, and were animated by a desire to amend Catholic institutions in conformity with liberal thought.

In the first place, the reformers aimed at restricting and bringing back to justifiable limits the authority of the Pope in the Church, which they regarded as exorbitant.   They rebelled against the oppression under which the Roman Curia weighed down the German episcopacy, and demanded the independence and prerogatives of the bishops with regard to the Pope.   They accused the Papacy of having in the past fraudulently usurped the sovereign power it had appropriated to itself by basing its claims upon the celebrated pseudo-Isidorian decretals.   In short, they asserted that the supreme authority over the Church was handed down, not to the Bishop of Rome, but to the Œcumenical Council.   This attitude led them, on the other hand, to show themselves, on the question of the relationship between Church and State, respectful towards the rights of the State. They aimed at freeing the national Church as far as possible from all outside influence. They acknowledged the right of temporal sovereigns to exercise an extensive superintendence and a considerable influence in the administration of the Church. Lastly, they endeavoured to reform Catholic theology in a liberal sense, and tried to introduce a more independent spirit and a more scientific method into the study of history, to simplify the ceremonial of the services, and to restrict processions and pilgrimages. They waged war against certain religious orders like the Jesuits and the mendicant friars. They denounced the ignorance of the clergy, and demanded that religious instruction should be freely distributed to the people. And they aimed at effacing or diminishing as much as possible the difference which separated Protestants and Catholics, especially from the moral point of view.

And during the second half of the eighteenth century, the Roman Catholic cause visibly lost ground. It is true that Pope Pius VI. succeeded in extracting a semblance of recantation from Johann Nikolaus von Hontheim (Febronius), the most famous representative of reform. But the liberal ideas, of which this man had made himself the champion, nevertheless made significant progress. The dissolution of the order of the Jesuits (1773) was an important victory won over the spirit of intolerance and of war to the death against reformation and rationalism. In Austria Joseph II. loosened the yoke of Rome by a series of bold reforms ; he appointed himself the head of the Church in his own empire, made enormous reductions in the number of monks, and by the Edict of Toleration of 1781 placed Protestants upon the same footing as Catholics with regard to civil rights and the holding of public offices. In Germany a few years later the three ecclesiastical electors, together with the Archbishop of Salzburg, proclaimed in the famous *Punctatio* of Ems (1786) principles which were identical with those circulated by Hontheim-Febronius on the independence of bishops in relation to the Holy See. The reform movement penetrated into most of the Catholic universities of Germany. The spirit of toleration spread further and further, and everywhere moderated denominational hostility. All propaganda for securing converts ceased almost entirely until the end of the century. The philosophy of Kant, which is inspired by an exceedingly Protestant spirit, found numerous disciples among Catholics. At this juncture the French Revolution seemed to level a decisive blow at Roman Catholicism in the very heart of Rome herself. In 1798 the Roman Republic was proclaimed, and a statue of Liberty with her heel upon the Triple Crown was erected. Pius VI., in spite of his eighty years, was carried into captivity at Sienna, and afterwards at Valencia, where he died in the following year. And his successor, Pius VII., was appointed by a conclave which met at Venice under the protection of schismatic Russia. At last, a few years later, the Recesses [1] of 1803 accomplished the definite ruin of the temporal power of Catholicism in Germany. The Church lost her sovereignty over a territory exceeding 1,700 square miles, containing a population of over 3,000,000 and producing a revenue estimated at over 21,000,000 florins.

[1] A Recess, it should be noted, is a resolution, decree, or act of the Imperial Diet of Germany.—TR,

At the end of the eighteenth century it looked as though Catholicism were on the eve of extinction. Spittler, a famous historian of that time, at the end of his lectures on the history of the Papacy, expressed his conviction that the celibacy of the priesthood and the use of Latin would shortly disappear, even in Austria, that the Catholic Church would cease to be Roman, and that the people would resume the rights of which they had been deprived by the clergy. And again, in 1799, Novalis wrote in a similar spirit : " The non-essential form of Catholicism is almost played out. The old Papacy is laid in the tomb, and Rome for the second time has become a ruin."

But after the last years of the eighteenth century there appeared in Germany a very strong reactionary movement in favour of " positive " forms of religion. This movement, which flourished at the expense of liberal ideas, proved above all advantageous to Roman Catholicism, and in a very short time succeeded in increasing to enormous proportions the influence of the Catholic Church, which seemed to be dangerously menaced.

The principal reason for this sudden change should apparently be sought in the impression produced upon German public opinion by the development of the French Revolution, which in the beginning had been hailed with enthusiasm by all the cultured classes in Germany, who saw in it the practical realisation of the philosophical theories of the eighteenth century and of rationalism and the doctrines of Rousseau. The Revolution had appeared in the light of a terrible experience sent to prove the organising power of Reason. It had solemnly recognised as its god, the god of the philosophers. People had

seen it celebrate the cult of the goddess Reason with
great pomp in Notre Dame, and proclaim by the
mouth of Robespierre that " without constraint and
without persecution all sects would of their own
accord become merged in one body through the
universal Religion of Nature," and it had instituted
in 1794 the public and official worship of this Supreme
Being.   But the excesses of the revolutionaries, and
the violence they displayed against their political and
religious adversaries, quickly changed into terror,
aversion, and hatred the feelings of admiration which
the Revolution had at first inspired.   And the more
severely people condemned the Revolution, the more
surely did they turn gradually away from its fundamental principle and from that religion of Reason
which was guilty, if not of having inspired the revolutionary crimes, at least of not having prevented them.
And they lent an ever more attentive ear to the assertions of the *émigrés*, who made " philosophy " and its
impious doctrines responsible for the great social
upheaval.

Thus in opposition to the Revolution and to
rationalism there gradually grew up a coalition of
the historical and traditional powers, the sovereigns
by divine right, the hereditary nobility, and the
Church—the alliance between " the Throne and the
Altar."   And was not the " Altar " above all per-
sonified by the Roman Catholic Church, which had
always with indefatigable consistency defended the
principle of authority against philosophical infidelity
and the sacrilegious usurpations of rebellious Reason ?
From the moment that the Revolution appeared
(whether rightly or wrongly, does not matter here)
as the practical realisation of the rationalistic ideal,
the terror it inspired logically turned to the ad-

vantage of the power which was the embodiment of the opposite principle—the Papacy; and this to the detriment of reformed Catholicism and of Protestantism, which were both under suspicion of having entered into covenant with the errors of the century, and of having allowed themselves to be led astray into making culpable concessions to subversive ideas. In the face of the revolutionary upheaval which endangered both the Throne and the Altar, these two rival powers made a truce to their differences. The everlasting conflict between the Papacy, which embodied the international power of the Church, and the temporal sovereigns who represented the national power of the State, became a secondary consideration. Reconciled by the imminence of danger, the two adversaries found themselves constantly united against the common foe, against the Revolution and its chief doctrine of rationalist "irreligion." Even among the Protestant princes of Germany it was possible in many cases to discern a certain sympathy for Catholicism inasmuch as it was a conservative force capable of holding the revolutionary spirit in check, and of inclining the people to docility and submission.

Nevertheless it was not at the hands of kings nor of the highest in the land that the Church found salvation. The renaissance of Catholicism also appears in certain aspects as an impulse towards "liberty" and as a popular movement. A glance at the position of Catholicism after the crisis of 1803 will help us to understand this fact.

The Recesses of 1803 had resulted in the disappearance in Germany of the last vestiges of theocratic government. If matters are regarded from this point of view, it is clear that the process of secularisation did great harm to Catholicism. It deprived the Church and her congregations of considerable wealth, and to a large extent diminished their material power. Above all it seemed to level a blow at the very independence of the Church, which was subjected much more directly than before to the frequently oppressive and officious tutelage of the temporal sovereigns and their officials. Historians with ultramontane sympathies have not failed to point out the precarious and dependent position in which the Recesses left Catholicism in Germany. Armed with overwhelming evidence, they have depicted the Church, stripped of her most necessary rights and liberties, the authority of the bishops annihilated by the power of the officials, who were chiefly Protestants or hostile to Roman Catholicism, the convents closed, their goods confiscated, and their wealth sometimes plundered. They have shown how the Church, deprived of the free administration of her own resources, was reduced to live by the charity of secular powers and subjected to the financial tutelage of the State, which was mean with regard to the expenses of public worship, and prevented many of the religious foundations from fulfilling their original functions. They complained that denominational impartiality was not preserved by the State, which systematically gave the preference to Protestants rather than to Catholics in all appointments in the army, the Civil Service, and the universities. They drew attention to the fact that public instruction, in every rank, was taken away from the influence of the Church, that even the services were restricted by the State, which, under the pretext of suppressing abuses, tried to diminish the pomp of the ceremonies, limit the

number of feast-days, prohibit processions and
pilgrimages, and even introduce reforms into the
liturgy on its own authority.

But it is also easy to perceive the extent to which
these grievances were specious and calculated to
win sympathy to the Catholic cause. Catholicism—
which we have just seen as an ally of royalty in
the struggle against the Revolution—now made its
appearance before the public as a victim of govern-
mental oppression. What did it demand, in fact, if
not the same as every Liberal and Radical : "liberty"
and emancipation from the tyrannical control of the
State ? The great principle of autonomy, which inspired all the claims of democracy against monarchical
absolutism, also appeared as the basis of the complaints raised by Catholicism against the State !

Its opponents, indeed, replied on their part by
denouncing the ambitions of the clergy. They
tried to prove that Catholicism was in reality in no
way oppressed either in its religious convictions or
in the freedom of worship, whilst the "liberty"
it demanded was, as a matter of fact, the right to
oppress its enemies and to be supreme in the State,
and that in the very heyday of modern life it was
endeavouring to realise its old theocratic dreams.
But they did not succeed in robbing Catholics of
the conviction that they too were champions of
the modern cause of autonomy, that they were
fighting against an officious State the good fight
of liberty, and that the emancipation of the people
must go hand in hand with the emancipation of
the Church. And it is for this reason that during
the nineteenth century the Catholic movement
proved not merely an anti-revolutionary manifestation, but also ever more and more distinctly

a popular movement and an impulse on the part of the " Christian populace " towards religious independence.

Another consequence of the Recesses of 1803 was the weakening of liberal and " national " Catholicism to the benefit of Roman Catholicism.

The powerful prince-bishops and the rich prelates of the old German Church, who had nothing to fear from the encroachments of secular influence, were in a much better position to defend the independence of the bishops and the rights of the national Church against the absolutist pretensions of the Papacy. " If the bishops," said Cardinal Pacca, at the time when the chief clergy were supporting the policy of Joseph II. against the Curia, " had been less rich and less powerful, they would have listened with more deference to the voice of the Supreme Head of the Church, and would not have tried to emulate the example of the proud and ambitious patriarchs of Constantinople and acquire an independence which was well-nigh schismatical." The Recesses, by reducing the temporal power of the bishops, also struck a blow at the head of the reform party. The new clergy, deprived of all real influence, and with their independence menaced by secular power, stood in much greater need than their predecessors had done of the support of the Curia, and quickly accustomed themselves to take the word of command from Rome with docility. Before 1803 a large proportion of the German bishops endeavoured, with the help of the temporal princes, to defend the prerogatives of the national Churches against the Bishop of Rome. After 1803 the resistance was less vital and more easily broken. The clergy found themselves gradually driven to fight, with the support and under the direction of the Pope, against the pretensions of the secular State. The Papacy appeared to good Catholics in the light of the surest guarantee of religious independence ; the sovereignty of the Pope alone, who was independent of any particular State, could guarantee the autonomy of the Church, and protect it from the attempts of the civil power to invade the domain of religion.

The ancient episcopal system had in the past presumed to lay down the law for the Pope. The new episcopacy did not take long to perceive that it had to choose between two alternatives : either obedience to Rome or slavery under the State. And it threw itself emphatically on the side of Rome. A modern historian of German Catholicism says that the Papacy appears as the emancipator of the Church in Germany.

At the same time as Catholicism disciplined its forces and concentrated them in order to reach out for power with redoubled energy, it also revealed itself as a spiritual principle capable of gaining the respect of men's minds, of inflaming their hearts, and of inspiring the imagination of artists. The romantic movement, which bound together about the beginning of the nineteenth century the highest intellects of Germany, resulted in an apotheosis of Catholicism. There is nothing more curious than to watch the transitions by which these free spirits passed from the most audacious and independent philosophical speculations to the strictest religious faith.

Romanticism first appeared as a protestation against the somewhat childish rationalism of the " era of enlightenment." The rationalists had deified and worshipped conscious organising in-

tellect, and had considered it capable of conceiving
and defining with perfect clearness God or the First
Cause of all reality, and able by its own light alone
to guide the conduct of individuals and of nations.
Romanticism, on the contrary, posited the existence
of other powers besides the intellect, such as moral
will, love, intuition, and poetic imagination, which
play a decisive part in the destinies of man. Continuing the work of Kant and Goethe, whom it
recognised as its masters, and inspired, moreover,
by Spinoza and Plato, Bœhme and Hemsterhuys,
it reached a new solution of the religious problem.
The power by which man attains the knowledge
of God was not, in its opinion, the intellect alone.
Kant had already founded religion, not upon
knowledge, but upon moral will, not upon theoretical,
but upon practical reason. Following in his footsteps, the romanticists proclaimed that the existence
of God could not be proved by rational arguments,
that religion was not a certain kind of knowledge,
and that it was not by intellect but by love, contemplation, moral will, and poetical imagination,
that man could find God.

It is true that at the beginning at least the romanticists were very far from wishing to do violence
to reason, to subordinate it to other faculties, or
to subject it to the authority of a supernatural and
historical revelation which it must accept without
reservation. They repudiated none of the modern
conquests of reason and science, they had no desire
to make man retrace his footsteps and return to
obsolete beliefs. They prided themselves, on the
contrary, on being in the van of thought, and presumed to be able to explore into new regions of
the human soul. Their ambition was not to contra-

15

dict rationalism, but to surpass it. They did not wish to correct the scientific conception of the universe by a religious conception; they merely affirmed that they each had their own value and mutually complemented one another. In short, they had their eyes fixed not upon the past, but upon the future.

Nevertheless, romanticism insensibly became more disdainful of the power of reason. Directed in the beginning against an imprudent rationalism, which exaggerated the power of the intellect beyond all bounds, it came gradually to place theoretical reason lower and lower in the scale of values and to treat it as an inferior and suspicious character, and finally as an enemy. As early as Novalis theoretical intelligence was regarded merely as a sullen and grumbling scribe, which with great difficulty succeeded now and again in incorporating some morsel of eternal Truth into its precepts, and became positively pernicious when it tried to rebel against the superior forces, such as love, wisdom, and poetry, which rule the world. According to Friedrich Schlegel philosophy was merely a barren attempt to explain the world without God, an illusion which made man imagine that he could draw from himself the virtues which divine revelation had planted in his heart, so that he regarded as the natural and normal products of human reason ideas which were in reality confused reminiscences of the word which God Himself once gave to sinful man. Speculative reason, which was for the rationalist an infallible guide to man, became in the end a mistress of falsehood and a creator of delusions in the eyes of the romanticists, who had recovered from the disease of intellectual pride.

And in proportion as rational truth went down in

the scale of values, specifically religious truth rose higher in their estimation. At the beginning they attached but small importance to the historical and positive elements in religion. Fichte, for instance, professed a pantheistic monism, which he thought identical in its essence with the Christianity of the Fourth Gospel, but which was in reality a philosophical religion containing the elements common to the various Christian denominations and destined in the end to reconcile them in one last synthesis. But if at first romanticism, far from being a denominational reaction, pushed toleration, indifference to dogma, and freedom in the matter of religious organisation to their most extreme limits, it came gradually to pay an ever more sincere and reverent respect to positive Christianity. All its thinkers, from Novalis and Schlegel, to Wackenroder and Tieck, waxed enthusiastic over the glorious history of Christianity in the past—the Middle Ages with their moving and pious impulse towards art and religion, the glorious days of the Crusades, when the whole of Europe shared one faith, and that golden age of Christianity when one grand common interest united the provinces of that vast spiritual kingdom. And finally Friedrich Schlegel, after burying himself in the study of languages, mythology, and the philosophy of the East, arrived at the conviction that " man did not begin his career without God." He taught that the evolution of the human species was inconceivable without the admission of a divine revelation at the beginning. We could find traces of this in the most ancient and venerable document we possessed on the origin of man—the books of Moses ; and we might hear the faint echo and discover more or less confused recollections of it in the ancient systems of the East. In the depths of mankind's past, therefore, there shone forth a supernatural light, and all our efforts should be directed to the sole end of finding once more by a pious study of the Bible that divine truth, which alone could secure our salvation.

Let us advance a little further along this path, and we shall also understand the growing sympathy of the romanticists with Catholicism.

If one is not disposed to eliminate from religion all its positive elements as being vain superstitions, if reason has no right to correct religious intuition, is one not in the end led to the logical conclusion that reform may, perhaps, be the first manifestation of that impious rebellion of reason against faith, and that the simplifications which Protestantism has introduced into the religion of tradition may perhaps level a blow at the very integrity of that religion ? The Protestant Novalis reproached reform with having broken the unity of Christianity, and accused it of being " a revolutionary government which proclaims its own permanence." And on the other hand he praised in Catholicism precisely those characteristics which rationalism condemned with the greatest vehemence. He extolled the Popes for having in their consummate wisdom opposed in the past " the insolent development of certain human faculties as well as premature and dangerous discoveries in the realm of knowledge." He also upheld the celibacy of the priesthood. He defended the Jesuits, in whom he saw an admirable creation on the part of the ecclesiastical spirit and a magnificent attempt to restore the Papacy to its pristine glory. And if a large number of romanticists, like Novalis, Wackenrode, Tieck, and Gentz, did not push their sympathy for Catholicism to the point of being publicly converted, others actually took this final step. Friedrich Schlegel roundly condemned the culpable indifference of lukewarm minds, who, under the pretext that the external forms of religion matter very little, were content out of laziness to remain true to the faith in which they had been brought up. Every man should be under the obligation to decide for himself the capital question as to whether the one immutable religious truth is to be found on the Protestant or the Catholic side. In Schlegel's opinion, by the abolition of the external forms of religion, reform had at the same time rejected the most essential and most sublime elements of Christianity. And he acted in accordance with his beliefs. Partly through his reasoned convictions as a historian and a critic, and partly as an act of faith, and the free choice of his deepest feelings, he became an official convert to Catholicism at Cologne on April the 16th, 1808.

And his was not an isolated case. Conversions of this kind became very frequent at that time. Men of science and learning, like the philosopher Möller, Rumohr the æsthcticist, the political economist Adam Müller ; authors like Zacharias Werner ; artists like the two Veits, Klinkowström, Overbeck, and the two Schadows ; statesmen like Platner and Eduard von Schenk ; publicists like Jarcke ; princes like Frederick of Hesse-Darmstadt or Adolphus of Mecklenburg-Schwerin, went over to Catholicism. The fact that " human " motives may have contributed to these conversions is probable and even likely. Political considerations or artistic dilettantism, the idea that Catholicism was an effective method of keeping nations under control, or that it was *par excellence* the æsthetic religion, the faith which inspired the great artists of the Middle Ages, and gave birth to the masterpieces of painting and music, was probably an important factor in the conversion of many individuals.  But, generally speaking, it is certain that their sincerity was above suspicion, and that they were simply induced to go to the extreme limit by the strong current which bore away the minds of men from rationalism and carried them imperceptibly towards religious faith.

Thus the cycle of the religious evolution of romanticism was completed.  Innovators and revolutionaries at the beginning, the romanticists wished at first to continue the work of the classical era, and to explore a domain of the human soul unknown to the rationalism of the eighteenth century.  We find them carefully fixing the limits of the religious sphere, attributing in the psychic life of humanity an ever greater importance to irrational elements, to mystic intuition, to sentiment and to love, and paying an ever more respectful attention to the historical data of religion.  From an almost entirely rational conception of religion, a sort of philosophical Protestantism stripped of every historical and dogmatic element, romanticism, after holding theoretical reason in ever lower esteem, finally ended in an idea of religion which was ever more and more " irrationalistic." Its sympathies increased in ardour for religious beliefs in which the superhuman element predominated.  It showed an ever more decided preference for Catholicism in which the ecclesiastical hierarchy and the strict discipline, the character of long tradition and authoritative principles, formed the most marked contrast with the rational religion of the Categorical Imperative.  The precept of autonomy, which pervaded the moral and religious doctrines of Kant, seemed thenceforward an impious belief inspired by a rash confidence in the organising power of human reason.  Rationalistic pride became merged in a respectful adoration of the impenetrable mystery of the universe and in a confession full of humility of the weakness and poverty of man.  The contrite and repentant romanticist, fallen from his high hopes and his arrogant pride, returned humbly to the school of divine revelation and sought relief for his anxiety and doubt at the foot of the Cross and in the bosom of the Catholic Church.

Thus we see the importance of the romantic movement in the development of Catholicism.  Obviously the adhesion of a few cultured minds or the enthusiasm of a few artists could not determine its success.  But it is none the less significant to find that Catholicism was able to regain its influence over the educated minority.  Rationalism was full of disgust for " superstition."  The German mind at the end of the eighteenth century treated the Catholic idea as a negligible quantity.  "The Church of Rome," said Herder, " is merely an old ruin into which fresh life can never be breathed."  But thenceforward this was not so.  It is true that positivism, true to rationalistic tradition, considered religious thought an anachronism which was destined to disappear.  But the cause of religion found at this time convinced and able defenders in the ranks of cultured men.  Romanticism considered that the highest step Reason could take was precisely to realise her own incompetence and *raise* herself to religion ; positivist rationalism, far from being the last stage in the mental evolution of man, was in its eyes merely a transitory and outgrown phase.

The romantic movement, moreover, was not a

mere stage which was quickly left behind in the evolution of the German spirit. It was prolonged throughout the whole of the nineteenth century with varying success, but without ever stopping. The early romanticism of Schlegel, Novalis, Schelling, Wackenroder and Tieck was followed by the romanticism of the Heidelberg, Dresden, and Berlin circles, then by the era of young Heine, the reign of Frederick William IV., the reactionary period which followed upon 1848, and lastly by the modern neo-romanticism of our own day. And throughout all these transformations it remained unchanged in all its essential characteristics. The religiosity which inspired Richard Wagner's doctrine of regeneration, and which is voiced in his *Parsifal*, is reminiscent in many respects of the early romantic school—even to the vague perfume of Catholicism, which Nietzsche thought he could detect in it.

In short, there is no doubt whatever that the philosophy and the religious psychology of romanticism, by lowering on the one hand the pride of our " little sagacity," [1] and on the other by representing Catholicism as perfectly compatible with the highest intellectual and artistic culture, largely contributed to the renaissance of the Catholic faith among the civilised nations of the world.

At the same time as it won over an important section among the cultured minority, Catholicism also imposed itself by a different process upon the lowest of the people. It conquered them by giving ample satisfaction to the somewhat ponderous

---

[1] This is an allusion to a distinction which Nietzsche makes between the " great sagacity " which consists of the instincts of the body and the "little sagacity " which is the mind. See *Zarathustra*, pp. 35, 36.—Tr.

appetite for the supernatural, which is always to be found in the breast of the multitude. During the nineteenth century the use of indulgences increased. In almost all the large churches in Germany to-day there is a " special altar " upon which the Pope has conferred the following privilege—that if a priest says a Mass before it for the soul of a Catholic who died in the love of Christ, that soul will receive plenary indulgence, and is immediately delivered from the torments of Purgatory. Similarly the worship of the saints took on a fresh development, and above all the adoration of the Sacred Heart of Jesus, which dates, it is true, from the seventeenth century, but only attained its complete significance in the second half of the nineteenth century. The idea of worship became attached even to the most external and material objects : Catholics were taught that consecrated incense had a " supernatural spiritual effect " and produced " an odour of sanctity," that vessels used at the services " had something of the divine " and ought therefore to be honoured by a sort of religious respect. The popular faith was exalted by the solemn exhibition of the relics of the saints. In 1844 1,100,000 pilgrims gathered from every corner of Germany and thronged round the Sacred Tunic of Treves in a fever of devotion, and with a thirst for miracles, which was somewhat disconcerting to the modern sceptic. From that moment spectacles of this nature increased in number, and miraculous cures, which were piously placed upon record, as in the case of Treves, or marvellous apparitions, which were regarded as adding to the glory of the Church, as at Marpingen, constantly kept alive and stimulated the old love of the people for the supernatural and for material miracles.

Lastly, the activity of Catholic propaganda among the masses was increased by the creation of an enormous number of guilds, brotherhoods, and religious societies, which were multiplied more particularly in the second half of the nineteenth century, and some of which contained thousands of German members. " All these associations and their members," says a recent historian, " live under the spiritual domination of neo-Catholicism and its ritual ; they are bound together by the special worship of the saint of their particular brotherhood, and carry out their obligations as citizens in the spirit of this neo-Catholicism. They take part in processions, and are sometimes honoured by being allowed to bear a banner or hold the canopy over the head of the priest, who carries the Host. Each one of them quivers with pious thrills inspired by the ritual, whether he mingles with the rest of the congregation or kneels before the special altar of his brotherhood, and they all live in the hope of obtaining the indulgences which, since the time of Pius IX., have been dispensed with the greatest liberality." The numberless associations, headed by the ordinary clergy and the Jesuits, and supported by an increasingly important religious press, have exercised a decisive influence over the destinies of German Catholicism. They have made the Catholic movement "democratic." The influence of the bishops and the high dignitaries of the Church, which was formerly exercised in favour of aristocratic principles, was considerably reduced at the end of the century—from the day on which the Pope, summing up in his own person the tradition of the Church, proclaimed his infallibility. It was by this means that German Catholicism has come at the present day to represent an essentially popular party, admirably organised, controlled and disciplined, which plays a clever and successful part in political struggles, fights eagerly for power, and obediently takes the word of command from the infallible Pope, who furnishes it with the general outlines of its policy.

Invigorated in this way by a number of favourable conditions which hastened its diffusion, both among the classes and the masses, the Catholic Renaissance proclaimed its existence after the first few years of the nineteenth century by a series of significant symptoms. In 1800 the conversion of Count Friedrich Leopold of Stolberg took place ; after long years of hesitation he went over to Catholicism out of disgust "for the pitiable condition of the Lutheran religion, which under our very eyes is melting into theism and atheism." This conversion was a sign of the times, all the more important because it was followed (as we have already seen) by a long series of similar conversions. Gradually, active centres of Catholic propaganda were formed. At Munster there was the group founded by the Princess Amelia of Gallitzine, at Würzburg and Eichstädt the Catholic circles directed by Bishop Zirkel, and at Vienna the Ultramontane Party organised after 1808 by Father Clemens Maria Hofbauer. After the concordat of 1802, concluded with Napoleon, which marks the first important victory of the Curia, the influence of Rome grew ever more important through the complicated negotiations which paved the way for the reorganisation of the Catholic Church in the west and south of Germany. The vehement and malevolent opposition displayed towards a Liberal prelate, like the celebrated Vicar-General Ignatius Henry of Wessenberg, whose deposition the Pope demanded in 1814, proves the weakness of the reforming party. Lastly,

the fall of Napoleon marked the decisive victory of
the Papacy.  In 1814 the triumphal entry of Pius VII.
into Rome took place, followed in the same year by
the restoration of the order of the Jesuits to their
old constitution and privileges, and shortly afterwards by the renewal of the Inquisition and the
revival of the Index.

And in 1832, in the Bull *Pastor Aeternus*, by which
he proclaimed his elevation to the pontifical throne,
Gregory XVI. launched a haughty declaration of
war against modern subjectivism :  " The cause of
the progress of unbelief and rebellion against the
sacred dogma of the Church is pseudo-science.  It
is the teaching and the example of the masters that
has turned away the hearts of the young, brought
about the defeat of religion, and the terrible decadence
of morals.  It is therefore needful, for the preservation of the Church from all these innovations, to recall
at once to men's minds that the Pope alone can decide
the doctrines and the government of the Church ;
the bishops must always agree with the Holy Father,
and the priests must obey the bishops.  The discipline ordained by the Church must never be called in
question, or above all be subordinated to the power of
the State.  It is absurd to talk about the regeneration
of the Church, and an abomination to attack the vow
of celibacy and to cast doubt upon the indissolubility
of the marriage tie.  Above all it is needful to fight
against indifference and the illusion that salvation
can be found in any creed.  For from this arises
that foolish error that every man has the right to
liberty of conscience."

# CHAPTER II

THE PROGRESS OF CATHOLICISM DURING THE NINE-
TEENTH CENTURY

## I

DURING the nineteenth century Roman Catholicism
met with two chief adversaries in Germany—reformed
Catholicism, on the one hand, and the secular State
on the other. But it obtained an almost uninterrupted
series of victories over them both.

The triumph of the Church of Rome over Liberal
Catholicism was complete and apparently decisive.
From the end of the eighteenth century the Church
entered upon a campaign of extermination against it,
which it continued from that time forward with in-
vincible pertinacity. As early as about 1794 complaints from the pens of Liberal writers are to be
found about the gradual disappearance of the progressive spirit. And the measures taken in the same
year against several Liberal professors in the Catholic University of Dillingen, of whom the gentle
mystic Sailer was one, prove the growing power of
anti-rationalistic tendencies. Nevertheless Liberal
Catholicism was still a power at the beginning of the
nineteenth century. Its principal supporters were
to be found among the superior clergy and in the
Catholic universities. Baron von Wessenberg, the
Vicar-General of the Bishopric of Constance, Christian
von Hohenlohe-Waldenburg, the Prince-Bishop of

237

Breslau, Count Spiegel, the Archbishop of Cologne, and numerous other prelates, like Bishop Frint at Saint-Pölten, Bishop Gruber at Salzburg, and Bishop Milde in Vienna, gave evidence of a wide Liberalism in their administration, and showed a more or less open sympathy with the idea of a national Church which should preserve a certain independence in its relations with the Chair of St. Peter. At the same time the Liberal spirit began to make itself felt in the Catholic universities. Professor Hermes of Bonn, the most famous representative of these tendencies, constructed a system which founded Catholic dogma upon the basis of Kant's philosophy. He succeeded in securing the triumph of his ideas among the faculties and seminaries of Treves, Cologne, Munster, Breslau, and Braunsberg. But Roman Catholicism was not slow to regain the upper hand. At the Congress of Vienna, as well as at the *Bundestag* of Frankfort, the organisation of the " Church of Germany," dreamt of by Wessenberg, failed to be carried out owing to the dissensions among the German states and the intrigues of the Ultramontanes. The overwhelming hostility with which Wessenberg met at Rome compelled him to retire in 1827, and death gradually freed the Papacy of its other adversaries in the ranks of the superior clergy in Germany. Finally, at the end of the 'thirties, after the death of Hermes and his protector, Count Spiegel, Hermesianism, which had been condemned by the Pope, was violently eradicated from the Catholic faculties, and after a futile resistance slowly died out. Thus the decisive blow was struck at the Reform Party, which, stripped of its influence over ecclesiastical education, found itself reduced to the alternative of a full and complete submission or to a fruitless struggle.

It was from that time forward condemned to impotence in spite of a few attempts at resistance, which did not seriously trouble the victorious Church of Rome. The campaigns against the celibacy of the priesthood, which for some time agitated Silesia and Baden, the movement in favour of a German liturgy and the simplification of the ritual, which gave rise to fairly lively polemics, the synodal agitation, which before 1848 demanded an equal distribution of power between the ecclesiastical hierarchy and the internal opinion of the Church, produced no result of any importance. The " German Catholic " movement, let loose by Ronge and Czerski at the time of the exhibition of the Sacred Tunic at Treves in 1844, and which resulted in the formation of one or two separatist communities, remained confined to a very limited circle, and had not the slightest effect upon the life of Catholicism as a whole. And when at last ultramontanism plucked the final fruit of its victory and proclaimed in 1870 the dogma of the infallibility of the Pope, the protestations of Liberal Catholicism in Germany were feeble and impotent. In spite of the great personal merit of the protesters, men like Döllinger, Friedrich, Schulte, and Reinkens, the " Old Catholics," who refused to acquiesce in the dogma of infallibility or to accept the complete domination of Rome, did not meet with any lasting success. Though they were able to offer a certain resistance, especially at Bonn and Munich, which were their chief centres of influence, and to organise independent parishes, and even in 1863 to appoint a special bishop, their numbers always remained insignificant. They never had more than 100,000 followers in Germany and Switzerland, and these gradually declined to less than 30,000. Everywhere the bishops, even those who had been hostile to the promulgation of the dogma of infallibility, bowed before the accomplished fact, and obediently proclaimed the new dogma in their dioceses, and succeeded, without meeting with any serious opposition, in making their well-disciplined flock of true believers follow in their train.

## II

Just as Roman Catholicism broke the resistance of the Reforming Party, it also vigorously opposed the pretensions of the State, and finally, after a great conflict, secured that Catholic "liberty" which it considered necessary for the independence of the Church.

It gradually forced the German states to loosen the bonds of dependence in which they wished to keep the Church. This design was already clearly outlined in the negotiations which led to the ecclesiastical reorganisation of Germany at the time of the Peace of Vienna. After having succeeded in preventing, both at the Congress of Vienna and subsequently at the Diet of Frankfort, the constitution of a " Church of Germany " capable of developing into an autonomous body independent of Rome, papal diplomacy entered into separate negotiations with the various German states, and concluded during the years between 1817 and 1821 advantageous concordats with Bavaria, Prussia, and the petty states of the South. The resistance of Catholicism to State control was afterwards accentuated when the controversy between the Government and the two Archbishops of Cologne and of Posen, respectively, took place on the subject of the Church's blessing on mixed marriages. This conflict was terminated by the almost unreserved capitulation of the Prussian

Government to the demands of the Church. In 1848 the Conclave of German Bishops assembled at Würzburg solemnly formulated the demands of the new German episcopate. They protested against the encroachments which, under the pretext of rights of patronage, the temporal princes had made upon the domain of the Church, asserted the privileges of the ecclesiastical hierarchy in connection with seminaries and theological faculties, claimed for the bishops the right of free communication with the Sovereign Pontiff, and rose against the exercise of the right of *placet* by the civil authority. Most of these demands, with the approval of the Pope, passed during the 'fifties into the legislation of Prussia (1848 and 1850) and of Austria (Concordat of 1855), who, after having been for a long time the stronghold of reform, became once more the central hearth of Roman Catholicism in Germany. About 1860 the hierarchy, relying upon the clerical democracy and the numberless Catholic associations, which had spread their roots through the whole country, had obtained from the secular powers throughout Germany a sum-total of concessions which went far to secure the independence necessary for the free exercise of Catholicism.

Nevertheless, a fresh conflict, more grave than all the preceding ones, was in course of preparation.

On the one hand the evolution of Ultramontane Catholicism produced its final consequences. A series of dogmatic decrees of capital importance—the promulgation of the dogma of the Immaculate Conception in 1854, the *Syllabus* of 1864, and above all the proclamation of Papal Infallibility by the Vatican Council in 1870—crowned the imposing edifice of the Romish system, and made the most rigorous absolu-

16

tism predominant in the Church. The authority of the Pope unequivocally proclaimed itself as the supreme tribunal of Catholicism, and exercised a direct influence upon the lowest masses of the Catholic democracy. The bishops, stripped of their autonomy, and held in check by the infallibility of the Supreme Head of the Church, were reduced to the position of docile intermediaries between the Pope and the " Christian populace." And on the other hand, to counterbalance this mighty spiritual power, which displayed ever more clearly its desire to dominate the civil power, the German Empire was brought to life once more in the very centre of Europe. But this Empire was not the restoration of the Holy Roman Empire which had existed before the Revolution, and it had not been formed under the hegemony of Catholic Austria. Fierce political struggles and two great wars had placed a Hohenzollern at its head, and the new Empire was dominated by Protestant influences. Thus the Roman Curia, despoiled of its temporal power by revolutionary Italy, also saw its influence in Europe menaced by the rise of a great Protestant State. From that moment it prepared itself for a struggle which it regarded as inevitable. In alliance with all the particularistic elements, which had been injured by the hegemony of Prussia, the Catholic democracy of Germany, under the able guidance of the Guelf Windthorst, mobilised its forces. A Catholic party, the Centre, which united the apparently most heterogeneous elements, in which Bavarian aristocrats, Prussian Junkers, and Polish magnates rubbed shoulders with Liberals and Radicals from the Valley of the Rhine, was formed during the elections of March 1871 for the defence of Catholic interests. Between German Catholicism hostile to the Empire and the Imperial Government very jealous of its power and resolved not to have the law laid down by a rival, war was inevitable. The *Kulturkampf* represented the duel between the Empire and the Curia.

On the question of the scope and significance of the *Kulturkampf* there exists a great difference of opinion on the part of historians.

Some of them depict Bismarck as having been surprised by the clerical aggression, which he had not foreseen, and in which he did not wish to believe. Driven by his too exclusively realistic nature into imagining that he would make an end of the clerical opposition by having recourse to police measures, he gradually learnt to realise the futility of his brutal policy. He therefore beat a retreat, in spite of his vow that he would " not go to Canossa," [1] and allowed the May Laws one after the other to fall into desuetude. And finally he found himself obliged to purchase, by means of concessions, the support of the Centre Party, which became the arbiter of the political destinies of Germany and the pivot of the Government majority.

Others represent the religious policy of the great Chancellor in a less primitive and more favourable light. They insist on the impossibility for Bismarck to come to any understanding by means of diplomatic negotiations, and through the instrumentality of a concordat with a Power which declared itself infallible and aspired to dominate every civil authority.

---

[1] Meaning he would not humiliate himself before the Pope. The mention of Canossa refers, of course, to the fact that the Emperor Henry IV. waited three days and three nights in a court-yard at that place for the pardon of Pope Gregory VII. (1077).—Tr.

They approve of Bismarck's policy of having, under
the circumstances, preferred to regulate the relations
between Church and State in an authoritative way,
by means of legislation, so as subsequently to be in
a position to negotiate secretly with the Head of
the Church, and gradually to modify the law in such
a manner as to make it acceptable to both sides
alike.  And they praise the Chancellor for having
carried out this delicate policy with marvellous skill,
for having fought with a warlike spirit and a vigorous
resolution the battle against clerical demagogy, and
for having afterwards, in his negotiations with the
Curia and the diplomats of Rome, shown a very
keen insight into the political necessities and possibilities of the moment.  And they give him credit
for having in the end succeeded in organising the
relationship between Church and State in such a way
as to provide sufficient safeguard for the rights of the
State, and at the same time with enough liberality
to give satisfaction to the Church and reconcile the
Catholic particularistic Centre with the new Empire.

In short, it is quite open to question who was the
real victor in this conflict between the spiritual and
temporal powers.  Events can be represented either
in the light of a triumph for Catholicism, which victoriously repulsed an awkward and brutal attempt
at oppression, or else as a success for the State, which
vigorously held its own against the particularistic
and clerical opposition directed against the Protestant Empire of the Hohenzollern.

In distinction to these two views the one thing
certain is that an understanding was finally reached
between the two adversaries, and that it was an
exceedingly curious evolution which rendered this
change of front possible.

There was, as a matter of fact, no necessary or inevitable antagonism between the Catholic Church and the German Empire. It required time for both sides to realise that a system of mutual tolerance and even of profitable co-operation was possible. But an agreement was eventually reached between them. The State learnt that it could with advantage give up the hostile legislation and severe measures passed at the beginning of the conflict, and little by little it laid down its arms. In 1879 Falk, who had directed the war against clericalism, resigned his ministry. Between 1881 and 1887 most of the regulations enforced by the famous " May Laws " were abrogated one after the other. And in 1904 one of the last vestiges of the *Kulturkampf*, the clause shutting out the Jesuits from German territory, disappeared. The Centre, for their part, realised that if they did not wish to condemn their party to an implacable and in the long run barren opposition, they must recognise the accomplished fact, frankly accept the new Empire, and rally round a national policy. They consequently succeeded very cleverly in moderating their particularistic tendencies, on the one hand, in such a way as not to lay themselves open to the suspicion of separatist ambitions, and on the other hand so tempered their ultramontanism as no longer to give any grounds for the reproach which had often been made against them of being an unpatriotic association. It is possible that this evolution was, as some have asserted, facilitated by the direction favourable to France and the Dual Alliance given by the diplomacy of Rome under Leo XIII. after 1890. This policy perhaps upset a number of German Catholics and led them, in their turn, to take up a more independent attitude towards Rome.

Under these circumstances an understanding could be cemented between the Centre Party and the Imperial Government. And this understanding was all the more obvious because, from the political point of view, the Centre had not and could not have any decided policy. We have already seen how Catholicism assumed a character at once Conservative and democratic, aristocratic and popular. The Centre was, therefore, quite logically able to contain, with a view to common action, feudalists, who were fundamentally Conservative and Liberals with very advanced views. It always avoided accentuating its attitude too violently in one direction or the other. At a certain moment in 1889 it seemed likely that under the guidance of the members of its aristocratic section—Count Ballestrem, von Huene, von Schorlemer, and von Frankenstein—the Centre would form an alliance with the Right for the purpose of introducing reforms of a Conservative nature into educational and religious legislation. But in spite of these considerations, from the economic and social point of view the Centre had no intention of making common cause with the agrarian feudalists. And in 1893, under the direction of Dr. Lieber, the balance of power inclined once more to the advantage of the Democratic Party. So that finally the sum-total of divergent forces, which were grouped in the Catholic Party, resolved itself into a slightly progressive attitude.

Thus the requirements of the Centre very naturally fitted in with those of the Imperial Government. In fact, the central authority considered that its mission was precisely the establishment of a sort of court of arbitration between the different conflicting parties and the discovery of some golden

mean between the various aspirations which appeared
in the country.  What, then, could be more natural
than for it to seek its chief support in a party whose
line of conduct was already precisely the result of
a compromise between Conservative and democratic
tendencies ?

The Centre knew very well how to adapt itself
to its new rôle.  A party of implacable opposition
until 1881, it began from 1881 to 1887 to take a
part in public affairs.  Then from 1890 onwards its
share grew gradually more active and more important.  From 1898 until the most recent elections
the President of the Chamber was a member of the
Centre, which was thus officially proclaimed the
most influential party in the Reichstag.  And,
as a matter of fact, it does possess considerable
authority.  Without binding itself to the Government it has, nevertheless, given its support to nearly
all the great legislative measures of the last twenty-
five years—the workmen's insurance acts, the
commercial treaties during Caprivi's ministry, the
Civil Code, and the laws on the increase of the navy,
which marked the evolution of Germany towards a
universal policy.  And its position is still extremely
strong to-day.  " Katholisch ist Trumph " is an oft-
quoted saying.  The Catholic Party has been able
to regard itself, of recent years, as the arbiter of
the political situation in Germany.  For the moment,
it is true, it finds itself once again thrown into
opposition.  The terrible rupture between the Centre
and the Government over colonial questions is well
known.  But the elections immediately furnished
the proof that the hostility of the Ministry had
in no way shaken the credit of the Catholic Party
among the electoral body.  And it may safely be

asserted, moreover, that the solidity of the Liberal-Conservative *bloc*, upon which the Government at the present moment relies, only inspires on the whole a fairly limited confidence. It therefore seems certain that the political power of the Centre has not received any mortal blow, and there is nothing to prevent its regaining in a more or less immediate future the decisive influence it still possessed a short time ago.

The almost predominant position of Catholicism in an Empire which is chiefly Protestant will seem less paradoxical if we examine the tendencies of the Emperor William II. with regard to religious policy a little more closely. A recent historian thought he could detect, among Protestants as well as among the most highly educated Catholics, the actual development of a disposition which might be termed " interdenominational," and which is calculated, if not to eradicate, at least to attenuate the differences either between the various shades of Protestantism or between Protestantism and Catholicism. In any case, it is certain that it is in this direction that the private religious sympathies of the Emperor are directed. His Christianity, which is exceedingly sincere and exceedingly " positive," is strictly inter-denominational. He not only shows for Catholicism that deferential toleration which the traditions of the Hohenzollern impose upon him, and which is natural in the lord of an Empire living under a system of religious " equality," but it is also plain that he does not consider himself *outside* the pale of Catholicism, but regards himself, inasmuch as he represents German *Christianity*, as a sovereign who is *both* Protestant and Catholic. This accounts for the attitude of William II. at the time of the Chinese war, to which he tried to give the complexion of a Crusade on the part of Christian Europe under the leadership of Germany against the yellow race. Hence his courtesy to the Holy See, his three visits to Rome, and his pilgrimage to the Holy Land. It is quite true of course that this conduct was dictated by political considerations. The Emperor does not only require the support of the Centre in the House for his parliamentary policy. He also relies upon the help of the Catholics to subdue the anti-German agitation in Alsace and Poland. He fully appreciates the importance of the support which can be given to the universal policy of Germany by an international power like the Papacy, especially in questions such as the protectorate over Christians in the East. Nevertheless the sympathy of William II. with Catholicism is very probably not only dictated by considerations of interest, but has its deepest roots in the religious nature of the Emperor himself.

Is the Catholic world inclined to respond to the imperial advances ? Some observers think they can see amongst German Catholics signs which indicate a new development. And it is certain that Catholicism increased, during the century, not only as a political, but also as a spiritual power. It numbers among its followers philosophers like Wilmann, historians like Janssen or Willy Pastor, and poets like Weber. It is a matter of constantly recurring controversy to decide whether Catholic culture in Germany to-day has regained or not the superiority which, by the common consent of all, it had allowed Protestant culture to win. It seems certain that Catholics—and as representatives of this tendency the names of such theologians are

quoted as Franz Xaver Kraus of Friburg, Schell
of Würzburg, Ehrhard of Strasburg, or historians
like Spahn of Strasburg—would like Catholicism to
rest satisfied with the strong position it has conquered, and to relax its combative attitude a little
and cease aspiring to political power, in order to
develop itself above all as a principle of the inner
life and as a religious ideal for modern man. Is
this budding opposition between political clericalism
and religious Catholicism destined to increase?
Will it be favourable, as the similar evolution of
Protestant pietism was, to the rise of that inter-
denominational Christianity which we mentioned
above? It is quite possible. At all events, it is
a fact that the " White Pope " and the " Black
Pope," the Sovereign Pontiff and the Head of the
Jesuits, are to-day notoriously well disposed towards
Germany, and inclined to march in unison with the
Protestant Empire.

Is this a fleeting phase in the history of the Church,
or is it, on the contrary, an important sign of the
times? Shall we, after a passing truce, see the
struggle between the German Empire and the Black
Internationalist reopened? Or shall we, on the
contrary, see the intimacy between the Pope and
the Emperor become again as close as it was in
days gone by? Shall we, perhaps, witness the
two great Conservative forces working in concert
for the solution of the social problem by means of
Christianity? These are questions which in the
presence of certain contemporary events one may
be allowed to ask, but to which the historian, of
course, is not able for the moment to give any
decisive answer.

# CHAPTER III

## THE PROTESTANT SPIRIT

### I

ROTHE, a Protestant historian of the reform movement, has described the evolution of Protestantism since the Peace of Westphalia as "the gradual decadence of Protestant Christianity as a Church, and its progress as a moral and political principle." And it is, indeed, true that the history of the Protestant *spirit* is infinitely more glorious than that of the Protestant *Church*. The one with a praiseworthy courage attacked the chief religious problem of the present day—the reconciliation of the traditional religion of the past with rational science. It is open to question whether it has finally attained its end ; it is, nevertheless, difficult to deny that, in the course of its development, it has accomplished a great work in the domain of history, philology, and religious psychology, and that it has produced men of exceptionally lofty moral attainments. The Protestant Church, on the contrary, holds its own with difficulty in the midst of almost universal indifference, and its decadence is so obvious that one merely wonders whether it is on the road towards transformation or towards evanescence. Whence comes this contrast between the destiny of the Protestant spirit and that of the Protestant Church ?

251

This is the problem I propose to examine when I put the question : What is the Protestant spirit ?

One of the first distinctive characteristics of the Protestant spirit is that it proclaims on principle the absolute independence of reason and faith and also the necessary harmony between them.

It would be well to point out here its fundamental antagonism in this respect to Catholicism, which denies and condemns independent science. The system of St. Thomas, which has been accepted and revived once more in the Germany of to-day by the neo-Thomistic School, is a combination of the two great factors in the spiritual life of the Middle Ages—the Catholic faith and the philosophy of Aristotle. It aims at proving that scientific truth and Catholic dogma do not clash, but are complementary to each other. Reason, by means of its own light, realises, as the Greek philosophers had done, that the ultimate cause of all must be sought for in an eternal Reason—that is to say, in God. It also demonstrates that although the specific dogmas of the Church cannot be derived from reason, they are at all events not contrary to it. But reason alone is not the only source of Truth. Above human science there is a superior truth derived from divine inspiration—revelation, which is the criterion of all truth. In the domain of faith the Church, guided by the spirit of God, is the supreme authority. And thus faith is made the crown and coping-stone of worldly science ; it is the human anticipation of the one universal truth which is to be found in God.

Now this Thomistic " semi-rationalism," to use Paulsen's expression, is absolutism in its strongest form. The principle of authority may have been proclaimed with greater insistence by some of St. Thomas's successors. Duns Scotus and Occam declared that no higher truths were capable of demonstration, and that reason must submit exclusively and without reserve to the authority of the Church in every matter touching the articles of faith. But this absolutist and ascetic Radicalism had its dangers. Reason, if violated and ill treated, runs the risk of being pushed into rebellion by the very excess of the despotism to which it is subjected. It may resign itself, for the love of peace, to acts of external submission, but it will emancipate itself internally in the depths of its conscience, and wait for a propitious moment in order to shake off the yoke that weighs too heavily upon it. It is better policy to give reason some partial satisfaction and allow it, as St. Thomas did, to have a share in the direction of life and in the elaboration of a general idea of the universe. By accustoming it to work in the second rank under the guidance of faith, by utilising its energies whilst forcing it to feel at every moment the limits beyond which it must not go, it is cajoled into submission and modesty, and made to play the part of an active but humble servant, a diligent and docile auxiliary to the Christian Faith.

As early as Luther Protestantism opposed the Thomistic semi-rationalism by a resolute " irrationalism." Far from wishing to make reason work under the control of faith, it aimed, on the contrary, at separating as completely as possible the domain of faith from that of reason, and at a radical denial of the power of reason in religious matters. The " Word of God " contained in the Holy Scriptures was the only source of faith. Now in relation to the Bible the work of reason was a mere formality—it simply had to decide the exact meaning of the sacred books. Theology was reduced to the philological interpretation of the Bible. As for the rational and philosophical proof of religious truth, this was neither necessary nor possible. Reason left to itself led to a mechanical or natural explanation of the Universe ; the supernatural was beyond its grasp. Separation was therefore necessary. Let reason abstain from opening its mouth upon sacred subjects into which it could only bring obscurity and confusion. In return it would be lawful for it to explain natural phenomena in its own way, and with perfect freedom ; faith had nothing to do with physics or cosmology.

The great religious crisis of Luther's life resulted in his liberation from scholastic theology and from semi-rationalism. It was, indeed, over the important question of grace that reason revealed to him its powerlessness in matters of faith. Reason, if asked what was necessary to salvation, would, in fact, answer that it must be won by works, or at least that good intention should be manifested in works, in which case God could pardon our shortcomings. This was the doctrine of the Church, and she exhorted her members to do good works. But Luther had learnt from his own experience that the soul does not attain ease by this method. He therefore concluded that reason was blind with regard to matters of faith, and the Church blind for having given reason so much credit. One of the principal causes of the corruption of the Church was, accordingly, in his eyes, the intrusion of reason into the realm of theology. The Church had set up as a Professor in all her schools and universities Aristotle, "that Greek who soweth illusion in all men's minds, that serpent with a thousand heads who brought forth the Scotists and the

Thomists, and who taught the vile doctrine that the whole of justice is in our own hearts."

Protestant irrationalism therefore resulted in an immense *simplification* of theological science. There were to be no more complicated speculations about the existence, the personality, and the attributes of God, or on " natural " religion and morality, but men were to return to the simple faith of primitive Christianity. Christ did not give humanity a theological system, but said to children and to the simple hearted : " Believe in Me and ye shall be saved." Men must once again forget the science of books and shut their ears to the babblings of the Doctors in the Temple and the Pharisees.

Protestant irrationalism may at first sight appear even more hostile than Catholicism to the development of any science not founded upon a religious basis. And it is, indeed, true that Luther occasionally hurled the most violent anathemas against the proud pretensions of reason, and that until quite recent times Protestantism has often shown itself full of mistrust and contempt towards the modern spirit and independent science.

Nevertheless, generally speaking, the sharp line of demarcation which Protestantism made between the domain of faith and that of reason was favourable to the development of science. In fact, if it imposed silence upon reason in the realm of faith, it left it, on the other hand, absolutely free in its own sphere, and allowed it complete liberty in its attempt to find a rational explanation for natural phenomena. The Catholic must always be ready to make his reason bow before authority. Reason always remains, in his eyes, in the position of a minor under the tutelage of faith ; he regards it with suspicion, and is per-

suaded that if it becomes emancipated and is allowed
to go its own way, it will separate man from God,
and lead him to pride and rebellion. Very different
is the fundamental conviction of Protestantism.
Firmly persuaded that religion has nothing to fear
from true science, that reason cannot separate man
from God as long as it is confined to its proper sphere,
Protestantism does not aim at exercising any control
over science, but leaves it entirely free to develop as
it pleases. The Protestant does not ever expect
science to support religious truth by its arguments,
but at the same time he does not see in it an enemy
against whom he should be on his guard—a source of
error and perdition. He holds out his hand to it
without fear. The Protestant is allowed, when he
takes up the study of nature, history, or philosophy,
to seek the natural truth without bias of any sort, and
without any preconceived desire to find in science an
apology for religion. He can consequently put himself into the position most favourable to scientific
research. The conviction that the unrestricted research for truth cannot possibly be bad or lead to
results contrary to those inculcated by religious faith,
is one of the ideas which showed themselves with
ever greater clearness in the breast of Protestantism,
and it made the reconciliation of the religion of the
Gospel with that of science an easy task.

This Protestant irrationalism is formulated with
the greatest clarity, and pushed to its extreme logical
conclusion in Schleiermacher's celebrated *Discourses
on Religion.*

In the first place, no one has recognised more frankly
than he the progress of modern culture and the
legitimacy of independent science. His *Discourses*
constitute a " defence " of religion. His apology,

however, is never made at the expense of science and secular philosophy. The author never addresses himself to the " despisers of religion " with any idea whatsoever of confuting them or of constraining them to abjure their heresies and submit to some superior authority. He does not attack either their metaphysics or their ethics, nor yet their conception of art. Schleiermacher had fully assimilated the most refined culture of his day, and was impregnated by the ideas of German classicism and by Kant and Goethe. But in his opinion this culture was not in any way irreconcilable with the religious spirit. He hurls no anathemas against the unbelievers who " in their sumptuous abodes have no other household gods but the maxims of the sages and the songs of the poets," who, full of love for humanity and their own country, science and art, have no room left in their hearts for the Beyond and for Eternity. He only asks of them one thing, and that is " to be fully and perfectly *cultured* in their disdain of religion." In short, he was persuaded that the irreligion of these intellectualists arose not from their positive culture, but simply from their ignorance of the true nature of religion, and consequently from a *defect* in their culture.

And this defect he undertakes to remedy by giving an exact definition of the domain proper to religion, and by showing that it is absolutely independent of the sphere of science and ethics.

According to Schleiermacher the real cause of the discredit into which religion had fallen was precisely the fact that this definition had not been made with sufficient care. Religion was very rarely to be found in all its purity, but was nearly always mixed up with alien elements. And this led to the belief that it consisted of a combination of certain meta-

17

physical conceptions—the idea of a Supreme Being, the First Cause of the Universe—together with certain moral principles—the idea of the law of duty. There was nothing more erroneous than the conception which turned religion into an aggregate of heterogeneous elements—a mediocre " chrestomathy for beginners." Religion had nothing to do with either metaphysics or morality. Metaphysics were the result of reflection, the image of the Universe reflected in our conscious thought. Morality appealed to the will, it aimed at extending indefinitely the Kingdom of Liberty and at making the Universe conform to the law it laid down. Religion was neither thought nor action : it was, according to Schleiermacher, *contemplation* and *feeling*. The moment the religious spirit ceased contemplating and feeling and tried to *define* the nature of the All, it could give birth only to a " vain mythology," a mass of dogmas, symbols, poetical images, and metaphysical concepts, which were devoid of any value either for science or for the religious consciousness. Religion, moreover, could not be a substitute for morality. Moral law in fact should regulate all our actions, and we should fulfil it with perfect consciousness, with calm and reflexion. Religious feelings, on the contrary, should accompany all our actions like sacred music, but it should not guide them. " Man should do everything *with* religion, nothing *through* religion." Perfectly distinct from both metaphysics and from morality, religion was an original and independent force, which possessed in every heart " a province which belonged to it alone, and in which it was sovereign." It was, together with speculative reason and practical reason, " the third necessary and indispensable element " in the human soul.

## II

If religion and science have each their distinctive sphere, where shall we find the domain proper to religion ?

When one tries to define in what the essence of religion in the eyes of the Protestant consists, one finds that he sees in it above all an intimate experience, an inner flame which is kindled in the heart of the believer.  Religion is the adhesion of the man in his entirety to the " Word of God " and to the Gospel Christ came to bring.  It is a mystic impulse of the heart, a state of the soul which requires to be *lived* in order to be realised, and of which no verbal description can give any adequate idea.

This inner experience was the great event in the spiritual life of Luther.  As a matter of fact, in his case we find at the basis of his doctrine of grace and predestination a mystic illumination which in a way formed the origin of his whole religious life.  When, from the depths of his cell in the Augustinian monastery at Erfurt, he sought in the agony of his heart for the road to salvation, it was not through reason or philosophy, nor by the discovery of a metaphysical theory or of a new dogma that he won peace for his soul.  It was the mystical doctrines of his friend Staupitz, the Vicar-General of the Order of St. Augustine, that delivered him from his doubts.  He was raised to a direct and lively faith in God who had promised men pardon through Christ, and gave it to them in spite of their state of profound and irremediable degradation, in spite of the radical inadequacy of their works, by virtue of a free and unmerited gift, without their being able to claim the smallest share in this work of grace. The immediate faith in the God of pity, the living consciousness of possessing Him—this was for Luther the very essence of religion. In the experience of the Protestant, therefore, faith is a certain state of feeling, a definite aggregate of subjective emotions, and not a doctrine conceived by the mind or a sum-total of clearly apprehended ideas to which human language can give precise expression.

From the historical point of view this mystic and individualistic element in religion shows itself more particularly in the vast number of very different manifestations which appeared from the seventeenth to the nineteenth century in the Protestant as well as in the Catholic world, in France and Holland, England and America, Germany and Austria, and which were designated by the common title of pietism.

Pietism was the ascetic and mystical reaction of religious feeling against the decadence of living faith and of the visible Church. It was a rebellion against the scholastic dogmatism which reduced religion to a mass of theological formulæ, and stirred up irritating and barren controversies in every department. In order to combat this parching intellectualism it endeavoured to stimulate religious feeling and imagination. It also condemned the dangerous alliance of the modern State with the official Church, and denounced the survival of Popery in the institution of State Churches. Abandoning the hope of organising the whole of society upon the basis of Christianity, it founded, either within or in opposition to the official Church, sects and pious conventicles where, in a narrower circle, a more sincere, efficient and intense Christianity might at least flourish.

The pietists thus voluntarily placed themselves

outside the pale of society, but they did not exalt their asceticism to a principle, or hurl forth anathemas against the world. They explained their attitude as a temporary necessity, and believed they were living at the end of the period of rebellion against God, which preceded the Second Advent of Christ. And in their struggle against scholasticism in dogma, and against the corruption of the official Church, they endeavoured to rekindle the flame of Christian mysticism and to found their religion upon the lively, intimate, and personal experience of divine grace. They wanted that inner illumination felt by Luther and the great mystics to be renewed in every Christian. And finding no food for their faith in the barren theological controversies of their day, they revived the taste for neo-Platonic and mystic literature, in which they found the religious psychology adapted to their needs, the description of mystic ecstasy and of gradual absorption into the bosom of Divine Unity. They plunged into the study of St. Augustine and St. Bernard, into the writings of anabaptists, spiritualists, and theosophists, in order, by contact with thought of this nature, to exalt their sense of religion.

This pietism was at once a reactionary and a progressive movement—reactionary because it tried to revive the old Christian and Protestant asceticism in all its rigour, and because it voluntarily associated itself with orthodox tendencies in matters of dogma; progressive, inasmuch as it developed religious subjectivism and was inclined to regard faith, not as the assent of a body of men to certain objective truths, but as the entirely personal experience of certain subjective emotions and the creation of the individual conscience.

Born amid the reformed circles of Holland in the seventeenth century, and imported into Germany during the seventeenth and eighteenth centuries, pietism developed more especially among the Lutheran communities, where, under Spencer and Francke, it became one of the most important elements in the religious life of the period. Then during the second half of the eighteenth century it lost ground. Mystic enthusiasm slowly died out and resolved itself into moral preaching and sentimental piety. It thus gradually lost its essential characteristics and became one of the elements of which the culture based upon rationalism prevalent during the era of enlightenment was formed.

After the end of the eighteenth century, however, it entered upon a fresh lease of life, especially among the southern Teutonic peoples, in Wurtemburg, Alsace, and Switzerland. At that time it welcomed to its breast all who had made a shipwreck of life— and their numbers during the period of strife and war were great, especially in the ranks of the aristocracy, who provided many recruits for the conventicles. From that moment pietism became an active factor in the spiritual life of Germany. It had its own writers, its own philosophers, and saints, like Hamann and Lavater, Claudius and Jung Stilling, Oberlin and Pfeffel, Jacobi and Novalis. And as a matter of fact it displayed some offensive characteristics at this juncture. The piety of these votaries often contained an element of moroseness, anxiety, and discontent ; it was narrow and had no broad outlook, and was too strictly immured within the intimate bounds of the religious life, too indifferent to public affairs, and too disdainful of scientific and artistic culture. At times it was even intolerant. A small group of ecstatic pietists and theosophists, during the era of reaction inaugurated by Wœllner in the reign of Frederick William IV., made the yoke of their demoralising despotism weigh heavy upon the necks of the Prussian clergy. But intriguing and ambitious pietism was still the exception. Piety was not yet turned into a career, and people did not frequent conventicles in order to insinuate themselves into aristocratic circles and push themselves on in the world. Pietism had many points in common with reformed Catholicism, and like it combated the dogmatic narrowness and the traditional formalism of the official Church. But it also held out its hand to Pestalozzi and his disciples, and supported them in the great work of popular education and the material and moral elevation of the lower classes.

Then came what is known as the period of the "Awakening." It seemed as though the temperature of the Protestant spirit had risen again. Pietistic tendencies mingled in a thousand different ways with the rousing of national feeling and with the political romanticism of the restoration. Hence arose a series of multifarious and diverse currents in the breast of Protestantism. Schleiermacher, as we have just seen, founded his religion upon contemplation and feeling, and led pious souls to approach as near to Christ as possible, in order, through His mediation, to succeed in themselves living the fundamental truths of faith and revelation. This grade of pietism, which was tinged with philosophy and literature, spread more particularly in the north and centre of Germany. Neander and Tholuck are considered its most typical representatives. In other quarters a simple piety based upon an unsophisticated faith in the Bible was spread abroad. It was to be found in the extreme north, at Kiel, where Claus Harms published in 1817, in honour of the anniversary of the Reformation, ninety-five theses against the modern Antichrist—that is to say, Reason elevated to the position of an infallible Pope. And similarly in Swabia and Bavaria there flourished an interdenominational pietism, in which the lay element predominated, and whose members held communion by personal faith in Jesus, the divine Saviour of men. The theological faculties of Tübingen and Erlangen, under Beck, Thomasius, and Hoffmann, were instrumental in spreading this particular form of Protestantism. In other quarters pietism allied itself with political romanticism, it spread among the aristocracy and the higher Civil Service, and even ended by ascending the throne in the person of Frederick William IV. Under this form we find it holding out its hand to orthodoxy, founding belief in revelation and the Scriptures upon the intimate personal experience of conversion through the Bible, and thus restoring the divine character of Holy Writ and favouring a conservative exegesis of the sacred text. This orthodox pietism, which was ambitious and militant, tried to impose its doctrine upon university professors and the clergy, and aimed at exercising a predominating influence over the official Church.

About 1848, however, rationalist ideas once more gradually took the offensive; they grew stronger and stronger, and even at one moment seemed upon the point of getting the upper hand in the sphere of politics. From that time the importance of pietism as a factor in the spiritual life of Germany also began to decline, Its alliance with orthodoxy became closer. In fact, among the professing Protestants of the official Church there existed a form of religion which was pietistic on account of its subjective character and orthodox because of the positive nature of the doctrines it professed. But on becoming an integral portion of official Protestantism, pietism also found itself involved in the decline of the State Church. It lost its practical influence over men's minds in proportion as it accentuated the reactionary tendency, the seeds of which it carried from its birth.

The pietistic spirit, at all events, is still to be found to-day, in quite different social strata, in which even now it gives proofs of vitality. Nearly everywhere the dissenting sects formed in England or America by pietism—the Methodists, the Irvingites, the Memnonites, the Baptists, etc.—carry on an ardent propaganda, and form in almost all parts of the world conventicles which sometimes live in good harmony with the official Church, but more often maintain a defiant and critical attitude towards the State clergy, and seduce from public worship precisely those natures in whom the need for religion is most strongly developed. Hence arose that popular form of pietism which now draws its recruits by preference from the lower social strata and harms the orthodox pietism of the public church. And the official clergy are filled with anxiety by this condition of things without, however, being able to protest overmuch. For these very sects and communities, which are independent and separatist, form an exceedingly ardent centre of Christian activity, and have given birth to a number of charitable works, teaching institutions, and home and foreign missions, which do honour to Protestantism.

We thus see, in rough outline, the part which pietism played in the evolution of Protestantism. It kept alive the religious spirit by insisting upon the necessity for every Christian to feel personally in his own heart that mystic impulse which raises man to God, and which was to be found at the beginning of Luther's religious life. By the very fact that it founded religion upon individual experience, it also tended to separate itself from the State Church— the official body which demanded from its members merely the external adherence to a certain creed and gave shelter haphazard to all those who subscribed to its doctrines, the religious and the lukewarm alike, the pious and the indifferent. Pietism formed conventicles in opposition to the Church, limited groups and guilds composed by the free membership of believers who lived in a real communion of feeling, and acted as a mutual control upon each other. Thus pietism also frequently appeared as a conservative force. In order to satisfy an exceedingly intense religious need it willingly inclined to the restoration of the positive forms of the old Protestantism, and made itself an ally and accomplice of the orthodoxy of which, in other respects, it nevertheless combated the formalist spirit and dogmatic dryness. And sometimes it presented itself in an aspect which astonished and shocked modern feeling, manifesting itself as a strict, narrow, and bitter piety, hostile to the world and wrapped up in itself, a blind and intolerant fanaticism, a mystic ecstasy which became inflamed to hysteria and nervous disorder, an extravagant form of superstition.

The part which pietism played in the heart of Protestantism has been compared to that of the

monastic orders in Catholicism. Like these institutions it was constantly reminding the Church
of her spiritual mission.  But whilst the monasteries
turned their backs upon the world in ascetic renunciation, and at the same time enrolled themselves
in the ranks of the worldly hierarchy of Catholicism,
the pietists, for their part, did not bow their individualism to any compromise, but continued,
although they too were animated by the spirit of
asceticism, to act in accordance with their age,
and on their age.  Thus pietism was an independent
spiritual force which periodically revived religious
subjectivism in the breast of Protestantism, constantly created new religious sects and rekindled
lively piety in the old ones.  It was an influence
which acted more particularly upon the lowest
strata of the nation, and satisfied their need of
religious excitement.  For this reason, also, it was
popular among the feudalists, who wished to keep
religion alive among the people.

But it was something more than all this.  It was
in fact the really living principle of Protestant
religiosity in its purest form.  It was the experiences
of pietism which made possible, in the breast of
the enfranchised Protestant conscience, the modern
science of religious psychology.  " All the theories,"
says Troeltsch, " which represent religion as being
essentially an emotion, a presentiment, poetry, a
symbolical representation of ideas which are active
in the subconscious depths of human nature, a
practical and active conviction, and a general condition of the soul—in short, the most precious results
of the modern science of religion have their root
in Radical pietism." It was upon pietism that
Lessing built his foundations when he realised that

feeling was the essence of religion and conceived the idea of his "eternal Gospel," which was destined to take the place of religion based upon dogma and authority. The religion of Kant was also, in the last instance, pietistic in postulating as a fundamental truth the "existence of practical reason," and thus founding religion upon the persevering effort of the Will to triumph over evil and be born again. Similarly in the religion of Herder, Jacobi, and Goethe—who were romanticists in their protestation against the dryness of rationalism and in the insistence with which they cast into relief the emotional, mystical, and voluntary element in religion, and the affinity between poetry and religion —it is easy to see the influence of pietism. And it appears most clearly in the doctrines of Schleiermacher, who defined religion as a mystic intuition of God, "a sense and love of the Infinite," as a vision of the universe and the emotion which accompanies this vision. It still lives to-day in the breasts of many German Protestants, and even among those of them who have no positive faith, but in whom the need for religion survives in the shape of a yearning of the heart towards the divine principle in the world, and a more or less joyous and confident adhesion to a universal order.

## III

The subjective and mystical character of the Protestant religion had as its direct consequence the gradual crumbling away of Christian dogma.

For Catholics religious truth is one, positive and unchanging. It has no longer to be discovered, but was found long ago, and received expression in

dogma, whilst the Church's mission consists in preserving this dogma in all its purity, and fighting
heresy wherever it appears. Dogma, in the eyes
of Catholics, is an aggregate of doctrines which
are objectively true, which are external to the spirit
of the believer and humbly received by him—an
organic whole, a synthesis which is either accepted
or rejected *en bloc*, but which allows of no discussion
in detail or any arbitrary eliminations.

Now Luther resolutely repudiated Catholic dogma.
Determined to bring back religion to its essential
principle, that mystic impulse of the soul illuminated
by the vision of the Divine, he was firmly resolved
to destroy the edifice of scholastic theology, and
put an end to dogmatic intellectualism in order
to substitute in its place " the Word of God " and
the " Gospel " of Jesus alone. It is true that Luther
found great difficulty in establishing a clear distinction between what was " Gospel " and what
was " dogma." And he ended—as we shall see
later on—in laying the foundations of a new dogmatism almost as complicated and intolerant as the
old one. But he had, nevertheless, levied a very
decisive blow at the ancient edifice of orthodoxy—
and the work of demolition was carried on after
his day. In fact, it was quite impossible for Protestantism, in consistency with its own principles, to
support the idea of an intangible dogma. If religion
is essentially a state of the soul, an intimate subjective
experience, it is evident that the categories " true "
and " false " have no application in matters of
faith. A man either feels or does not feel a state
of the soul, an emotion ; but such a state of the
soul or such an emotion is neither "true" nor "false,"
and cannot be brought home to the outsider. Dogmas

necessarily give only an inadequate and approximate and consequently provisional and changeable interpretation of the intimate, subjective experiences which constitute religion. From the Protestant point of view, therefore, it is illusory and iniquitous to gauge the " religion " of a believer by his acceptance of such and such a dogma—that is to say, by metaphysical and historical conceptions which belong to the realm of reason. Religion has its roots, not in the domain of intelligence and knowledge, but in a much more profound region of the human soul.

As early as the end of the eighteenth century the progress towards subjectivism had reached its furthest limits. Schleiermacher refused to admit that a dogma, or any metaphysical conception, could be an essential element of religion. It may be argued that faith in the Supernatural is necessary in the believer. But every contingent phenomenon is either " miraculous " or not, according to the point of view from which it is regarded, whether it is considered in relation to the Infinite or in connection with the finite world, with the eyes of the religious or of the scientific man. Or perhaps faith in the Bible is a prerequisite ? But the Holy Scriptures, far from being a code of intangible truths, form " merely a mausoleum of religion, a commemorative monument recording the fact that there once existed a powerful spirit which no longer lives to-day." Even the belief in God and the immortality of the soul have not, from the religious point of view, the importance which is generally attributed to them, and an " atheist " may have a profoundly religious nature, as, for instance, Spinoza, in whom Schleiermacher venerated one of the sublimest spirits, most thoroughly permeated with the divine, that has ever existed. One should even go further. A religion, inasmuch as it is a vision of the Universe, is an absolutely individual experience. No man can boast of possessing in himself alone the *whole* of religious truth. Religion is necessarily "infinite" and is the sum-total of all private religious experiences. Every one must feel conscious of the fact that *his religion* is only a fraction of the All, and respect the originality of every soul that has understood the language of the Infinite. True religion, therefore, is absolutely tolerant, as "in the bosom of the Infinite all things co-exist side by side in peace ; all is *one* and all is *true.*"

And just as Protestantism eliminated from religion all obligatory belief in a metaphysical idea, it also gradually stripped Christianity of its historical elements.

Here once again Luther set the example. By allotting to Reason the task of interpreting the Bible and of fixing its "true" meaning, and by thus instituting the critical study of the Holy Scriptures, he threw open to human Reason an enormous field for research. But this critical examination of the Bible, prolonged through centuries, from Reimarus and Lessing to Strauss and Harnack, has led in the present day to results which Luther certainly never anticipated, and which would have filled him with horror if he had foreseen them, but which are in themselves in no way contradictory to the spirit of Protestantism. In fact, from the moment that the Reformation recognised the right of Reason to submit the sacred text to its investigation, it also became impossible for it to assign any limits to these researches, or to fix the point at which criticism ceased to be " Protestant," and to pass sentence on principle against the results of that philological inquiry which it had itself provoked.

From the eighteenth century onwards, the criticism of the Bible boldly attacked the belief in the supernatural. In fact, the rationalism of the era of enlightenment was convinced that science and faith must inevitably agree. Philosophy and science led the man of learning to a " natural religion," which postulated the existence of a God, who was omnipotently good, powerful and wise, as the creator of the Universe. Consequently all well-conducted criticism of the Bible must necessarily lead to the same results. Theologians, therefore, tried to eliminate from the Bible everything that was irrational. For instance, they eradicated the miracles, which they explained away as illusions or pious frauds. They denied the divinity of Christ, Whom they no longer regarded as a God, but as a superior man, Who enunciated the moral law and deserved to have Christianity called after Him, though He Himself never had any such pretension. In short, they reduced the moral teaching of Christianity to a reasoned and somewhat prosaic moral eudæmonism. The supernatural was thus eliminated from Holy Scripture by means of " natural " explanations, which were often, it is true, puerile and devoid of all semblance of probability.

Religious psychology and the criticism of the rationalists were too inadequate for their interpretation of the Bible to survive for long. But the progress of the historical and philological sciences in the nineteenth century resulted in the birth of a Biblical criticism, which was infinitely more methodical, better informed, and more radical in its conclusions than the rationalistic one had been.

The criticism of the eighteenth century had eliminated the supernatural element from the Bible, but
it did not deny in any comprehensive manner that
the Bible records provided authentic sources of
knowledge which brought to our consciousness an
aggregate of facts which were historically true. It
was at this point that the higher criticism of the
nineteenth century stepped in to cast doubt precisely upon the historical value of the Scriptures.
Strauss, followed by Baur and the Tübingen School,
saw in the Biblical stories not historical records,
but myths. Regarded as historical facts, all the
positive data upon which the traditional faith
was based—the supernatural birth of Jesus, His
miracles, His resurrection, and His ascension into
heaven—were stripped of all likelihood. In fact,
they depicted for us, not the historical Jesus, but the
Christ of sacred legend, and were not the correct
records of chroniclers, but the products of the religious
imagination and the poetic myths brought forth by
the unconsciously creative fancy of the people. The
Bible narratives about the founder of Christianity
were simply legends which had their birth in the
primitive Christian community, and among the
various groups which sprang from it, and they clothed
in a pseudo-historical cloak the ideas and the sentiments which were active in these circles. The Gospel
stories did not form a biography of Jesus, but were a
sort of legendary poem breathing forth the desire
which the primitive community felt to glorify their
founder and the need they experienced of seeing the
idea of the Messiah realised. Thus the Bible, in which
the old believers saw a sacred book inspired by God
Himself, became in the eyes of modern critics a human
document, in which were reflected the thoughts, the

18

passions, and the hopes of a body of enthusiasts who formed the primitive Church.

Thus the progress of religion towards subjectivism was completed. The historical data of Christianity ceased, for the Protestant, to contain objective facts, which every Christian must accept. They were simply the poetical description of the religious experiences of the first believers. They too were the product of religious subjectivism, the figurative expression of certain states of the soul. In the present, as in the past, the essence of religion was the individual impulse towards the Divine. Christian history, or, more properly speaking, Christian legend was, like dogma, merely a provisional and imperfect transcript of the Christian conscience. To reconstruct by the light of the Gospel story the actual facts which gave them birth and the real life of Jesus, to find out history from the myth, which alone had come down to us, to unravel from all these subjective testimonies the consciousness which Jesus possessed of Himself—*das Selbstbewusstein Jesu*—became a hazardous enterprise, a problem which had a great attraction for Protestant critics, from Strauss to our own day, but of which they realised the insurmountable difficulties ever more clearly. So much was this the case that a Catholic historian of Protestantism, after pointing out the necessarily subjective character of these attempts, and the divergencies which existed between them, was able to wonder, without appearing paradoxical, whether Christ had not once more become for the scientific Germany of to-day that which He was to the Athenians in the time of St. Paul—" The Unknown God ! "

At the same time as Protestantism, by reducing religion to the rank of a mere matter of experience, cast doubt upon the *objective* nature of Christianity, it also called in question its *absolute* character.

In the Middle Ages, as well as in primitive Protestantism, there was *only one* true religion communicated to men by the miracle of divine revelation, which alone was capable of securing their salvation. Paganism was not a religion, but an error which had its source in original sin, and was punished by eternal damnation. Religion, therefore, was one and absolute, and outside its pale there was no possible salvation for men. The very notion of a history of *religions*, the attempt to conceive a general idea of " religion," and to explain by means of this idea the genesis of the various religious conceptions of humanity, would have been regarded as impious, and those who actually did attempt it, like Pic de la Mirandole or Erasmus, were the objects of general reprobation.

And thus, about the eighteenth century, there gradually came into existence, thanks to the efforts of English and French thinkers especially, a science of religion which made a comparative study of the various religious manifestations, from Christianity to the grossest superstitions of the most primitive savages, which endeavoured to unravel the laws governing this complex aggregate of phenomena and set itself the task of tracing the genesis of the " religious sense " of humanity. This science was based, not upon the Bible and the tradition of the Church, but upon the inner experiences by which the religious life is revealed. It regarded religious phenomena as a particular subdivision of psychic phenomena as a whole. It considered religious faith in the light of a spiritual activity, and drew up a classification of the objective contents of this faith and the positive dogma the " truth " of which was precisely the problematical point. In this way it enlarged our religious horizon considerably. The modern man gradually learnt to realise the small compass of Christianity in relation to humanity as a whole, and he accustomed himself to regard the various religions of mankind as identical in principle, and to utilise the same critical methods in the study of their myths and documents. He ceased to consider religion as an unchangeable and positive " truth." On the contrary, he acknowledged that religion was a thing which *varied* in different times and places, and which was subjected, like every other manifestation of life, to the great law of evolution. After the end of the eighteenth century the science of religion resulted in two opposing theories, which grew more and more divergent. Some critics, like Hume, saw in religious phenomena a characteristic manifestation of primitive human thought; they believed that religions were begotten by fear or by hope, and were exceedingly sceptical with respect to the " truth " of their positive contents. From this theory there was derived, during the nineteenth century, the positivist idea of the three epochs of humanity—the religious, the metaphysical, and the scientific epochs. This hypothesis, which resulted in the more or less open denial of the eternal value either of positive religions or of religious feeling in general, was fundamentally opposed to that German idealism which regarded the evolution of the religious sense as the central factor of psychical development as a whole, and even for some time agreed with Hegel in discerning in Christianity the highest form and the perfect bloom of the religious idea.

From that moment Protestantism was confronted with a grave problem. To what extent could it

assimilate the results of the science of religion ? To
what extent could it sacrifice the " absolute " character of religious truth ?

By virtue of its own fundamental principles, Protestantism was bound to be accommodating with
respect to these new ideas. And as a matter of fact
this was perfectly possible. In short, Protestantism
tended, as we have already seen, to minimise the
dogmatic and historical elements of religion as much
as possible. By the distinction it made between the
Christianity of the Church and the " Christianity of
Christ," by the contrast it established between the
teaching of St. Paul and that of Jesus, and by the
final reduction of the essence of Christianity to the
Gospel of Christ alone, it ended by so simplifying
the principle of that faith as to render it possible to
identify it with the fundamental principle of morality
and religion. The evolution of the Christian conscience thus seemed the final stage in the evolution
of the religious sense in the heart of mankind.

And inasmuch as Schleiermacher admitted religious
subjectivism, so also did he recognise that Christianity was not the *only* religion, and that, moreover,
it was not fixed once and for all. There were as
many religions as there were original intuitions regarding the universe and the Infinite. Religion *in
itself* was the aggregate of *all* the possible forms of
positive religion. And similarly no positive religion
could be the *whole* of religion—Christianity not ex-
cepted. The intuition upon which it was based was
on the one hand the eternal *contrast* between the
Finite and the Infinite, between imperfect and sinful
man and God, and on the other hand the eternal act
of *mediation* between the Finite and Infinite, salvation
by means of a number of mediators between the God-

head and man the sinner. Christianity was, therefore, in a certain sense, an eternal religion. Having
as its particular object the very history of religion,
the succession of the religious intuitions of the Universe, it was a faith which was capable of infinite
development, a " potential religion," a " religion of
religions." But Schleiermacher expressly stated that
although Christ was *one* admirable mediator among
many, He was not the *only* possible mediator. The
Christian idea continued to develop after Christ ; it
gave birth to new religious ideas, and would do so
again. But more than that ; it might even become
superfluous at a time when there would no longer be
any need for a mediator between the Finite and the
Infinite, and when religious truth would shine forth
upon all men alike. But he also thought that,
practically speaking, this state of holiness was still
in the dim distance, and that, in any case, it could
not last ; corruption would return unceasingly, and
consequently the necessity for redemption would
always make itself felt anew. Thus each epoch in
the life of mankind would be a sort of " palingenesis
of Christianity," which from time to time would reappear in a constantly more spiritualised form.

We now have a clear conception of the direction
in which Protestantism evolved. It tended to strip
religion of its objective, historical, and absolute
character. Christianity no longer appeared in the
light of an aggregate of revealed truths which were
external to the believer and in which he must have
faith, but as a state of feeling which every individual
must *live* for himself. It no longer demanded from
its followers a belief in the reality of certain historical
facts. Protestant criticism ended by discovering in
the Gospel narrative merely the mythical expression

of the religious experiences of the primitive Christians, and only allowed us to perceive, through a more and more impenetrable fog, the personality and teaching of the *historical* Christ. Protestantism, in short, tended to strip Christianity of its qualities as a revealed religion that was one and eternal. The Christian faith was merely one of the myriad manifestations of humanity's religious sense, an admirable manifestation certainly, a superior one maybe; but certainly not a unique or even, perhaps, an eternal one; and in any case it was subject to change. In short, Protestantism inclined towards instituting a Christianity devoid of dogma, which *developed* a subjective religion involved in an endless cycle of evolution.

## IV

Thus Protestantism, by its very nature, aimed at reconciling into a synthetic whole as perfect as possible the two great conceptions of the universe over which the mind of modern man was divided—Christianity and scientific rationalism. Whilst in Catholic countries, especially in France, the collision between religion and science resulted in an open and violent conflict between the Church and the philosophers, it was accomplished in Protestant Germany in the most peaceful manner. The two rival powers, instead of mutually exterminating each other, tried to come to terms and concluded an alliance.

In the eighteenth century the rationalistic deism of the era of enlightenment had already appeared as a preliminary attempt to reconcile these two conflicting principles. The identity between the system of nature constructed by the philosophers and the explanation of the universe taught by theologians was proclaimed. " Reason and revelation," said Wolf, " cannot be contradictory, since both come from God, the sole source of truth, who transmits it through these two channels." And as a matter of fact everything was arranged at the expense of a few concessions on either side. The philosophers proved by means of rational arguments the existence of an omnipotently good, powerful, and wise God, as Creator of the universe, and also the immortality of the soul. They insisted upon the harmony of nature, and asserted their optimistic faith in the indefinite progress of mankind. The theologians, as we have already seen, eliminated the supernatural from the Bible, toned down the pessimistic character of primitive Christianity, and promoted moral teaching to the foremost rank. And thus a religious philosophy was established, which gave satisfaction both to religious natures and men of science. It faced the " radicals " of both parties at once. It combated atheists and the despisers of " natural religion." It hurled its fulminations against Spinoza, who was the scapegoat that had to be cast forth into the wilderness in order to point out to those who believed in the philosophy of Descartes and Leibnitz the dangerous paths into which they must not stray. It condemned Voltaire, Helvetius, and the Encyclopædists, whose unbridled materialism was of a nature to alarm moderate spirits and throw them back into the arms of superstition. But it also, on the other hand, opposed the fanatical and ignorant sectarians of the " positive religions," as well as the intolerant and hypocritical members of the orthodox faith, the bigoted and narrow pietists, and above all the Jesuits, the invisible and omnipresent instigators of a colossal conspiracy against liberty and enlightenment.

There is no doubt whatever that rationalism rendered great services to Germany. Its generous faith in the power of the intelligent will, its attempt to smooth over denominational differences and to unravel from the positive religions a universal ideal for mankind, deserve admiration and respect for all time. And its action proved above all beneficial, inasmuch as it favoured the diffusion in Germany of a patrimony of ideas and feelings common to the whole nation. Accepted not only by men of high culture, but also by the clergy, and protected by the Government, rationalism was able to penetrate into the lowest strata of the people. By means of preaching, and through the elementary schools, it was able to spread its fundamental principles, liberty of thought and conscience, the free exercise of reason in all circumstances of life, the habit of reflection and of consciousness of self—even among the masses. It placed its seal upon a very considerable fraction of the nation, and it thus maintained a certain unity in the spiritual life of the country. Thanks to it the upper classes did not lose all touch with the religious ideal of the masses; and the masses were not entirely ignorant of the culture which had spread among the upper strata of society.

But it must, on the other hand, be confessed that this culture of the era of enlightenment was of a very mediocre description. Optimistic and dogmatic as it was, and convinced that it had explained the mystery of the world and found a solution for all great psychological, moral, metaphysical, and religious problems, firmly believing that through a precise science it knew the meaning of life, and peremptory in all its assertions, rationalism was a conception of life suitable to profoundly honest and respectable men, who were filled with no indiscreet curiosity of mind, who were not much inclined to any refinements of thought and feeling, and as little accessible to doubt or to uneasiness of conscience as they were incapable of any passionate religious exaltation. But it could not, in the long run, satisfy the cultured minority. Its psychology was, as a matter of fact, too rudimentary. In its shortsighted enthusiasm for reason and science it did not know how to estimate at their proper valuation the " irrational " forces in human nature. It either despised imagination or regarded it with suspicion ; it was mistrustful of sensitiveness and passion ; it thought it could reduce morality to a question of interest, and it almost eliminated the element of mysticism from religion. All these forces, which it opposed or despised—instinct, sensitiveness, creative imagination, and moral and religious faith—combined together to put an end to an unjustifiable domination which was becoming intolerable.

And at the same time it began to be realised that the attempted reconciliation between science and faith was no real solution, but a halting compromise which did not take long to dissatisfy everybody. Religious spirits saw in rationalism a thinly veiled atheism. As for the really scientific minds, they regarded it, like Lessing, as " a patchwork put together by clumsy pseudo-philosophers," and accused the champions of enlightenment of having " far too little of the theologian about them and not enough, by a very long way, of the philosopher." And if in our own days a Nietzsche has risen up with so much vehemence against Protestantism, which he calls " the

THE PROTESTANT SPIRIT 283

semi-paralysis of Christianity and reason," it is precisely on account of its capacity for producing bastard and misbegotten compromises like rationalism. Towards the end of the eighteenth century it was wholly discredited among the cultured classes of the nation, and melted away beneath a hail of scorn and ridicule.

Whilst worn-out rationalism gradually died beneath the scoffing of cultured Germany, a new and impressive attempt at reconciling science and faith was made through the instrumentality of Kant and of German idealism.

The rationalists had made themselves the champions of the rights of reason, or, more accurately, to use Fichte's expression, " of the natural intelligence which is developed outside all culture and all morality." German idealism, on the contrary, subjected these pretensions to a severe criticism, and put an end to the despotic sovereignty of theoretical reason.

Against the pure intellectualists, who asserted that the real dignity of man was to be found in knowledge, Kant proclaimed " the supremacy of practical reason." Man was not merely a thinking creature—he was above all an acting one. It was not by man's theoretical reason alone that he attained to certainty. In the existence of the consciousness of duty, which dominated our actions, we possessed a certainty as complete and as absolute—even more absolute—than rational certainty. But the moral law, if we analysed its premises, revealed to us the law of the Categorical Imperative of Duty—a law which was not imposed upon us from without, but which we laid down for ourselves, and which commanded us to do good, not with an eye to any particular advantage, nor for the attainment of any practical object, but in an absolute fashion simply because it was good. This law of duty was for Kant an absolutely certain truth, which admitted of no possible doubt. It was a postulate of practical reason. It was, in short, an act of faith, but one which provided us with evidence as startling as that of science itself.

And upon the basis of the " existence of practical reason " Kant built the religion of idealism. God existed because He was the necessary condition for the moral law. The existence of God was a postulate of practical reason, not a theoretical but a practical affirmation, which had its source in a moral need—a need, moreover, which was not merely an individual, but a universal one, as necessary as reason itself. We believed in God because we believed in the reality of duty, because without God the Categorical Imperative would cease to be conceivable as a real law of the human will. Thus religious faith, according to the doctrine of Kant, was a " rational belief " (*Vernunftglauben*).

Having thus demonstrated that the essence of the religious life of mankind was to be found in the eternal effort of the will towards regeneration and salvation, Kant unveiled for us the genesis of this religious ideal. As man was incapable of rising all at once to a clear consciousness of his destination and of his true nature, " rational faith " first manifested itself in the heart of the human species in the shape of a divine revelation, which authoritatively demanded belief as the expression of the will of God Himself. The visible Church, which was the vessel and guardian of this revelation, obliged the faithful to believe a certain number of historical facts, which they had to admit without discussion, and dogmas and statutes to which they were called upon to submit blindly. But these irrational elements in religion tended gradually to become spiritualised and absorbed. In proportion as humanity reached nearer to maturity it " rationalised " the historical elements of the ecclesiastical faith and learnt gradually to identify it with rational faith.

This identity was not only possible, but necessary. The faith in Christ Himself, in fact, was not belief in an historical fact. It was faith in the most ideal type of humanity, in man wholly regenerate, fundamentally good, and consequently the Son of God; it was faith in the possibility of our regeneration, in the reality of the law of duty and of our moral destination. Humanity, shaped in the school of the visible Churches, thus gradually tended to form a " Church invisible," in which there would no longer be any ecclesiastical hierarchy or revealed dogma, in which every believer would be a priest, and in which the historical faith in a divine revelation and unreasoning obedience to the orders of God would finally develop into an autonomous and conscious " rational faith."

The conclusion of all this was a general conception of life founded not upon intelligence alone, but upon human nature in its " completeness," and upon reason and the moral will in particular; a religion based upon the existence of moral obligation, and which gushed forth from the depths of the human soul, without being imposed upon mankind from without, through the channel of a supernatural revelation—a religious philosophy which bound the past to the present, and showed in the traditional religions the necessary stages by which man gradually raised himself to the consciousness of natural religion. Such were, apparently, the essential traits of German idealism. This movement thus revealed itself as an effort on the part of the Protestant spirit to provide a comprehensive interpretation of the universe, which should be in conformity with its own most fundamental tendencies, at once strictly scientific and profoundly religious, holding all the conquests of modern Reason in high esteem, and at the same time full of respect for the beliefs of the past. Contemporary historians of German thought are quite right when they agree as a rule in seeing in Kant the greatest modern representative of the Reformation and the philosopher *par excellence* of Protestantism.

It is obviously impossible for me to trace the evolution of German idealism in the space at my command. To give the narrowest interpretation of the term, it means the philosophical movement of which Kant, Fichte, Schleiermacher, Schelling, Hegel, Jacobi, and Fries are the best-known representatives. On the one hand, this philosophical movement was in intimate connection with the contemporary literary movement, with the classicism of Goethe and Schiller, and with romanticism. But, on the other, German idealism was not confined to the period between Kant and Hegel, and did not end with the dissolution of the Hegelian School and the crashing failure of metaphysical speculation. After a short interval of eclipse it came to light again in the second half of the century in the persons of Fechner, Lotze, Wundt, Eucken, and Bergmann. It brought forth a new idealistic philosophy, opposed the progress of materialism with the help of the tenets of Kant, and once more set flowing in literature and in art the modern idealistic and neo-romantic current of thought, which can be perceived side by side with realism and naturalism. It goes without saying that in the course of this long evolution German idealism clothed itself in the most diverse forms. Speculative and adventurous in the beginning, with the grandiose constructions of a Fichte or a Hegel, it became more scientific at the end of the century, and endeavoured to found an *inductive* metaphysics upon the solid basis of the exact sciences. In some respects it was very similar to pantheism and absorbed God into the universe. In others again it tended towards a religion of beauty and harmony and a restoration of the Hellenic ideal. But on the whole, under all its various manifestations, it preserved certain essential characteristics. It opposed the narrow dogmatism of the old rationalists, the scepticism or agnosticism of the pure empiricists, and the utilitarian materialism of the positivists. And above all, in spite of its independent and on occasion apparently irreligious airs, it remained conscious of its connection with Christianity. The philosophers from Kant to Hegel, the artists from Goethe to the romanticists, or Richard Wagner, all agreed in regarding modern " religion " as identical with the religion of Christ. And thus German idealism appeared in the light of a new combination of the two great elements of Western culture —the classical element and the Christian element— and as an ingenious and profound attempt to unite into one original whole the spiritualised religion of Christ and that of science and beauty.

This religion of the cultured minority, the influence of which spread far beyond the bounds of Germany, to France, England, and America, certainly possesses a far greater scientific interest than the rationalism of the eighteenth century which preceded it. But nevertheless it must be confessed that its sphere of action remained much more limited than that of rationalism.

It was never able, like the latter, to become a really popular religion, and never penetrated into the lowest strata of the nation. It was too intellectual, too complicated, and also too subjective. It demanded from its adherents too high a degree of culture, and above all it always remained indifferent to any kind of organised ritual. It had as its basis a popular religion, but it rose above the level of that faith, and it did not arouse in its followers the need of a common religious life or of public services. It remained in the condition of an entirely intimate and personal religiosity without resulting in any reformation of the existing Church. Schleiermacher was the only one of the great representatives of idealism who had the reorganisation of the Church really at heart. But the tendencies which came to light in his *Discourses on Religion* were never realised in practice. And from his time the idealistic Protestantism of the minority always remained upon the outskirts of the official Church, incapable of finding expression for its most intimate aspirations in the dogmas, the liturgy, and the ritual of the conservative *Landeskirchen*, freed from the worship of the Bible, which had ceased in its eyes to be the spiritual food *par excellence*, and, moreover, but little inclined to regard as a possible consummation an intimate and lively intercourse between the human soul and the immanent and impersonal God which it worshipped.

Hence also a certain impotence in the domain of actual life. This religion of metaphysicians, men of letters, artists, and speculators of all sorts was lacking in consistency. These idealists, conscious of their own intellectual superiority, were, with an incurable simplicity, periodically astonished at the successes won by the organised religions, by Catholicism or by a ponderous orthodox pietism. And thus, opposed on the one hand by the " positivists," who cast aspersions upon its pantheism and suspected the authenticity of its Christianity, and menaced on the other by materialism, which accused it of being lacking in scientific exactitude and won over innumerable converts in the capitalistic and labouring classes, German idealism remained a force which was held in esteem in the higher ranks of culture. But it had little influence over the lower strata of ordinary life, and but a small hold upon the mass of the people, whilst its power of attraction and organisation was not by any means considerable.

This does not mean, however, that this vanguard of Protestantism did not play an important part in the spiritual life of Germany. Naturally this small aristocracy of intellect, to whom it was very doubtful whether even the appellation of Christian could be applied, had no very great importance for denominational Protestantism as a dogmatic creed and as a Church. But none the less was it an exceedingly vital element of Protestantism ; it was the lever which made it a " progressive " religion, and prevented it from becoming petrified in the dogma and ritual of the past. If, in accordance with the positivist doctrine, universal evolution leads to the gradual disappearance of the feeling and need for religion, German idealism would be nothing but an interesting but barren period in the history of civilisation. It would only have served to delay the final dissolution of Protestantism by concealing the fundamental incompatibility between faith and science beneath specious though deceptive hypotheses, and thus keeping a certain number of good souls a little longer in captivity to an illusion of religion. But if the need of

19

religion is an integral element in human nature, if the " religion " of the future must grow from that of the past by a regular and progressive evolution, it becomes at once evident that German idealism has perhaps a great career before it. In this case, it is justifiable to ask whether it is not this minority—which is at once a reforming body, and one that believes in tradition—that is drawing up the table of values which will rule the society of the future. And without wishing to pass any premature verdict upon the solution which this problem may one day receive, it is possible, at all events, to assert that this idealistic religion, which is in high favour to-day in the cultured society of Germany, is a very characteristic manifestation of the German genius, which, in politics as well as in religion, shows itself to be distinctly progressive, though it is hostile to all revolutionary Radicalism, and is an advocate of historical continuity and a seemly compromise between the past and the future.

# CHAPTER IV

## THE PROTESTANT CHURCH

### I

PROTESTANTISM, as we have said, tended towards a subjective religion free from dogma. But at the same time it also constantly gave expression to the uncontrollable need of restoring a dogma and a creed in some shape or form.

We have already pointed out this contradiction in Luther. At the very moment when he was working with all his might to demolish the edifice of Catholic dogma, he was impelled by a sort of fatality which was almost tragic to formulate a new form of dogmatism. He wished only the " Gospel of Jesus " to remain standing. But how was the distinction between " Gospel " and " dogma " to be drawn ? The departure taken by Luther was upon many points an arbitrary one. He regarded as an integral portion of the " Gospel " some of the old dogmas, such as that of the Trinity and the twofold nature of Christ. Hostile towards any superstitious reverence for the letter of the Bible, he nevertheless did not refrain from constraining others to bow before the text of the Scriptures when this text seemed to him particularly important or convincing. Although he was an enemy of scholastic hair-splitting, yet he allowed himself to be inveigled into interminable controversies of a subtle description. And thus willy-nilly

291

he laid the foundations of a new dogmatism. After him Melanchthon furnished the Protestant faith with an ample basis of philosophical formulæ. In this connection he restored the philosophy of Aristotle, the very man against whom Luther had hurled his fulminations in such violent terms. From the seventeenth century onwards there was to be found in all the Protestant universities, as well as in the Catholic ones, a scholastic philosophy at the service of theology —*ancilla theologiæ*. And the theologians, taking up their stand upon these formulæ, vied with each other in drawing distinctions between Protestantism and Catholicism, and differentiating the various Protestant sects and in convicting each other of heresy.

Thus the idea of " orthodoxy " sprang up once more in the breast of Protestantism. A problematical and dangerous idea certainly ! For how was it possible to conceive of orthodoxy in the case of a religion which tended to suppress dogma in favour of religious intuition, a faith which was susceptible of variation ? What is orthodoxy if the " true doctrine " is not definite and unchanging ? And yet Protestantism necessarily tended, as every other religion had done, to set up a dogma. A religion, in fact, ought to be susceptible of communication, and should serve as a bond between all who have had similar religious experiences. Now it is evident that it is extraordinarily difficult for people to communicate intuitions, states of the soul, and emotions to each other ; and that consequently, in the case of a subjective religion, it is far from easy to know whether the faithful possess a communion of sentiment or not. Conceptions and ideas, on the other hand, are easily communicated, and from the practical point of view are more easily utilised as signs of recognition and as rallying-points. Hence the tendency, which Protestantism was clearly incapable of overcoming, to accept dogma to a certain extent as a substitute for religious intuition, and to allow intellectual conceptions to supplant and take the place of intimate experience, and to define, by means of metaphysical formulæ or historical assertions the essence of that " Word of God," that " Gospel of Jesus " which Luther regarded as the basis of the Christian religion.

In the nineteenth century the Conservative and orthodox tendency manifested itself with as much energy as the opposing Liberal one.

From the 'twenties, orthodox Lutheranism became a power in Germany. We have already pointed out how, in alliance with pietism, it ended by exercising a considerable influence over the public authorities and gaining the real supremacy in the official Church. The chief personage in whom this renaissance of orthodoxy became incarnate was the famous zealot Hengstenberg, the founder of the *Evangelische Kirchenzeitung*. He anathematised with the fury of a sectarian all the progressive tendencies of Protestantism, from the old rationalism of the eighteenth century to the subjective spiritualism of Schleiermacher and the idealism of Hegel. He levelled a fierce attack not only at doctrines, but also at men, and made an unscrupulous use of invective and denunciation, and of his own accord appealed to the authority of the Government against his religious opponents. This neo-Lutheran ortho-doxy originated in the reign of Frederick William III., and was predominant in Prussia under Frederick William IV. Driven back at the time of the Revolution in 1848, it regained its footing in the 'fifties, and denounced the subjectivism of Liberal Protestantism and the aberrations of " besotted Science " with redoubled energy.  Its power, moreover, made itself felt not only in Prussia, but also in the rest of Germany, and it celebrated its greatest triumph in Mecklenburg and the Electorate of Hesse.  Here, under Kliefoth and Vilmar, it did not merely confine itself to demanding a literal belief in traditional dogma.  It taught the miraculous and divine efficacy of the Sacraments, which were the veritable acts of God ; it proclaimed the direct action of supernatural powers upon human life, and especially that of the devil.  Vilmar asserted that he had with his own eyes seen the enemy of the human race with his horrible gnashing teeth.  And if to-day orthodoxy scarcely ever manifests itself in such superannuated shapes, it nevertheless remains a real power.  Not only does it maintain a compact group of convinced believers, but it is also considered the natural auxiliary of royalty in its struggle against revolutionary parties.  The alliance between the Throne and the Altar, once denounced by Schleiermacher as one of the Church's gravest dangers, still existed up to the end of the century.  Political conservatism and religious conservatism gladly made common cause against those who did not believe in positive dogma, whether religious or monarchical.

And it cannot be denied that for German Protestantism the conflict between the positive and the negative attitudes, between the denominationalism of the orthodox and the subjectivism of the " infidels," constituted a serious problem.  Critics hostile to reform have frequently pointed out the inconveniences and dangers of this position.

They depict for us the sorry condition of the

parson, who during his sojourn at the university had assimilated contemporary religious science. Such a man no longer believed in dogma or in the historical elements of Christianity. But he found himself constrained to preach this dogma in his parish, to explain and to comment upon the great events of sacred history. Under these circumstances he could only get out of his difficulties by means of equivocation, mental reservation, and tricks of symbolical interpretation, which perpetually exposed him to the degrading taunt that he did not believe in the truths he preached to his parishioners. We find Protestantism obliged to enforce a uniform liturgy in the ceremonies of baptism, confirmation, and ordination, and to demand, under certain circumstances, the use of the apostolic symbol. And on the other hand, the " modernists " showed their repugnance to having forced upon them a public adhesion to dogmas which, in their eyes, no longer expressed the essence of the Christian faith, which were liable to be incompatible with their deepest beliefs, and which in any case dealt a blow at private conviction.

They insist more especially upon the embarrassing problem with which Protestantism was faced in connection with religious teaching in the universities. The German parson was the pupil of professors of theology, criticism, and ecclesiastical history, who often belonged to the most advanced wing of Protestantism, and destroyed in him all belief in the positive and historical elements of religion. He was subjected, on the other hand, to Civil Service authorities, who thought it important to maintain, at least nominally and on principle, a more or less strict orthodoxy, and endeavoured to eliminate

from the service of the Church all who were too
audaciously heterodox or too avowedly sceptical.
Between the intellectual minority who ruled the
universities and shaped the minds and consciences
of the future clergy, and the mass of believers,
together with the official authority which ruled
over the Church, there existed profound and
permanent dissension. The drawbacks of such a
situation are patent, as well as the difficulty of
remedying them. What could the authorities do,
placed as they were between the representatives of
orthodoxy, who denied that infidels had any right
to administer a parish of Protestants who believed
in tradition, and the modernists who demanded
liberty of conscience and the rights of independent
science ? Should they regard the claims of the
believers in tradition as null and void ? But in
this case they would run the risk of wounding the
sincere convictions of the most zealous majority
of believers, and that in order to keep at the head
of a parish some free-thinker, who perhaps no longer
had the right to the name of " Christian " ! Ought
they to take severe measures against the advanced
thinkers ? Ought they to expel infidel professors
from the universities ? But then they would put
themselves into conflict with the essential principle
of Protestantism, they would lay violent hands
upon the independence of scientific teaching, and
they would lay themselves open to the reproach of
wishing in the name of religion to place fetters upon
free research. In order to avoid this twofold danger,
the Government endeavoured to manœuvre tactfully
between the two parties, and not to quarrel irrevocably with either the one or the other. And it
thus involuntarily favoured a spirit of equivocation

and compromise, to the detriment of honesty of opinion. It created thorny cases of conscience and false and painful situations for precisely the most interesting among the clergy—those who would not agree to any compromise upon the subject of scientific, moral and religious honesty.

We thus see the formidable dissension in which the evolution of the Protestant spirit in Germany resulted. The picked intellects of Protestantism ended in conceiving and professing a purely subjective religion, which no longer demanded from the believer an obligatory adhesion to any metaphysical, moral or historical dogma. Between the idealistic Protestantism and the positive Protestantism of tradition ever more fundamental divergences came to light. So much was this the case that it was possible to wonder, on occasion, whether the Protestant spirit were capable of creating a " religion," a faith *common* to the whole aggregate of believers, or whether it were not merely a dissolvent which gradually eliminated from Christianity every positive element, until at last it faded into a vague religiosity which was stripped of all power of attraction and was incapable of becoming the guiding principle of any genuine religious body.

## II

We have just seen the difficulties experienced by Protestantism in formulating once and for all a creed common to all believers. The internal dissensions of Protestantism will appear more clearly than ever if we examine the evolution of the Protestant Church.

The Middle Ages saw in the Church a supernatural and miraculous institution created by God Himself for the salvation of sinful man. The religious orders, who alone were expected to observe in all its severity the rule of life laid down by Christ, constituted a grand hierarchy, which was subjected to one of the most severe systems of discipline that history has ever known. In both the parallel groups of the regular and the secular clergy the religious orders were always bound to the duty of the strictest obedience. The bishops and the Heads of Orders themselves bowed before the supreme authority of the Pope, who was the chief head of Christianity and the Vicar of God upon earth. Separated from the clergy by a strong barrier, the mere laity, who remained " in the world " and obeyed the laws of a morality which was simply "adequate," were in perpetual tutelage. The priest, upon whom the Sacrament of Ordination conferred a sacred character, was the only depository of true doctrine, and he alone had the right to read and interpret the Bible. The faithful remained for ever dependent upon dogma, the priest and the ritual. They could gain salvation only in and through the Church.

But Protestantism, as Pariset has pointed out, tended from the beginning to reverse this wise organisation of the Church. By denying the authority of the Pope and the bishops, it at once ruined the whole hierarchical edifice. And on the other hand it abolished the distinction recognised by Catholicism between the priest and the congregation, between the " religious " life and the " worldly " life, between the higher morality and the adequate morality. It is true that it allowed a body of clergy to survive, in the pastors. But the latter did not constitute an organised and hierarchical body. Distinctions of rank were almost entirely done away with. All the pastors were equal with regard to discipline, and the conditions of life were almost identical for each. And, moreover, no barrier separated them from their faithful flocks. The sacerdotal sacraments were abolished as well as the vows which made the Catholic member of a religious order a being set apart. The pastor was free to take a wife and found a family. He was not even master in his own church, since he was assisted in his ministry either by a body of laymen, as in the case of the Presbyterian consistories, or by State officials in the Government consistories. Consequently there no longer really existed, according to Protestant ideas, either a close body of clergy, a special organism, or a Church which had a life of its own and formed an independent power.

In distinction to the Catholic conception of a Church with a strict hierarchy which led up to a theocracy, Protestantism upheld the idea of a universal priesthood. Every believer was a priest. The Church was wheresoever any two persons were assembled together in the name of God, and wheresoever any believer in his solitude addressed his prayer to the Eternal Father. We find this idea formulated with the most perfect clarity by Schleiermacher. The ideal Church, the " City of God," as he called it, had for its object the fruitful exchange of religious impressions and communion in religious emotions. " Every man is a *priest* when he can draw others to himself into the domain which he has especially appropriated, and in which he can demonstrate his virtuosity. Every one is a *believer* when he submits to the direction and guidance of another in order to penetrate into regions of religion with which he is unfamiliar." There was in the City of God no caste and no ecclesiastical despotism ; it formed " a priestly nation," an ideal republic in which every man was a leader or a subject by turns.  In it there existed no advantage for one sect over another, as the groups formed in it by the free play of natural affinities did not tend to fall apart, but were bound to each other by imperceptible transitions.  In the bosom of the ideal Church men lived peacefully side by side without attempting to convert each other.  They were conscious of all participating in the religion of the whole community, in that "infinite religion" of which all particular religions were so many subdivisions, but which no man could embrace in all its entirety.

Thus Protestantism tended towards the ideal of a religion without priests, and instituted a universal priesthood.  But in practice no religion can exist without some ecclesiastical organisation.  Consequently a Protestant Church was formed.  But the strange phenomenon occurred that in Germany, and especially in Prussia, this Church was in many respects contradictory to the most profound tendencies of the Protestant spirit.

It must be remembered that at the beginning Protestantism admitted, just as much as Catholicism, the supernatural character of the Church, as well as the idea of a Christian community, a *corpus christianum*, which should be the outcome of the harmonious co-operation between Church and State.  But, in addition to this, Protestantism, by renouncing the hierarchical Catholic system, contracted with the State a union much more intimate than Catholicism had ever consummated.  In fact, it confided to the sovereign authority of the Christian princes the mission of safeguarding the existence of the Christian community.  And never for one moment did it doubt that these sovereigns would remain effectually impregnated by the purest Christian spirit and not fail conscientiously to carry out this task.

The result of this abdication by the clergy of their organising power was the supremacy of the State in the government of the new churches. In Prussia especially, where a strong monarchy was established during the eighteenth century under the Hohenzollern, the Church, according to Pariset, fairly quickly developed into a regular State institution. The King of Prussia considered himself the supreme head of the churches in his dominions. He had the title of Supreme Bishop (*summus episcopus*), and in this capacity he administered and protected the Church, regulated the lives of the clergy and ecclesiastical discipline, kept a strict superintendence over everything which in the life of the Church emanated from the free initiative of the faithful, and restricted the shreds of an authority which ancient customs had left to the clergy and the ecclesiastical bodies. Thus the State became the guardian of the Church, and the clergy acted in the capacity of royal officials and collaborators of royal officials in education, the public service, and the administration of justice and even of the Church. For they were occasionally called upon to publish edicts, and were obliged to pray publicly for the King and preach obedience to his commands. The Prussian State, which concentrated the whole of public life into itself, thus ended by monopolising even the Church and by creating, with its support, a sort of State religion. Obedience to Prussian discipline, which was accepted as a dogma by Protestantism, was elevated to the rank of a supreme virtue and a religious conviction for the sovereign as well as the lowest of his subjects.

This intimate alliance between the Throne and the Altar, between the Prussian State and the Protestant Church, was the source of some advantage to the

Church and country, and, above all, to the State. The Church thereby found security, wealth, and material power. By associating itself with the royal family of Prussia the triumphs of the latter were its triumphs. For the country also this intimate union between the spiritual and temporal power was in certain respects beneficial. In Catholic countries where the State and the Church are independent and sometimes rivals, there may, on occasion, arise in the consciences of the faithful a conflict between religious and civic duty. Nothing of this kind was possible in Prussia, where the national feeling was never at variance with religious and moral faith, and where the people, in the decisive crises in the life of the country —in 1813, and also perhaps in 1870—were able, without any hypocrisy, to feel convinced that they were fighting both for God and the King. In short, in the case of the Prussian monarchy the support of the Church was a most valuable resource, and it utilised the authority of religion for the maintenance of public order. It charged the clergy to preach obedience, resignation, and submission to the powers that be, and to fight the spirit of discontent and revolt in the breast of secular society. It thus tried to make the Church auxiliary to the police, and to enrol the clergy in the ranks of the Conservative party.

In the long run, however, this association between Church and State could not last ; and this for an exceedingly fundamental reason. The State gradually became secularised. It ceased to be " Christian," and no longer put before itself the task of realising the will of God upon earth. It set itself up as an independent sovereignty, and knew no other ends than the increase of its own temporal prosperity and the attainment of power. And this power it desired for its own purposes and not for the sake of placing it at the disposal of the Church and its spiritual ends. Thus the Church and the State broke their time-established alliance and followed each its own path. The Church aimed at establishing its spiritual kingdom, whilst the State consecrated its energies exclusively to its own task and dissociated itself more and more from the destinies of the Church. It ceased to intrude itself upon the internal life of the Church, and was no longer concerned with maintaining orthodox doctrine in all its purity. It proclaimed its neutrality from the religious point of view, practised toleration, and secured liberty of conscience and freedom of worship for the various denominations. It continued, moreover, to exercise a superintendence over the Church, though it did so no longer in the interests of that body, but on its own behalf, aiming at making sure that the Church did not stand in the light of its own designs or trouble the public peace. Otherwise it no longer meddled in ecclesiastical matters. It left the Church to itself, and allowed it the liberty to follow its own ends in any way it might deem advisable.

This evolution came about by a gradual process. Even to-day it is not complete, and has only reached its final development in America. But, in any case, it is evident that the idea of the sovereign State, which aims exclusively at the development of its own independent power and is indifferent on principle to every religious ideal, is imposing itself more and more forcibly upon the modern conscience even in countries like Germany, for instance, in which the traditional bond which united the Church and the State has not yet been finally broken.

This novel attitude on the part of the State brought in its train a new conception of the mission and nature of the Church also.

In proportion as the idea of a sovereign State was elaborated in modern society and the notion of religious subjectivism was developed in the Protestant conscience, the conception of the Church also underwent a radical transformation. In the eyes of Catholicism and of primitive Protestantism the Church was a divine institution, an absolute miracle. For the modern Protestant it became more and more evident that the religious " miracle " was no *external* fact, such as the constitution of a Church which could dispense eternal salvation, but on the contrary, the absolutely *internal* fact of " conversion," of private religious illumination. From the Gospel of Jesus there emanated a principle of life which, spreading from man to man, gradually grouped an ever-increasing number of disciples into a more or less complete spiritual communion. Identity of certain religious experiences created the community, and the community created the Church. The Church thus gradually ceased to be considered a supernatural body. It was a human institution, susceptible to variation and capable of development just like the religious feeling which gave it birth. It was an association of individuals who felt themselves united by one religious sentiment and formed free groups in order to communicate to each other their impressions and emotions. It was a guild formed by the spontaneous adhesion of the faithful, and capable of assuming as many shapes as there were different shades in men's ideas of Christianity. Consequently there was no longer *one* Church established by God and working with the State for the development of the Christian life. There were a *multitude* of churches corresponding with the *diversity* of private religious experiences, and were all of them imperfect human attempts to fix in a concrete and precise form the undenominational idea of Christianity in its pristine purity.

Thus the Church was both one and infinitely diverse. As Schleiermacher would have said, it should be neither a State institution nor a multiplicity of small sects strictly differentiated from and hostile to each other. Just as religion was one, continuous and infinite, so also the Church would never be a real school of religion until the day when, instead of breaking itself up into a series of separate individual institutions, it became " a fluid and amorphous mass, without any definite outlines, and of which each part found itself now in one place and now in another, whilst all its elements mingled peacefully together." Thus the conception of an official State Church gradually gave place in the Protestant conscience to the idea of Free Churches.

Of course this charge was not consummated in a day, or all of a sudden. The official Church did not cease to exist in Germany, it merely found itself imperceptibly gliding into a position opposed to the Protestant spirit.

The princes tried to conciliate to the best of their ability their temporal mission as monarchs of a secular self-governing State and their spiritual mission as chiefs of the national Church. But it gradually became apparent that they were above all secular sovereigns, who were imperceptibly subordinating religion to the service of the State, and that the spiritual authority of the Church was thus gravely compromised. At the end of the eighteenth century

20

Schleiermacher eloquently denounced the sacrilegious compact by which it was bound to the State. " Would to God," he exclaimed, " that the chiefs of the State, the experts and artists in politics, had remained for ever shut out from the remotest intuition of what religion means ! Would to God that no man among them had ever been gripped by the power of that epidemic of enthusiasm, when once they ceased to know how to separate their own individuality from their duties as public officials ! . . . You wish that the hem of a priestly robe had never swept the floor of a royal apartment. So be it. But allow us in our turn to wish that the royal purple had never kissed the dust before the altar. A prince should never have been allowed to cross the threshold of the temple without having laid aside the fairest ornament of his royal dignity, his cornucopia of favours and distinctions."

The alliance with the State, continues Schleiermacher, perverted the Church, which allowed a political and social mission to be imposed upon it incompatible with the pure manifestation of the religious sentiment. The State relieved itself by placing upon the shoulders of the Church the duty of providing the education of the people through giving them elementary instruction and inculcating upon them some notions of morality. It profaned the symbolical acts of the Church—Baptism, Communion, Marriage, and Extreme Unction—by connecting them with civil acts. It arrogated to itself the right of filling ecclesiastical posts. And inasmuch as it expected from the clergy services which had nothing to do with religion, it ended by excluding religious men from the government of the Church. In short, it stripped the Church of liberty and self-government, without which she remained for ever incapable of

fulfilling her real mission, which was to prepare souls
to receive the revelation of religion.

Thus the divorce between the religious spirit and
the official Church was consummated. The modern
German Protestant is a subjectivist. In his eyes the
true Church is not a political and social institution,
but the " City of God " of which Schleiermacher
dreamt, the ideal Church which groups into one
spiritual community all those whom the same mystic
impulse of the soul draws towards God. And this
ideal Church should receive a practical incarnation
in an infinite variety of free Churches, composed by
the spontaneous membership of the faithful. The
official Church, when it became simply a conservative
organ of the State, appears, from this point of view,
an anachronism, a survival of the old system which
has no meaning in the present day. Everywhere a
growing dissatisfaction with it is to be found among
the people. The large towns had become " spiritual
cemeteries." Outside the official world, which, following the example of the Emperor, professed a strict
Evangelicalism, there were hardly any believers.
The enlightened middle classes, out of respect for
tradition and as a matter of form, associated religion
with the most important acts of their lives, and found
in it a salutary curb to keep the masses in subjection.
But they had lost all lively faith and any real need
of religion. As for the working masses, fermented
as they were by Socialism, they displayed merely
indifference or hostility. They were quite ready to
suspect the parson of being in league with the
police and the Church, " of working for the safety
of the Throne and the security of wealth much more
than for the glory of God." And in the country
districts as well it seemed that the preaching and

teaching of the clergy had almost no hold upon the minds of the peasants or over public morality.

In short, a diminution in the vitality of the official Church was everywhere apparent. It was kept alive artificially, thanks to the energetic support of the Government, in the midst of a society which was indifferent to its practices. The Prussian princes, especially, continued to take their functions as *summus episcopus* of the Kingdom very seriously. They endeavoured to maintain in the Protestant Church a certain cohesion and a certain unity. Frederick William IV. succeeded in establishing in his dominions the union of all the denominations which were the outcome of the Reformation, by decreeing certain compromises between them on matters of dogma. And similarly the Emperor William II. took the interests of Protestantism actively in hand. In the course of the debates upon the *Agenda*, he intervened personally in favour of the divinity of Christ ; in a famous telegram he denounced the political and social intrigues of the " Christian Socialist " party, and attempted to combat religious indifference by increasing the number of churches in Berlin. But all these efforts did not avail to infuse fresh life into the official Church. It seemed more and more of an anachronism and a bar to the normal development of Protestant principles. The Protestant spirit continued its evolution during the nineteenth century, by making the idea of religion ever more spiritual, by giving birth to a science of the Bible and a new theology, and by endeavouring with indefatigable ingenuity to reconcile science and faith into one bold synthesis. And in proportion to its progress it felt itself constantly fettered by the rigid framework of a State Church, the creation of a bygone age, which no longer satisfied the modern mind. The result is that the Church is to-day nothing but a body without a soul, a showy edifice whose imposing exterior but poorly hides its real organic ruin.

It is therefore probable that the ecclesiastical organisation of evangelical Germany has not yet found its true form, but that it is at present going through a period of transition from the system of State Churches (*Landeskirchen*), to that of Free Churches (*Freikirchen*). Not only do we find to-day in Germany a very large number of sects which have sprung from the pietist movement and which have free self-government, but the official Church itself is also aspiring towards enjoying a rather more independent existence. The constitution of 1873–76, by developing synodic institutions, gave congregations the opportunity of expressing their opinions fairly freely upon matters connected with the life of the Church. It is true that even to-day the Evangelical Church, which is subjected to the *placet* of the Government in all its internal legislation, is perhaps less free than the Catholic Church, which was liberated from this necessity as a result of the *Kulturkampf*. Nevertheless it cannot be denied that the first steps towards the independence of the Church have been taken. How far will Germany go along this path ? Will the Protestant Church and the State one day enter upon the perilous venture of a complete divorce ? There is nothing to show that this radical solution will be tried in the near future. Even among the " modernist " Protestants there are those who believe that a synodic system would put more fetters upon the audacities of free theological research than State administration, and therefore feel a certain sympathy for the system of *Landeskirchen*. Yet,

generally speaking, recent historians of religion are
quite ready to admit that, to use Tröltsch's words,
" Protestantism on the whole, as a spiritual principle
and as a Church, is involved in an evolution whose
essence is the idea of *independence*."

This situation is not without its inconveniences
and dangers. It reveals once more the fundamental
contradictions which we have already pointed out in
Protestantism. The Protestant faith is progressing
towards a purely spiritual and internal religion,
without dogmas, priests, sacrifices, good works, or
external ceremonies. And yet, apparently in order
to have a tangible existence and an outside influence,
it cannot avoid promulgating a creed and binding
itself to the historical and traditional past of Christianity and constituting itself as a Church. It is
obviously open to question whether on the one hand
the Protestant spirit will not necessarily feel itself
cramped in any Church, and on the other whether a
religion without a Church is not sheer nonsense.

Naturally upon this question opinions are divided.
Some, like Goyau, insist upon the impossibility of
reconciling the religious feeling of the few with the
religion of the masses. They point out the growing
gulf between the mental outlook of the enlightened
Protestants who are capable of making their own
belief, and the crowd of the mediocre, the lukewarm
and half-hearted believers who do not *make* their
Christianity, but *submit* to it and thus remain attached
to the old forms and the ancient practices. And from
this they draw the conclusion that Protestantism
contains a contradiction within itself which is destined
to become ever more intolerable in proportion as it
develops, and will entail the more or less fatal dissolution of the Protestant Church.

Others, on the contrary, are of the opinion that Protestantism will know how to put an end to this contradiction by a series of successive compromises, and that it will give birth during the course of its evolution to provisional types of organisation which will be adapted to the various states of conscience and the degrees of culture through which the Protestant soul will pass. And they see in this capacity for change the real greatness of Protestantism. From this point of view a religion is not something absolute and unchangeable, but something which *becomes*—the product of human striving after perfection, the fruit of painful and ceaseless groping. And, like religion itself, the Church also must evolve and be transformed. The difficulties with which it meets, the contradictions which are set before it, arise from the very nature of circumstances. Protestantism will show its value, not by finding *the* solution of the Church's problem—which is impossible—but by raising itself step by step to ever less imperfect forms of religious association.

The discussion finally resolves itself into the question of ascertaining whether the specifically Protestant idea still possesses sufficient vitality to exercise a *real* influence over the life of to-day, whether it is capable of producing fresh compromises between religious traditionalism and wilful rationalism, and of rallying around its dogmas a sufficiently large and compact body of adherents. Catholics, as a rule, do not estimate its power of attraction very highly. And even in the Protestant world there are some who ask themselves to what extent the existing organisation of Protestantism is still a *living* principle of life and an *effective* organising force. And they do not blink the fact that in any case the Protestant Church is going through a crisis the end of which is not yet in sight.

On the whole, however, there is a tendency to be optimistic with regard to the result of this crisis. It is recognised that the problem of the maintenance of Protestantism is exceptionally complicated and difficult at the present moment, based as it is upon the lowest layers of the nation, upon a *crowd* which needs, above all, an organised religion, a Church with rites, doctrines, and traditional ceremonies. As for the cultured few, they are emancipated from all dogmatic belief, and live on the outskirts of the Church, picking out their path in perfect independence, allied with all the idealistic energies of the day in their struggle against scepticism pure and simple, as well as against the utilitarian realism which has no higher aspirations. That such incongruous elements sometimes find it difficult to agree, is not surprising. But the strength of Protestantism lies in the very fact that it unites these *two* elements. It has more fundamental vigour than purely idealistic philosophy, as it thrusts out its roots into a popular religion and relies upon an organised Church. And it carries the day over authoritative religions inasmuch as it blossoms into an idealistic faith which is purely human, and because it is, according to its followers, the only religion by which the modern man, who is an individualist and in love with liberty, can live. The members of the Protestant camp are therefore confident of the future. They feel that the German genius, which is at once conservative and progressive, will prove supple and resourceful enough to maintain indefinitely, without having to subject it to irreparable humiliation in either one direction or the other, a religion so well adapted to the fundamental tendencies of the race.

# CHAPTER V

## FREE THOUGHT

### I

In the course of the last chapter we described the prodigious effort made by idealism to reconcile reason and faith, and to elaborate a general conception of the universe which should be in harmony with the conclusions of the positive sciences and yet of such a nature as to satisfy the traditional religious needs of the modern mind. We shall not recur in the present chapter to this exceedingly original creation of the German spirit, although it was obviously the outcome of free thought. We shall only occupy ourselves with the attempts on the part of the German mind to emancipate itself completely from religious tradition and to constitute outside Christianity, or even in conscious opposition to it, an idea of the world and a rule of life which should be purely rational, or, at all events, " irreligious."

In opposition to Christianity, and in direct antagonism with it, the nineteenth century witnessed the development, in the first place, of a vigorous militant materialism which was absolutely confident of the soundness of its doctrines and numbers its adherents to-day by the million.

Fostered during the 'thirties and 'forties by the antichristian sensualism of Young Germany and the apostles of the rehabilitation of the flesh, by the theological radicalism of men like Strauss and Baur, by the philosophical and political radicalism of men after the stamp of Ruge or the Bauer brothers, and by the naturalism of Feuerbach, materialism dominated German thought during the 'fifties and 'sixties in the persons of Karl Vogt and Moleschott, Büchner and Czolbe on the one hand, and Marx and Engels on the other. The triumph of Darwin's ideas on evolution in the sphere of natural science accentuated its success still more forcibly among the representatives of modern culture; whilst in the domain of actual life, the diffusion of Socialism, and with it of Marxian materialism, among the masses, won over numberless followers to its cause.

Energetically combated after 1870, in the name of Kant's philosophy, with its theory of knowledge on the one hand, and later on also by the representatives of neo-romanticism, materialism certainly lost much of its credit among the cultured minority. But the enormous success of Haeckel's works, which were circulated by the thousand, clearly proves that it kept its hold over a very important fraction of the educated public. And its power of attraction over the Socialist masses does not seem to have diminished. It is true that the programme of Erfurt proclaimed that " religion is a private concern "; and the Socialist Congresses have on many occasions thrown out motions aimed at making the party leave this position of neutrality and take up a more militant attitude against religion. But if, out of consideration for political tactics, the party refuses to inscribe Atheism on its programme, so as to avoid compromising its success among certain elements of the population, the bulk of its adherents are nevertheless converts to Marxian materialism. On account of the philosophy upon which its programme is based Socialism is radically opposed to the idea of religion, and the mass of its followers—as is evident to all—is quite ready to admit with Bebel that " Christianity and Socialism are like fire and water together." And apparently the efforts recently made to prove that Socialism is not necessarily allied to the economic materialism of Marx, and can equally well find its justification in the doctrines of Kant, have not modified the position the least bit in the world.

We must therefore examine what this spread of materialism means.

Its success is due in the first place to the fact that it is regarded as the philosophical doctrine which co-ordinates the results of natural science. It inspires confidence because its champions, men like Karl Vogt and Haeckel, for instance, are at the same time naturalists of great merit. As they possess the right to speak in the name of science, they derive the benefit, in their capacity as philosophers, from their very legitimate authority as scientists. I have already had occasion to point out several times how, in consequence of the marvellous progress made during the nineteenth century in science and rational technical processes, the conviction grew up that science was capable of solving the riddle of the universe, fixing standards of conduct for men, and leading humanity to the attainment of happiness. Preached by a certain number of scientists, and accepted by the bulk of the public as *the* scientific philosophy *par excellence*, materialism benefited by the enormous prestige in which exact science rejoices at the present day. Like the materialism of Democritus, Epicurus and Lucretius, and that of

Lamettrie and Baron Holbach, modern German materialism was born from the enthusiasm for the great scientific discoveries of the age, and the belief that it was quite easy to found upon purely scientific bases a metaphysical explanation of the universe.

Materialism arose, in the second place, from the general evolution towards realism which is one of the characteristic features of the modern world, and which has its source in the development of the spirit of capitalistic enterprise. Just as Germany aimed more and more consciously, as the century advanced, at the conquest of economic and political power; just as the middle classes, especially, consigned to the second place their desire for culture and political liberty in order to concentrate all their energies upon the attainment of wealth; just as art evolved from romantic subjectivism to modern naturalism; so also, in the domain of philosophy, external and material realism carried the day over ideas. The representative of modern capitalistic enterprise is incessantly absorbed in calculations of interest; he is jostled by the increasing rush in which life is lived, accustomed to regarding existence as an unceasing and endless race for wealth, driven to considering feverish work and *business* as an end in itself, and shaped to a purely utilitarian morality which in everything values only immediate tangible and solid success and holds in esteem only those qualities which lead to it. Consequently, in the domain of thought he feels himself peculiarly in touch with materialism which seeks for fundamental reality, not in any spiritual principle, but in concrete and palpable matter. And similarly he is quite ready to admit the theory of evolution which raises to a universal law the struggle for existence, that law of

competition which holds supreme sway in the world
of enterprise.

And at the other end of the social ladder the
populace who labour hard and ceaselessly to gain
their daily bread, who see their happiness, and even
their very existence menaced by forces over which
they have no control, who live in poverty or at best
in humble circumstances, whilst under their very
eyes and in their immediate neighbourhood they
have the enormous material resources of urban life,
agree with the capitalists and tend to turn life
and the world into purely materialistic conceptions.
The aristocratic materialism of the great capitalists
is balanced in the lower social scale by the levelling
and boundless materialism of the socialistic masses.

But there is yet another and rather more curious
reason which has contributed to the diffusion of
materialism among certain minds, and that is a kind
of pessimism which has sprung up in our day with
regard to the demands of sentiment.  Humanity
hitherto has found consolation in the religious hypothesis, in the idea of the immortality of the soul, in
the hope of a celestial justice which will make good
the inequalities of life and fate, in the faith in a
God of mercy and goodness who will keep watch
over His children and have pity upon their sufferings.

But there is no doubt that the modern man, at
the same time as he learnt no longer to trust his
reason, learnt also to feel greater suspicion with
regard to the demands of his heart.  Not only did
the consoling hypotheses of Christianity no longer
appear to him *ipso facto* true, but he also developed
within his breast a sort of ascetic honesty which for-
bade him to indulge in any longings for a Beyond,
and inclined him to take sides with the theories that

most rudely contradicted hopes which from that moment were regarded as illusions. A materialist like Czolbe, for instance, was convinced that the demand for eternity necessarily had its source in a certain weakness of soul, and scientific and moral honesty commands the man of to-day to resign himself, once and for all, to look life in the face and to limit his desires to existence upon earth. Regarded from this point of view, materialism appears in the light of an effort towards intellectual sincerity, and as a determined desire no longer to be the dupes of the illusions in which men found joy for many centuries.

And lastly, materialism is also the response of the modern spirit to the attacks of the champions of religion.

We have already seen how Roman Catholicism hurled its fulminations against "pseudo-science," how it violently stifled the rationalistic tendencies which made their appearance in the bosom of Catholicism, and how rigidly it made human reason bow before the principle of authority. But orthodox and pietistic Protestantism nourished almost as much suspicion as Catholicism with regard to independent science. The representatives of religion evidently showed an inclination to treat reason with suspicion or as an enemy. And when they were in power they did not hesitate to oppose it not only with spiritual weapons, but by force, and by appealing to the authority of the State to stamp out heresy. The persecutions of which such men as Fichte and Strauss, Büchner and Moleschott, were the victims, the innumerable annoyances to which the universities were exposed, during the Restoration period as well as during the reign of Frederick William IV., and the reactionary era which followed upon 1848, and the ill-will of orthodox pietism in connection with many a representative of German intellect, gave rise, in a certain section of public opinion, to profound irritation, and spread in it the conviction that between religion and science there existed a normal and necessary antagonism.

The Church gave rise to even greater hatred, as it so often appeared as the ally of the monarchy against revolution, as the enemy of the democratic movement, as the great conservative power which, by means of fallacious promises, kept the people in obedience, made them bow before authority and tradition, preached to them a cowardly resignation in their troubles, and turned them away from the energetic demand for their right to happiness. Thus materialism seemed to many the most radical form of anti-clericalism, as the declaration of a loyal and resolute war against the feeling of oppression which the Church and religion aimed at imposing upon the consciences of men. I do not mean to say, of course, that antagonism between religion and science is really a necessity, or that the Church must inevitably be a tyrannical and reactionary power. I merely wish to point out that in the course of history it has frequently proved intolerant and oppressive, and too friendly with the powerful in the land. Materialism is, in some respects, the classical form which the anti-clerical and anti-religious reaction, provoked by this attitude, assumes.

Materialism, however, seems recently to have lost some of its prestige in Germany, at least among the cultured classes.

Its "heyday" was during the reactionary period inaugurated after the upheavals of 1848. This was the time when Karl Vogt made fun of the " collier's faith " of his colleague, Rudolf Wagner, who tried to prove the existence of a vital energy and of a soul-substance. The protagonists of materialism showed themselves so superior to their philosophical and scientific adversaries that the Government, in order to reduce them to silence, could find no better course than that of driving Moleschott and Büchner from their professorial chairs. The publication of Darwin's *Origin of Species,* in 1859, seemed to give the death-blow to the spiritual theory. And D. F. Strauss, breaking his last ties with Christianity, announced by his book *The Old and the New Faith* (1872) his solemn adherence to the doctrine of evolution and materialistic monism.

But by the time Strauss's book appeared the reaction had already set in. A Kantian Renaissance could be discerned, and a really scientific criticism of knowledge which was of high philosophical importance was elaborated. And by the light of this criticism materialism was soon shown to be a metaphysical dogma quite as unproved and quite as undemonstrable as any idealistic system that had ever existed, a hazardous hypothesis in connection with problems about which human reason should make up its mind to a definite *ignorabimus.* Materialism, consequently, was not able to make itself, as it aspired to do, the scientific philosophy *par excellence.* There is no serious thinker to-day who does not frankly accept *all* the conclusions of the exact sciences and loyally aim at giving them as satisfactory an interpretation as possible. The materialists were foolish in arrogating to themselves a monopoly in this respect. The whole point is to know which explanation best covers the facts. Now the materialistic explanation from the neo-Kantian point of view had one grave defect—it ignored the positive and certain results of the criticism of knowledge. And it had therefore to be rejected as inadequate. The materialist was a dilettante at philosophy who ventured upon ground with which he was not familiar and where he went grossly astray.

Opposed on the one hand by the school philosophers in the name of the principles of criticism, materialism found itself, on the other hand, discredited in the eyes of the representatives of neo-romanticism. *The Old and the New Faith* by Strauss was greeted by the strident shriek of Nietzsche's terrible pamphlet against the " Philistine of Culture " and the " Socratic " rationalism of the modern world. Materialism had once seduced men's minds by its radicalism. It was now outgrown and contemptuously cast aside by a new radicalism which was even more uncompromising, which was pessimistic to the point of nihilism, sceptical by the very power of its intellectual consciousness, immoralist and antichristian through the extreme refinement of its moral honesty. Materialism had once gained adherents on account of its democratic tendencies, because it took in hand the cause of the people and dreamt of the establishment on earth of a social state which would secure comfort and happiness for all. Now it was decried as Utopian and foolishly optimistic. Its faith in the omnipotence of science was derided, and it was denied that science could ever be in a position to bring back paradise on earth. The materialists got to be suspected of intellectual mediocrity or moral dishonesty because they refused to understand, as Nietzsche would have had them do, that the slavery and poverty of the multitude is

21

the shameful and lamentable side of every civilisation, and because they tried to hide the bankruptcy of their beautiful promises by extolling the dignity of work, and proclaiming that it was nobler to earn one's bread by the sweat of the brow than to live in idleness. Banned by the official representatives of philosophy as not sufficiently scientific, materialism was rejected by advanced philosophers as being tainted by cowardice and " Philistinism."

Yet it is true that its credit is not ruined—very far from it. It keeps its hold over the Socialist masses, and from this point of view it remains an important factor in the spiritual life of Germany. Moreover, at intervals it springs to new life in a rejuvenated form, and the immense success which the works of Haeckel have attained among the bulk of the public is a sure indication that materialism has preserved considerable influence over a very large number of minds. But it must at the same time be pointed out that this triumph from the point of view of circulation is not accompanied by any success in philosophical " estimation." However sympathetic and respected the personality of Haeckel himself may be, scientific criticism has passed very severe judgment upon the work of that great populariser. It has been treated as a " philosophical cypher " ; and *The Riddle of the Universe* is mentioned in much the same tone as certain widely circulated novels, the material triumph of which is placed on record, whilst it is pointed out that this circumstance does no credit to the German reader, but merely proves the poverty in philosophical culture of the bulk of the public. Generally speaking, it may, I think, be said that materialism still exercises a fascination over the masses but has scarcely any hold over German intellect, which is, apparently, far more severe upon it than French public opinion. The German mind has no great respect for any conception of the universe which it regards as out of date, unscientific, pretentiously mediocre, and at best only suitable for the illiterate masses, or the half-educated, who hastily accept the oracles of a sham science.

## II

Hegel claimed to have given an explanation, in his system, of the rational evolution of the universe. Convinced of the identity of thought and being, persuaded that ideas do not merely correspond with reality as the picture does to the model, but that ideas *are* the very essence of reality and that the science of thought or logic is one and the same thing with the science of being or metaphysics, he thought he could give a fundamental and perfectly satisfactory explanation of the mystery of the world. By retracing the evolution of reason which raises itself from logic to the philosophy of nature, then to the philosophy of the subjective spirit (psychology), and subsequently to the philosophy of the objective spirit (philosophy of law and of history) till at length it reaches the philosophy of the absolute spirit (philosophy of art, religion, and philosophy) he thought he had given a complete description of the process by which the spirit becomes conscious of itself and also of the origin of the universe itself.

In opposition to this metaphysical dogmatism modern positivism came into existence and agreed with materialism in substituting for the speculative method of idealism the empirical method of the positive sciences, in order to cast doubt upon the identity of thought and being, and to deny any objective value to the grandiose and fragile constructions of speculative reason.  But whilst in the place of the idealistic dogmatism of Hegel materialism provided a naturalistic dogmatism which was quite as peremptory in its assertions and claimed in its turn to give a metaphysical explanation of the world, positivism brought a radical scepticism to bear against all metaphysics, and proceeded to a general liquidation of the philosophy of the past, rejecting as defective and devoid of scientific value all former attempts to give a comprehensive interpretation of the universe.

It tended, in the first place, to supplant in philosophy the speculative method of the great representatives of idealism by the scrupulous objective examination of reality—the empirical method, which, when applied to natural science, had produced such magnificent results.  And thus there grew up during the nineteenth century a psychology which became every day more strictly empirical.  The way for it was paved by Herbart, and above all by Beneke, and during the 'fifties and 'sixties it was placed on its feet by the fundamental works of Ernst Heinrich Weber, Lotze, Helmholz and Wundt, and afterwards matured in the writings of men like Ebbinghaus, Lipps, Mach, Rehmke, Hœffding and Paulsen.  To-day it is a flourishing science based upon an immense number of exact observations, and is still accumulating an ever greater mass of materials, descriptions and positive facts, with the object of instituting a complete natural history of psychic phenomena.

And at the same time as positivism is aiming at turning philosophy into an empirical science it also tends, on the other hand, to make a clear distinction between problems which are capable of receiving a scientific solution and those which remain for ever inaccessible to reason, and thus to define precisely the limits beyond which it is impossible for human knowledge to go. With this object in view it revived the criticism of Kant, whose wise prudence it contrasts with the rashness of the speculative philosophy of the epoch that followed him. The "return to Kant" was announced in 1847 by Christian Hermann Weisse, preached in 1862 by Eduard Zeller, and afterwards by F. Albert Lange, Otto Liebmann and Kuno Fischer. From this time forward a Kantian criticism arose which was as precise and detailed as the criticism of Goethe ; it had a review of its own, the *Kantstudien*, which has been its organ ever since 1896, and since 1900 the Berlin Academy of Sciences has been bringing out a monumental annotated edition of Kant. At the same time a neo-critical school has been organised. Following in the footsteps of Kant it enunciates the principle that for man there is, properly speaking, no knowledge outside the bounds of experience, and that consequently no scientific assertion is possible about things in themselves or on anything transcendental. It thus rigorously proscribes all metaphysics, and tends to assign to philosophy, as its essential task, the criticism of knowledge and the determination of the first principles and postulates upon which the exact sciences are founded. Among the neo-Kantians some, like Lange, Liebmann, Hermann Cohen and Alois Riehl, remain fairly faithful to the teaching of the master. Others stray further from Kant's philosophy. Some, like Laas, Schuppe, Rehmke and von Schubert-Soldern, follow both Hume and Kant. They have much in common with phenomenism, and aim at proceeding to an analysis, which shall be as exact as possible, of the immediate phenomena of consciousness. Others like Avenarius and E. Mach, sketch out an " empiro-critical " system which is rigorously hostile to all metaphysics, which regards " pure experience," the facts of our immediate experience, as the only basis of a science of objective reality, endeavours to replace man in the midst of nature and, finally, attempts to project some light into the darkness of the future towards which our species is evolving.

Positivism is certainly far superior from the scientific point of view to materialism. Idealism generally reproaches it with being too sceptical with regard to reason and too severely suspicious with respect to metaphysics. It accuses positivism, on the one hand, of not always succeeding in making clear the difference between that which is a certain fact, a demonstrable truth, and that which is a speculative addition, a mere hypothesis. And on the other hand it blames it for its critical asceticism, which leads it to barricade itself behind a cautious agnosticism with regard to the questions which most interest mankind. If one is to believe the idealists, mankind is impelled by an irresistible metaphysical necessity to fashion for himself at all costs some comprehensive conception of the world. But the positivist *abstinence* which refuses to satisfy this legitimate desire thereby does violence to an instinct which is deeply imbedded in human nature. Positivism therefore cannot be the last word in wisdom, but is perfectly explicable as a reaction against the intolerable dogmatism of Hegel. It will, however, remain incapable, according to the idealists, of stifling the need for metaphysics in the breast of man. The very success of materialism, which is a metaphysical hypothesis—

while it is in the eyes of the idealists a depressing
symptom of the mediocrity of the philosophical culture of our day—is at least also an indication that
the necessity for metaphysics has not been abolished,
but that it has taken on a fresh lease of life, and
seeks to satisfy its needs by producing at all costs a
comprehensive interpretation of the universe.

Thus positivism, it is said, will inevitably remain
the property of a small group of distinguished minds
in whom the critical faculty has been abnormally
developed.  More vigorous temperaments and the
mass of the people will always be incapable of taking
refuge in agnosticism, and will of necessity, at some
given moment, feel the need of quitting this over-
negative and over-cautious position in order to
hazard some more or less speculative hypothesis regarding the riddle of the universe.

The Radicalism of our own day, moreover, sees
in this positivist abstinence a last remainder of Christian asceticism.   Nietzsche, who is so hard upon
materialism, is on the other hand full of respect for
the positivists.   He feels no contempt for " these
deniers, these lonely ones of to-day, . . . these hard,
severe, self-denying and heroic spirits, who do honour
to our time, . . . these last idealists of *knowledge*,
in whom alone the intellectual consciousness of our
day resides and is incarnate."   He thinks very highly
of the laudable philosophical abstinence actuated by
such a belief, of this "intellectual stoicism which ends
by denying itself the *Nay* as severely as the *Yea*,
this determination to hold by positive reality, the
*factum brutum*, the *petit fait*—this renunciation of all
interpretation, of all that savours of violence, shuffling,
abbreviation, omission, addition, poetical development
and falsification—in short, the renunciation of all that

constitutes the essence of every art of interpretation."
But he also maintains that this will to *truth* at all
costs, this belief in the absolute and unqualified
value of science is nothing else than the infinitely
refined, subtle and sublimated form of the ascetic
Christian spirit. " Our faith in Science," he con-
cludes, " is still founded upon a *metaphysical* belief ;
and we too, we thinkers of to-day, we atheists and
anti-metaphysicians, we too believe in this faith
which inspires us to that form of incendiarism which
the belief of ages has kindled, to that Christian
religion which was also the religion of Plato, that
God is Truth and that the truth is *divine*. . . ."

Thus it is clear that for Nietzsche the uncompromising scientific honesty of the positivists was
simply the ultimate manifestation, spiritualised and
scarcely recognisable, of the religious instinct.
These " free spirits " were still at heart Christians,
as they had not yet called in question the value of
truth itself. And if not every one will hasten to agree
with Nietzsche that they are not yet sufficiently
" freed," yet, on the other hand, this affords a simple
explanation of the fact that German positivists are,
on the whole, less hostile to Christianity than the
materialists, and are fairly frequently inclined to
admit the possibility and the desirability of an agreement between Faith and Science.

### III

In addition to materialism and positivism, pessimism is undeniably one of the characteristic
tendencies of the second half of the nineteenth
century.

As a philosophical doctrine, the pessimism formulated by Schopenhauer was, as we know, derived from the teaching of Kant, and is thus connected with the great movement of German idealism. The author of *The World as Will and Idea* professed a monistic metaphysics with idealistic tendencies. But he definitely separated himself from his predecessors by denying most emphatically that reason could be the fundamental principle of the real, and that the Absolute was identical with Being. The essence of the world was according to him the Will—but not that free will whose evolution towards consciousness Fichte delighted in describing. The Will which Schopenhauer placed at the base of the world, which he recognised as one and the same in every being, which he saw asserting itself with painful energy in the whole of creation, was the independent Will of time, space and causality, the unconscious Will without a purpose, which strove and desired without ceasing, but which could never find lasting satisfaction. This Will became concrete in phenomena, and grew ever sharper, more selfish and more formidable in proportion as it attained to higher forms. Until at last, when it had reached the supreme heights of consciousness, the Will realised that its blind effort resulted of necessity in universal suffering, and perceived through the illusion of individualisation the fundamental unity behind all phenomena, and thus felt all sorrow as pertaining to itself. It thereby came to the conclusion that nonentity was far preferable to living, and by one supreme effort was converted, abdicated the will-to-live, and sought in the great peace of Nirvana the only refuge to be found from the unending torture of life.

This pessimism has been interpreted, not without some plausibility, as the last legacy of Christianity

which was on the point of dying out. The great task
of Christianity had been to provide an absolute
meaning and goal for life. The desire for the Kingdom of Heaven and the salvation of the soul had
become the rule of life for the Christian. But gradually faith in this goal and in this rule of life grew
weaker in men's minds, and they ceased to believe
in the " glad tidings " brought by Christ. But although this faith in the promises of religion slowly
died out, there still survived in the Christian heart
an intensely painful need to find a meaning for life
and to assign to it a definite goal towards which it
might progress. This ardent desire for an absolute
purpose, combined with the radical scepticism with
regard to the real existence of any sort of purpose,
had its logical conclusion in the pessimism of Schopenhauer, and the hypothesis of a meaningless will-to-
live that is condemned to eternal torture.

It was only in the second half of the century that
pessimism found a favourable soil for its development. It is well known that Schopenhauer's chief
work, *The World as Will and Idea*, published in 1819,
remained without any influence over public opinion
for thirty years, that it was ignored by the bulk of
the people, and despised by the scientific world. It
required the wreck of Hegelianism, the bankruptcy of
speculative philosophy and of optimistic rationalism,
the epoch of depression which followed the failure
of the Revolution of 1848–49, and the trials of all
kinds to which the reactionary period exposed the
intellectual minority of Germany, but, above all,
the sufferings which the development of the system
of capitalistic enterprise entailed for multitudes, the
profound uneasiness which the economic upheaval,
the increase in the pace of life, and the growing

complexity of psychology, produced in modern humanity, for the publication in 1851 of the *Parerga and Paralipomena* to draw the attention of the world upon the misanthropist of Frankfort.

But from that moment pessimism rapidly gained ground, and spread the dark waters of its rising tide far and wide over Germany and the whole world. It invaded philosophy, literature and art. The doctrines of pessimism were elaborated after Schopenhauer by Taubert, Bahnsen, Mainlænder, and Venetianer, but above all by Hartmann, whose *Philosophy of the Unconscious* (1869) won a brilliant success as soon as it was published, though after a short interval it fell into almost entire oblivion. The most illustrious representative of pessimism among the poets was Heine, who at the very end of his days descended to the weary nihilism of the *Romancero* and the *Last Poems*. In these verses which vibrate with the keenest emotion he celebrates the inevitable defeat of all beauty and of all grandeur, and finds his only semblance of comfort in a piety in which the sneers of a bitter and exasperated irony are mingled with a bottomless despair. During the 'sixties Leopardi became one of the favourite poets of the rising generation. But it was above all Richard Wagner who appeared in the light of a living incarnation of this new tendency in the German mind. An optimist and a disciple of Feuerbach before 1848, but after that year rapidly disillusioned by the failure of his revolutionary hopes, he found in the perusal of Schopenhauer the revelation which enlightened him upon himself and his own inclinations. And from that moment absolute renunciation, the abdication of the selfish will to live, the religion of suffering and pity became the deepest sources from which his inspiration was derived.  In *Tristan*, the desperate desire of the modern soul to reach Nirvana and the Night that sets it free, the great peace of death in which all the painful illusions of the day die away, where all the vain torments of this terrible life are ended, was expressed with tremendous force and undeniable sincerity.  And in *Parsifal* Wagner chanted with equal fervour the ineffable victories of the Will over itself, the infinite value of redeeming pity and the hope for a regeneration of sinful man through resignation and asceticism.

Little by little, however, the spiritual atmosphere of Germany cleared.  The military successes of 1866 and 1870, the magnificent economic rise of the country and the advent of a great imperialist and universal policy gave birth to fresh developments in men's minds.  The period of depression was followed by a joyous striving for power.  The exaltation of the spirit of enterprise no longer allowed the world to be regarded as a meaningless wilderness.  Action was considered of higher value than contemplation, and thus pessimism gradually became obsolete.  It was not merely opposed by optimists of every kind, by the disciples of the religion of progress, by those who laboured with Marx for the advent of an era of happiness and justice among men, and by all who believed that life could have a meaning and humanity a mission.  It was rejected, or rather " outgrown," by the very minds which showed the least disposition to accept consoling hypotheses and optimistic interpretations.  Nietzsche placed the problem of the value of existence in a fresh light.  For Schopenhauer, life, since it had neither a meaning nor an object, was something absolutely detestable and bad.  He felt in the pre-

sence of the will-to-live that instinctive horror which
certain delicate and timid natures experience before
any manifestations of elementary life. He had not
the smallest comprehension of that festive joy which
others feel in similar circumstances. Nietzsche, on
the other hand, had learnt from Darwin the great
*fact* of universal evolution. He thereupon saw in
the idea of an ascending evolution of the human
species a conception which allowed him to say " yea "
to life without on that account necessarily believing
in the existence of a final aim. Life is holy, not
because it tends to any particular end, but *in itself*,
because it grows and increases and amplifies itself.
Far from regarding it with repulsion, like Schopenhauer, he loved it with a joyous and almost mystic
exaltation. He saw in it a magnificent festival, an
incomparable adventure, a marvellous joy. In his
poet's imagination, the Darwinian theory of evolution was transfigured into that vision of an infinite
ascent to power which he celebrated in all his work
with such splendid lyric beauty.

What became of pessimism on this hypothesis ?
It was nothing but a disease, or, more correctly
speaking, the typical symptom of decadence. There
was according to Nietzsche a " pessimism of strength"
which points out the road to power and beauty
through suffering. But the weary pessimism which
will not suffer any more and which casts aspersions
upon life is the conception of the decadent in whom
the vital instinct is weak, and who no longer feels
within himself the creative force to beget anything
new. The pessimist is a degenerate, a sick man,
who must either get well or go away, but has no
business to poison the existence of healthy men, to
demoralise the powerful and to calumniate life.

Christianity, the democratic movement, Schopen-
hauerian pessimism, and Wagnerian romanticism,
were in Nietzsche's eyes so many manifestations of
this decadence and this weakening of vitality. And
he combated them not as one would refute an error,
but as one fights a disease. The triumph of pessimism
he would have regarded as the signal for a great
retrogression on the part of humanity. According to
him it was necessary for the present day to eliminate
this poison with which it was infected, to recover
the health and the joy in life, and to learn to say
" Yea " to life, to the *whole* of life, including suffering and evil.

And gradually towards the end of the century the
worship of life spread further and further. The idea
that life by its very essence and on account of its
fundamental energies is something which is capable
of eternally " surpassing itself " and of evolving ever
higher forms, the faith in the development which is
not necessary, but quite possible, of the type man,
and the will to participate as energetically as possible in this ascent to power are becoming more and
more prevalent among modern men. These tendencies found their most fundamental and characteristic poetical and philosophical expression in the
doctrines of Nietzsche, about which we must now
say a few words.

## IV

" We immoralists," said Nietzsche in his *Will to
Power*, " we are *the most advanced*." And he perfectly well understood that this " magic of the
extreme " was doubtless the subtle and somewhat
perverse charm which drew to him the spirits of his
contemporaries.

Nietzsche was the incarnation of that profound mistrust experienced by the nineteenth century for every religious interpretation of the universe and for all the comforting hypotheses in which humanity had till then found consolation. The modern man is afraid of being deceived ; he will not allow himself to be taken in by his desire for beauty and goodness, kindness and happiness ; he aspires to look reality in the face without any illusions. Nietzsche experienced this feeling in the highest degree. He endeavoured not only to form a theoretical conception but also to *realise* and *live* in spirit by the hypothesis, which was most diametrically opposed to the Christian idea and to every optimistic philosophy—the hypothesis that " God is dead," the nihilistic idea of a universe without a God, without unity, without law, and without any permanent substance—an absolute phenomenism in which the only reality is a process of Becoming which is quite callous and devoid of meaning. The psychological penetration, the superhuman energy and the concentrated passion with which he gave himself up to this formidable task, are his titles to a great and important position in the history of thought during the nineteenth century. It is possible, of course, to " lay a wager " against the nihilistic hypothesis, as Pascal and Fichte, for instance, did. It is also possible to condemn the solution proposed by Nietzsche in order to escape from pessimistic nihilism. But the most elementary intellectual honesty commands us at least to examine this possibility in all its bearings, if only in order to win the right of rejecting it with a full knowledge of the subject. Whatever objective value we may assign to Nietzsche's theories, we can but render homage to the bravery with which he threw himself

entirely, heart and soul, into the hazardous intellectual adventure which ended in that most tragic
catastrophe, the loss of his reason.

Moral optimism demands that the universe and
humanity should have a law, a final goal towards
which they should progress; and man, by virtue of
time-established custom, has learnt to rise in his
own estimation in proportion as he conforms his
actions to this law and thus feels himself a collaborator with God. But, according to Nietzsche, this is
an illusion which is gradually dissipated as man
grows more self-conscious. In the beginning man
believed that at the head of the universe there was
a supreme legislator, and regarded the moral law as
the expression of the will of the Lord of the world.
Then gradually he arrived at the conviction that
" God was dead " and that the world had no master.
Whereupon he searched feverishly for a substitute
for God, for some power that was capable of laying
down the law and of authoritatively imposing a
mission upon man. Instead of a personal God he
tried worshipping the " moral consciousness " and
its categorical imperative, or Reason, or the " social
instinct " of " history " and the laws it contained ;
he found a goal for human life in " happiness," or
in the " happiness of the greatest number." Or,
again, he resigned himself to agnosticism, maintaining all the while that evolution must " lead
somewhere, no matter whither." Finally, after one
deception and another, man discovered that Becoming led nowhere, but merely unfurled its infinite
and senseless combinations by pure chance. At
the end of this path nihilism stared him in the face :
" Life—something which *understands* its nothingness,
and in the end suppresses itself."

Scientific optimism posited harmony between thought and reality, and demanded for man the hope of being able to form a more and more satisfactory image of the universe. "Illusion again," answered Nietzsche. Becoming is *unthinkable*. There is in reality neither a thinking "subject" nor "things" thought, neither "identical things" nor cause and effect, nothing stable, permanent or regular. All our knowledge of the universe is founded upon a series of fundamental errors, upon an aggregate of fictions which are useful to life, upon a tremendous falsification of reality. But the instinct for knowledge, which in its extreme form is the will to truth at all costs, becomes, when it tries to dissipate this useful biological phantasmagoria, a power which is destructive to life—a form of nihilism.

Metaphysical optimism asserted that behind "the world of phenomena," behind the stream of Becoming there lay a "true world," the final home and last refuge of the human soul. But soon this illusion too was dissipated. Man confessed that he himself, through his desire for eternity, was the author of this "true world," and that he had fashioned this life merely in order to believe himself immortal. And from that moment intellectual honesty compelled him to forgo all faith in a metaphysical reality or in things or in himself, and he knew no other reality but Becoming.

Thus we see what nihilism meant in Nietzsche's eyes. Man began by distorting reality in conformity with his own needs. He wished the world to develop towards an end appointed by God; he wanted it to be subjected to fixed and well-organised laws, an immutable eternal substance free from change and death. And he *saw* and imagined the universe

22

as he wished it to be. He valued reality in proportion as it corresponded to this conception of his mind. And then gradually he realised that he had been the victim of an illusion. He therefore corrected the image of the world he had made for himself, and stripped reality of the qualities with which he had authoritatively endowed it. But the universe immediately lost its charm. Man loved the lie to which he had given birth. Reality—Becoming in eternal motion, changeable and void of sense—seemed hateful to him. Whereupon he was faced by a formidable dilemma and he found himself, to use Nietzsche's expression, obliged " to destroy either his table of values or himself." For, if the table of values by virtue of which he loves a fictitious world and condemns the real world is correct and legitimate, it is obvious that the nihilist should logically detest and try to destroy this bad reality. But if on the contrary the table of values is a fictitious one, it is none the less evident that the judgment passed by it upon reality is also erroneous, and should be rejected ; in this case he must revise his table of values from top to bottom, he must proceed, according to Nietzsche's celebrated formula, to a " transvaluation of all values."

This transvaluation Nietzsche urges men to make. The hypothesis he proposes to induce them to do so is well known.

The table of values in the name of which the nihilistic *pessimist* condemns reality and adores fiction is the product of " decadence." The belief in a metaphysical world beyond Becoming, the faith in a world of Being, of finality and of unity—in other words the *Christian* faith, for according to Nietzsche it is Christianity that embodies this conception of life

—is essentially a consolatory fiction by means of which a crowd of degenerates, weaklings and wretches have provided themselves with a plausible interpretation of their sufferings, and have hidden from their own eyes the sight of their weakness and decay. Take away this " vital falsehood," place them face to face with reality with all its ugliness and misery, and these people would succumb to despair. Very different is the outlook upon the world on the part of the *Strong*, who have a superabundance of health and energy. Why should the spectacle of Becoming without end inspire them with fear and horror ? If the decadent rejects it with terror, it is because, conscious as he is of his own degeneracy, he feels the need of thinking himself a collaborator with God, in order to believe his own value ; because he has not the strength to give a meaning to life and to lay down his own law. But the Man of Power who feels his own creative energy and knows that he is able to give a form to the " chaos " of Becoming, and can impose *his own* law upon a callous life-force, who has faith in his will to organise the universe, can also accept without revolt the idea that universal evolution should be meaningless in itself. His nihilism, instead of being *pessimistic*, is *Dionysian*. The spectacle of Becoming, the hypothesis of eternal recurrence, which is so crushing for the weak, becomes a triumphant and intoxicating vision for the creator who has succeeded in giving a meaning to life and in saying " Yea " to the eternal recurrence of Becoming.

In short, European nihilism was, in Nietzsche's eyes, a decisive and salutary crisis. By dissipating the mirage with which Christianity and Christian philosophy had surrounded reality, it acted in the capacity of an extremely powerful selective agent.

It was the touchstone by which to test the strong and the weak, healthy men and decadents. The latter it would break, and help them to disappear more quickly, which would be an advantage alike to themselves and to the world at large. But it would inspire the courage of the others and fill them with fresh enthusiasm for the conquest of power and for the infinite development of the type man.

Thus we see how, in the philosophy of Nietzsche, the principal tendencies which predominated in the nineteenth century are asserted and exalted.

The modern man believes in the organising power of the human will and intelligence. Nietzsche proclaims that the man of genius is the creator of all values, that he determines good and evil, that he creates " truth " itself and gives a meaning to Becoming. Superman takes the place left empty by the death of God : " Superman is the meaning of the world," says Zarathustra. " Your will should say : Let Superman be the meaning of the world." [1]

The modern man has learnt to disbelieve in miracles and grows more and more sceptical with regard to the Christian conception, which subjects man and the universe to the will of God, and he is also exceedingly doubtful about a Church in which he sees a power which is supremely hostile to human freedom. Nietzsche loudly proclaims his uncompromising hatred of Christianity. God is only a creation on the part of human suffering and weakness, a mirage which will vanish as soon as man has regained his

---

[1] For the benefit of all those who are unacquainted with Nietzsche's philosophy it should be noted that behind the idea of the Superman no new physiological species was anticipated by Nietzsche, but merely a " Ruler-man "—a man superior in spirit and will to his fellows and with power and capacity to govern them.—TR.

health and learnt to realise the energies he hides within himself. Christianity is the great conspiracy of the miserable and the " physiologically botched " against the strong and powerful ; it is the gigantic lie by means of which decadents have attempted to poison the intellectual and moral atmosphere of Europe ; it is the terrible virus which, if its effects became universal, would turn the world into a lazaretto ; it is, in the scornful words of the *Antichrist*, " the one immortal blemish of mankind. . . ."

The modern man is inclined to intellectual and moral scepticism ; he is a pessimist, full of suspicion with regard to all consolatory hypotheses, and he remains in a state of perplexity before the threatening problem of suffering. Nietzsche pushes his scepticism to the point of nihilism. He professes the most radical form of phenomenism. His " immorality " realises that vices and virtues proceed from the same source ; that man, in order to develop, must inevitably grow both in good and evil, just as a tree plunges its roots all the more deeply into the ground the more proudly it lifts its branches in the air ; that the superior type of the human race is not the " good " man of the old traditional morality, but the powerful man who can endure without being broken " that tension of the antagonistic elements " in human nature, and sums up in his own harmonious and complex personality the two contradictory aspects of life, its creative force and its destructive power. Lastly, Nietzsche is a profound pessimist inasmuch as he holds an essentially " combative " and " tragic " view of life. But his Dionysian nihilism, instead of allowing itself to be depressed by the formidable vision of senseless Becoming and eternal human suffering, finds in this very spectacle a cause of enthusiasm. His " pessimism of strength " recognises that suffering and evil have no need of justification, and that evil is the necessary " complement " of good. And he finally ends by the *whole-hearted* acceptance of human destiny, and with an enthusiastic hymn to life, with all its magnificence and cruelty—prolific and devouring life, which incessantly and without pity destroys its own creations, and yet remains ever-lastingly the same, indestructible, constantly reborn, eternally young and fair.

## V

The influence of Nietzsche upon the German thought of to-day has been considerable. The nobility of his moral nature, his magnificent intrepidity of thought, his infectious passion as an apostle and a prophet have won respect from all. Even those who were most diametrically opposed to his tendencies, the Christians and the Socialists, could not refuse to grant him their esteem, and brought themselves at least partially to assimilate his ideas. A Protestant pastor has written *Zarathustra Sermons*, and a militant Socialist has endeavoured to adapt to the needs of the people the aristocratic thought of the three great hermits of art and philosophical meditation—Schopen-hauer, Wagner and Nietzsche. The prophet of the Will to Power and the Superman is not only admired as a great poet, a psychologist of the first rank, and a profound connoisseur of the human heart, but he has also had great influence as an initiator into the life of the spirit.

Yet to what extent has this influence been a pro-found, a widespread and durable one ? It is, in my opinion, very difficult to decide this point as yet.

The outside observer is clearly convinced that Nietzsche cannot stand as the typical mouthpiece of the aspirations which are to-day predominant in Germany. He is a brilliant exception, an extraordinary " case " which is studied and admired. But I should be very much surprised to find that the number of those who go to him for rules of conduct and an interpretation of life is very great. It seems to me that he is still or has once more become " out of season," to use his own well-known expression.

" Modern Germany," says Nietzsche, " represents such an enormous store of inherited and acquired capacity, that for some time it might spend this accumulated treasure even with some prodigality. It is no superior culture that has ultimately become prevalent with this modern tendency, nor is it by any means delicate taste, or noble beauty of the instincts, but rather a number of virtues more manly than any that other European countries can show. An amount of good spirits and self-respect, plenty of firmness in human relations and in the reciprocity of duties ; much industry and much perseverance, and a certain inherited soberness which is much more in need of a spur than of a brake. Let me add that in this country people still obey without feeling that obedience humiliates. And no one despises his opponent." [1]

What has this modern Germany, which is by no means decadent, this somewhat ponderous, robust, and well-disciplined Germany, with her magnificent army, her solid administration, her strong organisation of scientific work, her powerful industrial and

[1] This English rendering is taken from Dr. Oscar Levy's Authorised English Translation of Nietzsche's Complete Works. (See *The Twilight of the Idols*, p. 50).—Tr.

commercial activity, her great schemes of insurance and social forethought—what has she to do with Nietzschean Radicalism ? Nietzsche, who had small admiration for the new Empire, said about it : " Power stupefies." And this new Germany on her part pays but scant courtesy to the Superman. At times she rejects Nietzsche with horror. At others she despises him as a " dilettante " who did not master any science fundamentally and in detail. Or else she politely pays him the tribute of homage due to a national celebrity, but seeks elsewhere for inspiration and guidance. She disapproves of the uncompromising thoroughness with which he pushes his ideas to their most extreme logical conclusions. She sees in him a romantic exaggeration with which a few idealists and men of letters can toy, but which remains extremely problematical and has no future before it. At heart this practical and positive Germany seems but little disposed to indulge in any extremes, either in the domain of action or of thought. We have already seen how in politics she sought out moderate solutions, provisional compromises between the monarchical and democratic principles, between nationalism and imperialism, between the interests of the agrarian Conservatives and the industrial middle classes, between those of capitalistic enterprise and the working masses. By its very nature, this Germany is not, apparently, " Radical," and it seems to me, that in the spiritual sphere as well, any extreme solutions, such as those advanced by Nietzsche, appear picturesque but improbable in her eyes, and she does not take them altogether seriously.

We have already seen, on the other hand, how the Germany of to-day, which is so realistic, so tenacious in her struggle for power and wealth, has proclaimed a fresh return to idealism, a new aspiration for a high culture, and a will for social justice and charity. But this reactionary movement against the utilitarian realism of the second half of the century is not apparently tending in the direction of Nietzsche's ideas. It is true that the poet of Zarathustra is in a certain sense a " romantic," an opponent of intellectualism and even, in spite of his atheism, a highly religious nature—" the most pious of all them that believe not in God," as Zarathustra says. And in this respect he is certainly a representative of the new idealism. But, on the other hand, it must not be forgotten, that this romanticist has judged and condemned romanticism with the utmost vigour, that this profoundly religious spirit has proclaimed with all the energy at his command and with passionate conviction the absolute bankruptcy of Christianity and every religious ideal. And on this point he has not been followed by his countrymen.

On the contrary, the characteristic feature of the last few years seems to be a renaissance, in Germany, of a certain religious mysticism, which is revealed by a series of significant symptoms : the victorious resistance of Catholicism to the *Kulturkampf*, the political triumph of the Centre ; the growth of a new Catholic literature and philosophy ; and in the Protestant camp the success of the " social evangelical " party and its effort to fashion out of Christian thought some principle of social policy. And the renewal of the vitality of the churches is not the only symptom of this movement. The lay world is also lured into participating in this new tendency. A breath of vague and mystic idealism suffuses novels and plays, from Hauptmann's *Sunken Bell* and

Sudermann's *Johannes* to Rosegger's *Gottsucher*. As was the case at the beginning of the nineteenth century, men are apparently seeking a " new God." Criticism is plunging with growing curiosity into the history of German romanticism and is analysing its religious idealism with a sympathetic spirit. And the bulk of the public is seeking food for its need of religious emotion in books like Harnack's *Essence of Christianity*.

And what precisely does this neo-romanticism which is not peculiar to Germany, and the symptoms of which are to be found everywhere in Europe, signify ? Is it a sincere revival of traditional re-ligious beliefs—a vague homesickness for the lost paradises of faith ? Or is it something less than this—a mere literary vogue which will die like the fashion for naturalism and symbolism ? People will lean to one or other of these interpretations in accordance with their own convictions and impres-sions. But the significance of this movement, especially in Germany, can certainly not be regarded as negligible. It is clear, at all events, that this neo-romantic atmosphere is not favourable to the diffusion of an anti-Christian radicalism. Germany seems quite as little inclined to cast Christianity finally aside in the spiritual domain as to reject the monarchical principle in the sphere of actual life. She seeks to amend rather than to destroy. She is of the opinion that each of the two antagonistic principles contains an element of truth, and en-deavours to reconcile them rather than to eliminate one by an arbitrary and violent process of simplifica-tion.

And it is for this reason that I am doubtful whether Nietzsche, in spite of his admirable moral nobility

and his genius, is really, in the eyes of the present
generation in Germany, the prophet of a new era.
People believe in the advent of a new idealism.
They believe that Germany, after her military and
economic successes, is to-day marching towards an
artistic, philosophical, and moral renaissance. They
hope for the swift return of an epoch of " classical "
culture, which will be steadier and more balanced
than the age of feverish and hasty transition in
which we are at present living. After the violent
and often anarchical struggle of the individual
towards power, wealth, and scientific utilitarian
rationalism, men began to aspire towards a new
" order," more stable in all its departments, in the
domain of actuality as well as in that of thought.
Average public opinion in Germany does not demand
war to the knife against the old powers, but rather
a happy compromise between the tendencies of the
past and the present.

Under these circumstances, the master whom
those who have undertaken to draw up the balance-
sheet of the century proclaim most loudly is Goethe.
To the radically uncompromising attitude and the
" combative " philosophy of the prophet of Superman they prefer the rule of tolerance, fair intellectual
and moral equilibrium, and the marvellous self-
possession of the sage of Weimar. It is under his
patronage that they would place the German culture of the future. And indeed they could not find
a better one. Let us accept the omen and wish, for
our part also, that the Germany of to-morrow may
become more and more a Germany " according to
Goethe."

# BOOK IV

## *EVOLUTION IN ART*

# CHAPTER I

## THE VALUE OF ART

### I

At the same time as the anti-rationalist reaction which set in towards the end of the eighteenth century gradually gave religious sentiment the precedence of theoretical reason, it also tended to place art at the head of the tables of values.

The era of enlightenment had but a mediocre comprehension of the nature of art. Absolutely persuaded of the sovereign power of reason, it saw in art, not an end in itself, but merely a convenient instrument for communicating to the multitude certain philosophical or moral truths in an agreeable form. And, moreover, it formed a mechanical and, as a rule, somewhat primitive conception of artistic creations. It compared the poet, the painter or the musician to clever craftsmen who fashion more or less successful articles according to whether or not they have imitated good models and used the best means prescribed by their craft. Hence the presumptuous indiscretion with which the critic allowed himself to domineer over the artist, to formulate theoretical rules for the creation of masterpieces, and to judge whether the works were beautiful or not—that is to say, whether they were in conformity with these rules.

351

But modern subjectivism repudiated this mechanistic interpretation. Like the majority of the great creations of the human spirit, like religion and language, morality and law, poetry and art did not seem to it the products of reflection and intelligence, but were rather organisms which were born and developed, which prospered or died by virtue of the germ of vitality within them, organisms which demanded care and respect as living entities, and which must only be touched with a wise precaution, if they were not to wither away immediately. The work of art, therefore, was no longer regarded as a product of human industry. Quite the contrary. The work which seemed to be the fruit of a too self-conscious art, that was over-clever in calculating its effects, was now condemned. A masterpiece was not *made*, but *born*. It was a living organism brought into the world by the genius, in virtue of an inner necessity. In the act of artistic creation the genius was unconscious and in a sense passive. He was compared to the woman with child, to the bee that secretes honey, to the bird that sings, to the somnambulist who succeeds in his perilous climbing. Hence also the predilection of the age for works in which the art was quite spontaneous and even anonymous, and which seemed to be the creation not of one individual but of an epoch, a race, a tribe ; hence the taste for popular poetry—whether real or spurious—for Macpherson-Ossian as much as for the old English and Scotch songs, for Homer, or the poets of the Bible.

At the same moment as the Germans learnt to conceive of art as a living organism, they also discovered in ancient Greece the classic land of beauty. The old humanism had set itself the task of continuing the work of classical antiquity and of Roman antiquity in particular, and thus of making the student capable of writing and philosophising like the ancients. Neo-Hellenism in the form in which it was revived in the German universities of the eighteenth century under the guidance of such masters as Gesner and Heyne, had very different aims. It no longer wished to imitate antiquity ; it simply aimed at understanding and savouring it, and at moulding the minds of modern men, their tastes and judgment by contact with the most perfect works which the human genius had ever produced. And in this form it obtained considerable success. Not only did it triumph in the universities from the end of the eighteenth century ; not only did it, from the beginning of the nineteenth century, inspire the reform of secondary education with its spirit ; but it also spread beyond university centres, and won over the educated public. Winckelmann opened out fresh horizons for his contemporaries on the subject of Greek art by showing that the masterpieces of Greek sculpture were not the artificial products of academic æsthetics, but the natural and spontaneous fruit of the Hellenic genius. Lessing opposed the dramatic æsthetics of the French with Aristotle and the true dramatic doctrines of the ancients. Herder represented Greek civilisation as the age of the radiant adolescence of humanity, and proclaimed that no nation was superior to the Greeks, among whom for the first time mankind was raised to clear self-consciousness. William of Humboldt maintained that " no people combined such great simplicity and naturalness with so great a culture." And lastly Frederick Augustus Wolff regarded the study of Hellenic civilisation as the best introduction to the

23

knowledge of man, and taught that Greece alone among the nations " afforded us the spectacle of a people which had developed organically till it reached its full bloom." He asserted the independence and self-sufficiency of philology, which had till then been considered an auxiliary science to jurisprudence and theology, and raised it to an end in itself and almost a religion for humanity.

With the great classicists of Germany, therefore— with Goethe, Schiller and Humboldt—there came into being an idealistic conception of Hellenism which ended in a veritable religion of beauty. Hellenic civilisation was in their eyes the period of synthesis which followed upon the wane of Asiatic and Egyptian civilisation. It seemed to them that the soul of humanity had in a sense concentrated all its energies in order to create this marvellous bud which summed up and gave expression to the whole of the Indo-European culture of the past and the future. In fact, the chief characteristic of the Greeks was that they were the epitome of mankind as a whole and realised as individuals that ideal of harmonious abundance, of " completeness," which used to hover before the mind of Goethe. They had the unique privilege of condensing every human energy into one perfect whole, a marvellously refined sensitiveness, a lucid intellect, a magic imagination and a powerful will. All these diverse gifts were in their case harmoniously welded and authoritatively combined in each individual unit. The Greek soul was in a sense the primordial and superior prototype of the human soul. It was really divine, because humanity is nothing less than the manifestation *par excellence* of the divine in nature.

And this splendid efflorescence of Hellenic culture

was a unique period in the annals of humanity. To
the epoch of *contraction* which had given it birth
there succeeded in fact a period of *expansion*. In
modern nations also the ideal image of the species
could be found. But this image instead of being
manifested *in its completeness* in every man was now
only *partially* realised by the individual. The beautiful synthetic unity of ancient Hellas had been shattered. Modern man developed his faculties one by
one, and he never developed them all ; he was, generally speaking, merely a fragment of humanity.
Chained to some strictly circumscribed task, riveted
to a particular point in the great social mechanism,
he was shaped or rather deformed by his duties. He
was no longer a " man," but simply a special wheel
in the vast machine. The same applied to nations
as to individuals. Greek culture had been perpetu-
ated in modern countries, but each nation displayed
the exaggerated development of a particular characteristic of the Hellenic genius. In the Roman the
practical wisdom and the solid reason of the Greeks
lived again ; in the Italian their sparkling imagination ;
in the Spaniard that inclination towards exaltation
which he held in check with so much care ; in the
sentimental Englishman that sweet melancholy which
enveloped the whole of Greek life like a light veil ;
in the Frenchman, the sense of beautiful form ; in
the German, profundity of thought. Thus modern
culture regarded *as a whole* was certainly the blossom
of ancient culture ; but the Eternal-Human was
no longer realised in its entirety, either by an isolated
people or in an individual.

The task of the future must therefore be an effort
in the direction of concentration. The era of disintegration through which humanity was at present

passing must be again followed by a period of synthesis.   And for this the Greeks must be studied, not, indeed, with the object of returning once more to Hellenic culture, but in order to " give birth to a new Greece," and restore the complete image of Humanity —of a Humanity, moreover, which would be richer and more complex than that which once flourished in Greece, a Humanity that had assimilated the results of two thousand years of culture.   This was the ideal towards which a Faust or a Wilhelm Meister aimed.   And the great representatives of classicism were persuaded that, of all the nations of the world, the Germans were predestined one day to attain this ideal.   They possessed a suppleness of mind which helped them to comprehend all foreign productions, an instinctive impartiality which rendered them capable of understanding and judging other nations from an absolutely objective standpoint, and a certain universality in their gifts and abilities which explained why their national genius did not present such accentuated features as that of other countries, but which permitted them, on the other hand, to assimilate the fruits of the most diverse cultures. The Germans were, in a word, " the most human of all the nations," and consequently the best fitted one day to realise that harmonious synthesis of all the elements of human nature of which the Greeks set the example, and which was the goal towards which modern times were tending.

The high position which art holds in the conception of life as it was pictured by the great German classicists is evident.   The end which they assigned for humanity was the imitation of the Greeks, the æsthetic culture of the ego.   Knowledge, in Goethe's eyes, was not merely theoretical and rational, it was

also intuitive—it was the result not only of abstract
thought, but also of the direct and concrete vision
of things. The Good, according to Schiller, was not
simply the outcome of the absolute triumph of
practical Reason over the inclinations, as Kant taught;
but " beautiful souls " could realise in themselves
the perfect concord between natural impulses and the
moral law. In the eyes of both Goethe and Schiller
moral superiority consisted in the harmonious development of all the energies which the human microcosm
contained. Art thus led to the True and the Good.
And the Good and the True in their turn, when they
attained perfection, would blossom into Beauty.

And this religion of Beauty exercised a profound
influence upon the thought of the whole of the nineteenth century. It is to be found in the great representatives of philosophical idealism. Fichte saw, in
the mists of the future, beyond the era of Science,
in which Reason and her law are perceived with
perfect clearness, a period of art in which humanity,
by the exercise of the perfect liberty which it will
realise at the end of its evolution, will again clothe
truth and science in beauty. Schelling maintained
that art, in which the complete balance between conscious and unconscious activity is revealed, is the
most perfect expression of the ego. He admitted the
fundamental identity of genius and nature ; the ideal
world of art and the real world of objects are the
products of one and the same activity, which, in its
unconscious action, creates the real and visible world
of things, and in its unconscious manifestation gives
birth to the æsthetic world of art. The world taken
as a whole, therefore, is a work of art ; it is " the
still unconscious poetry of the Spirit." Art reveals
the identity of the real and the ideal, it is the key to

the mystery of the world, it shows how the ideal becomes incarnate and how intelligence is the creator of nature. For Hegel, art, religion and philosophy were the three degrees that could be distinguished in the sphere of absolute Spirit : Art was the absolute Spirit *perceiving* its own essence in complete freedom, it was Spirit penetrating matter and transforming it into its own image. With Schopenhauer genius was the marvellous gift, imparted to a small number of the elect, of rising to the disinterested contemplation of things ; and the work of genius, art, had the privilege of " reproducing the eternal ideas which it had conceived by means of pure contemplation—that is to say, the essential and the permanent among all the phenomena of the world."

The romanticists in their turn vied with each other in proclaiming the sublime mission of art. Friedrich Schlegel transfigured in his own way in the domain of art the idealism of Fichte, which showed us the ego opposing to itself the non-ego in order finally to realise the identity of the ego and the non-ego. He compared the creative act of the ego, such as Fichte described it, to the act of artistic creation. The poet and the artist created a fictitious world ; but, at bottom, this world had as much reality as the external and so-called real world. The only difference which existed between these two worlds was that the latter was an *unconscious* creation of the ego, whilst the former was the *conscious* creation of the same ego. We merely attributed an independent existence to the non-ego by virtue of an illusion which would disappear with the progress of consciousness. Thus, in proportion as we came to see more clearly into ourselves, we should perceive more and more distinctly the identity between the world of reality and that of poetry, and the fact that the universe was the work of art of the supreme ego and that the real artist was a creator of worlds.

Novalis, in his theory of magic idealism, pushed to its most extreme consequences this paradoxical comparison between the poetic genius and the creator of the real world. Art seemed to him the liberating power by which the ego would gradually raise itself to omnipotence. The artist of to-day created partial illusions by making use of such and such an organ, of which he disposed authoritatively. Thus the painter, who by means of his palette called a whole world of dreams into being, in a certain sense exercised power over the organ of sight; similarly the musician disposed of hearing and the poet of the imagination and the sentiment. Now imagine all these partial geniuses synthetised into one unique and supreme genius, who moulded a universe according to his fancy, and created *his own* particular world, complete in all its parts, instead of having to submit to contact with a strange reality, and the type of the magic idealist was obtained. Art was thus the first stage in the conquest of the world by the ego at which the mystic aimed. And the supreme victory of idealism, the advent of the " Kingdom of Eternity," would also be the apotheosis of poetry. When the Kingdom of the Sun together with the reign of dualistic illusion had been annihilated, Fable would take the place of the Parcæ, Poetry would replace Fate and weave the woof of universal destiny. Really happy life did not mean, as philosophical idealism would have it do, the reign of absolute Reason; it was also the triumph of Beauty, it unravelled itself freely, like a harmonious poem or a divine dream.

And if all romanticists do not go to such lengths

as Novalis in the deification of art and the glorification of its magic power, they were all artists at heart and inclined to identify art, philosophy, and religion. They regarded the mission of the artist as that of a priest, and sought in poets, painters, and musicians the most profound revelations concerning the mystery of the universe, looking up to them as seers who expressed by their poetical, musical, or plastic symbols truths of a superior order to which the intellect by its own unaided efforts could not rise.

This cult of art continued to exist, roughly speaking, throughout the whole of the nineteenth century. It is to be found (to give two examples only) in two of the greatest artists of modern Germany—in Hebbel and Richard Wagner.

In agreement with the romanticists, Hebbel proclaimed that, in order to attain to a consciousness of human destiny such as it really is in its tragic necessity, man can choose two paths, that of the intellect and that of intuition, the path of science or the path of art. In common with them he was also persuaded of the inferiority of the conscious intellect as a means of knowledge, and deeply convinced that the most complete image of reality could only be attained by intuition, by that " inner illumination " which sprang up in the soul of the poet. Art was, in his eyes, the continuation of the act of creation; it was the expression at once private and symbolical of universal Becoming; it was the sublime sob of human pain, the moral consciousness of humanity, the living proof of philosophy, and the highest form of life.

And in Wagner's case also, art was the liberating principle *par excellence*. The artist, in the ideal images he created, made man perceive by direct intuition the goal towards which he was aiming in every branch of his activity. Whilst the man of science and the philosopher endeavoured to understand the universe and to formulate *by means of* the intellect and *for the sake of* the intellect the physical and moral laws of the world, the artist through his symbols translated for the *complete* man the purely theoretical and abstract conception of the man of thought. Whilst the " religious " man regarded the conversion of the selfish will as the final goal to which all the efforts of humanity should be directed, the poet conjured up before our eyes the consoling image of our future victories and the radiant spectacle of regenerated humanity. The work of art, Wagner proclaimed, was " the living representation of religion." The fictions of artists, like the religious allegories of priests, were symbolical images of that eternal truth which eluded all direct representation. Music especially, which Wagner agreed with Schopenhauer in regarding as the *direct* expression of the will, was marvellously adapted to tell the tale of the great tragedy of the fall and the redemption of man as it really was in its most fundamental reality. A symphony by Beethoven was a higher and purer revelation of Christian faith than all the dogmas of the priests. Modern religious faith was tired of the traditional religious allegories, which were so touching in their simplicity and yet so imperfect, and which became lies as soon as an attempt was made to impose them as historical or metaphysical dogmas. It was in the great creations of a Sophocles, a Shakespeare or a Beethoven, and above all in musical drama, that superior form of symphony, that we found the highest expression of the religious sentiment, the religious myth in its modern shape.

Thus throughout the nineteenth century we find under various forms the fundamental conviction of the infinite value of art and of the superior mission of the artist. Whether it regards a beautiful existence as the final end of human culture, whether it identifies artistic creation with the creative act from which the world has proceeded, whether it attributes to the poetical interpretation of the universe a degree of " truth " as great as, or even greater than, the scientific interpretation, or whether it sees in the artist the successor of the priest and the best authorised interpreter of our religious faith, German thought at all events assigns to art an exceedingly high position. For it honours in art a power of the same rank as science, morality, or religion.

## II

The development of the system of enterprise levelled a serious blow at this modern religion of art and a high level of general culture.

In the first place, it had the result of putting the problem of culture in an absolutely positive and prosaic light. For the modern commercial mind, culture was merely a commodity which was valued very highly by an ever larger section of the public. The production of culture was accordingly regarded as an industry, and a flourishing industry. And indeed with the general growth in wealth there was a very large increase in the number of those who could lay claim to a finished education, and especially in the number of intellectual workers who were in a position to devote themselves exclusively to a profession which was not directly useful to material existence. Under these circumstances people aimed

at producing culture " wholesale." And during the
nineteenth century the tremendous extension was
witnessed in all enterprises calculated to spread
culture in every shape and form among all ranks of
the nation.

Firstly, public education was developed to considerable proportions. A few figures will give a
rough idea of the progress made. In 1882 Prussia
had 20,440 primary schools with 1,427,045 scholars ;
in 1901 she had 4,413 schools with 35,733 classes in
the towns, and in the country 32,332 schools with
68,349 classes and a school population of over
5,680,000 scholars. Secondary education increased
in similar proportions : in 1835 Prussia had 136
grammar schools and preparatory schools ; in 1905
she had 363, to which must be added 335 technical
schools and colleges. Not less striking, in spite of
the marked falling off in the faculty of theology,
which during the course of the century lost almost
half its numbers, is the increase in the total number
of students at the universities, which from 15,870 in
1830 and 12,426 in 1850 rose to 37,677 in 1905. The
expenditure on public instruction and culture in
Prussia grew from about 10 millions of marks in
1850 to 185 millions in 1905.

In every respect the progress was remarkable.
Not only were the institutions and the old type of
teaching developed, but during the course of the
nineteenth century a whole host of new creations
came into existence—schools, superior technical,
agricultural and commercial schools, technical and
commercial colleges, classes for adults and professional
instruction of all kinds, popular universities, free or
paid lectures, public libraries, collections and museums
of all sorts. The school population and the teaching

staffs increased enormously at the same time as the professional capacity of these teachers was also improved. The total amount of instruction dispensed to the nation showed a prodigious increase. Germany, as we have already seen, prides herself upon marching at the head of the civilised nations of the world with regard to the organisation of education; and she applies herself with jealous care to the task of not allowing herself to be out-distanced, in this sphere, by rival countries.

Second in importance to the schools are books. Germany, as is well known, is the greatest book-producer in the world. At the beginning of the century the number of new works published was not more than 3,900 a year. It rose in 1900 to 24,792, in 1905 to 28,886; whilst France, which holds the second place as a book-producer, only reached in 1904 a total of 12,139 works. If the average number of books in an edition is placed at 1000, it has been estimated that Germany prints every year about one book to every two inhabitants! The book trade is in the most flourishing condition: it possessed in 1905, 7,152 establishments, and exported abroad 290 millions of marks' worth of goods. It seems, moreover, that the production of books is assuming a more and more *industrial* character. The author— even in the case of scientific works—is tending to become nothing more than a kind of executive agent, almost completely subordinated to the publisher, who commissions him to produce such and such a work. The multiplication of dictionaries, encyclopædias, " collections " and libraries of all sorts, and of books that come out in parts, etc., clearly proves that the majority of works actually published have their origin in speculation on the part of the publisher rather than in any artistic thought or scientific idea.

Germany is inundated with books, whilst newspapers and reviews swarm in even greater numbers. As early as 1825 Goethe hurled his fulminations against journalism, with its " disintegrating criticism " and its blustering publicity—which, it is true, spread among the masses a sort of semi-culture, but " was for all creative talent a fatal fog, a seductive poison which blighted the young shoots of the imagination, stripped it of its brilliant foliage, and penetrated into the depths in which the vital spunk and the most delicate fibres lay hid." Now, about that time there were 845 newspapers in Prussia. In 1869 there were 2,127. In 1891 the number of papers subjected to the postal tax reached 7,082. And the circulation of all these papers increased to most formidable proportions. During the last twenty years the number of newspapers which have passed through the post has almost trebled, rising from 500 millions in 1885 to 1,500 millions in 1905. Complaints against the abuse of journalism and against the mediocre quality of the semi-culture which these papers pour forth in floods among the public have not ceased since Goethe's time. But the evil—if evil it is—has only grown worse. And like the book trade, the trade in news, propagated either by means of print or pictures, has acquired a more and more colossal circulation.

Under these circumstances artistic production in its turn tends more and more to become industrialised. Concerts, theatrical representations, and artistic exhibitions of all kinds show a ceaseless increase. From 1882 to 1895 the number of people earning their livelihood as musicians or in connection with the theatre rose from 46,508 to 65,565, thus showing an increase of 41 per cent., whilst in the same lapse of time the population only increased by 14 per cent.  We know the loud anathemas which Richard Wagner hurled, in the middle of the century, against the "selfish" art which sprang from the capitalistic system, the art which was vitiated and perverted in its essence out of covetousness for "golden guineas" —the venal and artificial art destined not to satisfy the instinctive need of beauty, which always lies dormant in the hearts of the people, but the fictitious and demoralising need of luxury, or the unhealthy thirst for distractions and pleasures which tortures the rich.  In their romantic exaggeration Wagner's diatribes express an undeniable fact, which is that under the impulse of the spirit of capitalistic enterprise art tends less and less to become a disinterested and idealistic effort to attain beauty, but develops into the methodical and organised exploitation of the need of luxury and adornment, of distraction and amusement, not only among the rich but also among the mass of the people.  There is no doubt that great theatrical and musical enterprises, exhibitions of pictures or decorative art are *above all* of the nature of industrial enterprises.  Just as the "man of science" sometimes appears as the mere paid craftsman in some great publishing venture, so too the "artist" often becomes merely a purveyor to the theatre, the review, or the library, and works, not in obedience to his inner "genius," but simply to satisfy some well-known and undeniable public taste.  There exists to-day a trade in the theatre and in novels, in opera and singing, in pictures and statues; and every day it becomes more difficult to decide where *industry* ends and *art* begins, and to fix the limit which separates the manufactured article devoid of all æsthetic value from the superior work in which is embodied a disinterested attempt at beauty.

At the same time as the change, the general character of which I have just sketched, took place in the domain of culture and art, the position the latter held in the scale of values was also modified.

From the moment that the will to power and to wealth became the dominating instinct, and the pursuit of the useful tended, in an ever more marked fashion, to take the first place in public estimation, it was also natural that culture and art should lose their prestige. Classical or romantic idealism saw in the free play of the spiritual energies of man, in philosophy, art, poetry and religion the highest form of human activity, and proclaimed with Friedrich Schlegel : " The highest good and the only thing in the world that matters is culture." The realistic and positive spirit of the nineteenth century soon contradicted this verdict. As early as Goethe this change of opinion was announced in the *Travels of Wilhelm Meister*. In distinction to the ideal of a complete culture and the harmonious development of all the energies of the ego, Goethe insisted upon the necessity for specialisation which alone would make the individual a useful member of society : " To know and do one thing well secures a higher development than to do a hundred fairly well." The first duty of man was to learn one trade well. For mediocre spirits this trade would remain a trade ; in the case of superior natures it would become an art. And the genius himself would see in the one thing he did to perfection, the emblem of all that was well done, the symbol of every really fruitful and useful activity. The exercise of some activity that was practical and useful to society was thus imposed by Goethe as an

obligation upon every man, even upon those belonging
to the highest society. Far from being sacrificed or
subordinated to general culture, the useful, on the
contrary, was the only path which led to the true
and the beautiful.

And this conviction grew stronger and stronger in
German society during the second half of the century.

The progress of industry and commerce, the rise of
Bismarckian realism in politics, and the development
of materialistic and positivist ideas in philosophy,
had as their corollary a recrudescence of the utilitarian spirit. In the scholastic domain this tendency
was manifested by the creation, in addition to the
classical system of education, of a modern type of
instruction in which science and modern languages
played a greater part, which was more " practical "
and consequently better adapted to the needs of
the industrial and commercial middle classes. The
" culture " which developed in modern Germany upon
the basis of the natural and historical sciences is
not, perhaps, above criticism. We know the anger
and contempt which Nietzsche poured forth in his
*Thoughts out of Season* upon the civilisation dear to
the Philistine of Culture, the *Bildungsphilister*—that
" Socratic " civilisation founded upon the instinct of
knowledge and ignorant of the necessities of life,
trivially optimistic, full of mistrust of genius, and a
slave to routine as well as intolerant in its mediocrity. One remembers the invectives of Zarathustra
against the " civilised " men of to-day who have the
presumption to say " we are entirely *real*, free from
all belief and all superstition," and who are in reality
" tattooed with the symbols of the past," " moulded
out of colours and out of glued scraps," and present
to our gaze a miscellaneous aggregate of features

borrowed from all the civilisations in the history of the world through which they have been hurriedly led by foolhardy educators.

But it must be recognised that if this prudently utilitarian culture, so odious to an aristocratic temperament like Nietzsche's, is perhaps lacking in prestige and grandeur of style, it is yet the normal production of the general evolution of the German mind. It may be urged that it is not very interesting in itself, but none the less did it inspire the men who won Sadowa and Sedan. And the very vehemence of Nietzsche's attacks shows that he felt isolated and " out of season " in his antipathies. And I doubt whether, in spite of his enormous success, he is really much less " out of season " to-day. In spite of his passionate outbursts against the abuse of history, against philological erudition, against abstract science and specialisation, against cheap social optimism and the belief in the continual progress of humanity, the *average* culture of modern Germany is apparently still chiefly historical, philological, scientific, utilitarian and optimistic, suspicious of extreme solutions, always disposed to resolve by means of more or less happy compromises the great conflicting principles which present themselves to our era, and practical rather than æsthetic in its essential tendencies.

Under these circumstances it is impossible for art to enjoy the unique position which it held in the estimation of the country at the beginning of the nineteenth century. The progress of imperialistic rationalism was a menace to both religious and æsthetic faith. Contemporary positivism does not hesitate, occasionally, to contest the value of art. It foresees that, in the life of future generations, art and poetry will perhaps occupy but a very small space.

24

It points out that the natural development of man is from instinct to knowledge, from spontaneous emotion to reflective judgment. It proclaims that artistic intuition is a confused perception, inferior in value to rational ideas. And it predicts that scientific observation will continue to prevail more and more over the imagination, that the man of culture will consecrate himself ever more exclusively to science, and leave the arts and poetry to the more emotional fraction of humanity, to women, youths and children.

And contemporary naturalism shares to a certain extent the doubts felt by utilitarian positivism. Nietzsche subjects to the most ruthless criticism the religion of art of the classicists and the romanticists. Naturally artists would like to persuade us that they are the oracles of a superior wisdom which is inaccessible to the vulgar. They believe, as Zarathustra says, " that the dreamer that listeneth, lying in the grass or on the slope of the lonely vale, getteth light upon those things that are between heaven and earth." But this is merely a pose, says Nietzsche. A sincere psychology of the artist dissipates the glorious halo with which he delights to adorn his brow. It is not true that genius is a miraculous gift from heaven ; it is, on the contrary, a " long patience," and we know to-day, from Beethoven's note-books, that his most sublime melodies, far from being improvisations, were the result of a long process of pruning and of severe selection. It is not true that the work of art possesses that character of " necessity " proper to living organisms : those alone can go into ecstasies before the " superior reality " of a poetic creation who see in the real man merely a silhouette and not the *unique* incomparable individual that he really is, every one of whose manifestations is necessary. The artist is not a sincere man, a " conscientious man of the spirit " : he does not fight for truth, but for those interpretations of life from which he can obtain the most beautiful results. He is not a seer who presents us with the symbolical expression of truths that he foresees by virtue of his divining instinct. Far from being a pioneer of culture, he is a man behind the times, an epigone, a " raiser of the dead," who puts a little colour into pale and faded institutions and artificially revives obsolete modes of thought. Art blooms when religions are losing ground and when their dogmas are dissipated and overthrown by criticism and inspire insuperable suspicion. Then feeling which is chased out of the religious sphere by the progress of enlightenment flows over and finds an opening for itself in the domain of art. The artist becomes the successor of the priest. It is the artist who, when the shades of evening are falling about religion, revives and keeps alive the sacred flame of enthusiasm, consoles humanity by giving it in its turn a fictitious explanation of suffering and evil, and relieves it for the moment without, however, curing it, by means of palliatives and narcotics. But the reign of art is as ephemeral as that of religion. The appetite for knowledge, which grows ever more imperious, pushes man inexorably towards the science of nature and historical research. Even now men regard art simply as an emotional remembrance of the joys of youth, as a magnificent legacy of the past, as the fascinating reflection of a sun already set, whose rays no longer reach us directly, but which still lights the sky of our life and sets it aglow, although we can no longer see it ourselves.

From yet another point of view the time in which

we live reacts against the romantic cult of art. We have just seen that it definitely repudiates the pretensions of art to set itself up as a rival power to Science and to represent the work of art as an interpretation of reality endowed with a value as great as that of a rational representation. Similarly it deprives art of all pretension to rise above the real. Art cannot " excel " life or correct it ; on the contrary it is never greater than when it is *at the service of* life, and endows it with beauty and makes it more worthy of being lived.

From this point of view, once more, certain of Nietzsche's ideas seem to me to have a value which is not only an individual but a typical one, expressing some of the deepest tendencies of the soul of modern Germany. We know that, in his eyes, all higher art had its origin in Dionysian intoxication, in the feeling of increased strength and of superabundance of life which impels man to enrich all that surrounds him by his own plenitude, and to transform all things until they become the reflection of his will to power. Man *creates* Beauty by instinctively projecting into things his own perfection, by making the superabundance of that vitality which he feels bubbling within himself overflow into nature. He is the cause and the measure of all beauty and all ugliness. The Beautiful is the sovereign joy which the triumphant and magnificent will to power feels when it contemplates in itself and outside itself the image of its glorious perfection. The Ugly is degenerate man, it is the weakening of the will to power. Beauty is a tonic and a cordial ; ugliness lowers and depresses. Thus in the eyes of the true artist, art becomes an auxiliary to life. Before trying to create a work of art properly so called, before preaching the " art of works of art " he will labour to *embellish life,* to make man tolerable and, if possible, worthy of love from man.  He will aim at refining him, polishing him, teaching him courtesy, elegant manners and tact.  To ennoble human life by endowing it with beauty, such is the colossal and glorious task of true art, of healthy art, which has its source in exuberant life, and which tries to make life better worth living.  The production of works of art is only the last efflorescence which springs from an exceptionally rich and fruitful nature.  The superior genius, who feels within himself an excess of beneficent energies, ends by unloading himself of his superabundance by giving birth to the work of art, the apotheosis of full-blown and harmonious life.  It is this rich and really classic art which radiates in the works of Homer and Sophocles, Theocritus and Calderon, Racine and Goethe—a really superior, healthy and beneficent art, in which an exceptional will to power discharges its superabundance and blossoms into a flower of miraculous beauty for the joy and happiness of men.

This idea that art should not barricade itself in disdainful isolation, that it should not reduce itself to being only a precious recreation for a small symposium of refined spirits, that it cannot with impunity detach itself from reality, but that on the contrary it should work for the benefit of life, has been widely spread in Germany during the last few years.  Not that " art for the few " is repudiated, or that the boldness and refinements of modern impressionism, especially in the domain of lyrics and music and even in painting, are condemned.  But a fairly well defined reactionary movement against " decadent " art and against the exaggeration of neo-romanticism can be observed. More and more numerous voices are making themselves heard, demanding a "return to Goethe." And by this a restoration of the hellenising æstheticism of the eighteenth century is certainly not meant, but rather an attempt towards a new "classicism," a healthy and harmonious art which proceeds from exuberant health, and which sets itself the task of making life more worthy of being lived. And this same tendency is to be found even more clearly in the development that has taken place to-day in art industries, which aim at evolving a style for the modern dwelling, and thus at trying to beautify the surroundings in which everyday life is spent.

And at the same time as art places itself at the service of life it seems also to aim at becoming more democratic. Nothing in this respect is more characteristic than the example of Wagner. An irresistible need impelled him to *communicate himself* as liberally as possible to the outside world, to the crowd. He aspired with all his energy to a popular art similar to that which blossomed in Greece in the drama of the classic period, and in Germany in the *Volkslied*. He wanted art to respond to a *need* really experienced by the nation, instead of being a pastime at the disposal of a few rich idlers, or a recreation for the capitalist, or the man of enterprise tired out by the mad rush for wealth. He worked with superb enthusiasm to create a "communist" drama, by organising a brotherly collaboration between the arts, the co-operation of the poet, the performers and the public. And this feeling of human solidarity which moved Wagner to descend from the empyrean of ideal art to the people, as Lohengrin descended to earth from the serene heights of the Holy Grail to help Elsa in her distress, was shared in the nineteenth century by a number of artists. Painters and poets vied with each other in drawing near to the masses, in tracing in detail the destinies of workers in towns and dwellers in the country, in describing with scrupulous fidelity popular life in all its diverse provincial and local aspects ; in short, at making known, in a shape directly accessible to all, the life of the German people of their day. Architects and decorators, on their side, resolutely attacked the difficult task of providing healthy and comfortable homes for the people, and thus putting a little beauty into the daily life of the poor. There is certainly some romantic illusion in most of these attempts. The immense majority of the works produced were " popular " only in appearance, and really appealed only to a more or less limited minority. And if one considers the gulf that exists to-day between the culture of the masses and the culture of the refined, one may well ask to what point the advent of an *authentically* popular art, capable at once of pleasing the masses and of satisfying the exigencies of an educated taste, is possible at the present time. But it must at least be acknowledged that the *desire* to find the formula for this art does exist, in a very sincere and very active form, in the breasts of many German artists.

It must also be noted that this impulse on the part of the artists towards the people was answered by a powerful effort on the side of the people to attain culture and art. The Socialist movement resulted in awakening scientific curiosity and a taste for the beautiful in the hearts of the masses. And there can be no doubt that Socialism expects from the society of the future only the free access of all to the domains of the True and the Beautiful, that magnificent intellectual and artistic efflorescence which is the final goal in which social evolution should find its consummation. It believes that social revolution alone can give the people free access to high culture. But in the meantime it aims in the domain of education as well as in that of economics to ameliorate the condition of the masses at once. Just as it endeavours, even within the confines of middle-class life, to make the conditions of life pleasanter for the worker, it also tries to raise the intellectual level of the labourer. And to a large extent it succeeds.

Certainly the effort of the Socialists to attain culture is not altogether disinterested. They realise that science is a formidable instrument of power, and that, in the words of Bacon, " knowledge is power." And they also reckon that, in order to attain power, workers should not only have regard for the maintenance of their physical strength, but also make their brains ever more capable of reflection and reasoning, and stock them with as large an amount as possible of solid and well-classified knowledge. But they do not confine themselves to seeing in culture an efficient weapon of war ; they have also gradually come to esteem it for its own sake. A sincere and disinterested scientific curiosity is developing among the working classes. The most intelligent Socialists are not merely interested in the economic doctrines of their party, but also realise that Marxism rests upon a general conception of life, and consequently look out for opportunities for becoming acquainted with the general results of the natural and historical sciences. Hence the success of enterprises which aim at diffusing culture among workmen—debating and reading clubs, lending libraries, scientific and literary lectures, associations for study like the *Workmen's School* at Berlin. And just as the worker desires instruction, he also claims the right to artistic culture, he wants "art to belong to the people." He hurries enthusiastically to see plays performed at popular theatres which put within reach of the working classes the masterpieces of social drama, the plays of Ibsen and Hauptmann, Tolstoi and Gorki, and of the "realistic" school of modern German writers. He reads with interest some of the German classics, especially Heine, who is held up by Socialist writers as one of the champions of German democracy. The fine arts also begin to have a fascination for him, and it is an ascertained fact that numbers of working men buy the excellent cheap reproductions of the masterpieces of painting which certain art publishers put on the market nowadays.

Under these circumstances, the democratic movement, it seems, need not necessarily be regarded as a menace to art. Since the time of Heine and Nietzsche, Socialists have frequently been represented as "barbarians at heart," and as destroyers of all superior civilisation. This is, apparently, an injustice and an error. There is probably to-day as much scientific and artistic idealism among the masses as among the middle classes in Germany. On the other hand it must be confessed that for the time being the alliance dreamt of between the masses and modern art scarcely exists except in the shape of more or less confused aspirations and desires. With what luck will the movement that is being inaugurated to-day meet ? Shall we one day see rise up, face to face with our arts of luxury, a national art in the real interpretation of the word, veritably upheld by the intelligence and the enthusiasm of the masses ?   There is nothing to prevent our desiring and hoping for it ;  but I do not see how the historian can make any sort of positive statement in this connection.   The future alone can decide.

# CHAPTER II

## ROMANTICISM, REALISM AND IMPRESSIONISM

### I

AFTER having indicated the general aims which art in Germany is following, I should now like to give a summary of the fundamental tendencies which are to be found in the history of German art during the nineteenth century.

To proceed in accordance with historical sequence, it is " romanticism " with which we first meet at the dawn of the century, and which I shall begin by describing. It must be clearly understood that in this category are included not only the groups of writers and thinkers which historians of literature as a rule designate by the name of first and second romantic group, but, more generally speaking, the whole aggregate of writers and artists in whom a certain " romantic " turn of mind predominates, the chief tendencies of which I will try to define.

When the romantic movement came into existence in the last years of the eighteenth century it did not rise up in rebellion against classicism, as French romanticism afterwards did. The adversaries whom it riddled with its sarcasms were the majority of self-satisfied and overweening mediocrities, the last champions of the era of enlightenment which was tottering to its fall. Now the philosophic and literary classicism of Germany had itself just issued from a movement of reaction against degenerate rationalism with its withering intellectualism and its dull utilitarianism. The romanticists, in the beginning, had no other ambition than to carry on the classical tradition. When they made mock of Nicolaï and his laboratory for concocting anti-philosophical elixirs, when they hurled polemics against the " harmonious platitudes " of self-satisfied Philistines and against the puling utilitarianism of the " moral economists " who reduced life to a calculation of interests and saw nothing beyond an exceedingly virtuous, regular, and narrow middle-class existence ; when they made fun of the literary mediocrities of the day, men like Lafontaine and Clauren, Iffland and Kotzebue, Voss and Schmidt von Werneuchen, they felt they were conducting the campaign of *making healthy* the German Parnassus inaugurated by the *Xenien* of Goethe and Schiller. For a long time the romanticists and the classicists were in alliance and held each other in mutual esteem. The romanticists loudly proclaimed themselves the followers of Kant in their philosophy and of Goethe in literature. Only gradually did they come to distinguish clearly the differences which separated them from their models and to take up their stand against the classicism whose standpoint they had outgrown in the course of their evolution.

The romanticists, therefore, were in the beginning innovators in open revolt against senile intellectualism, over-cautious wisdom, and the dull common-sense of a worn-out rationalism, which, unconscious of its own nullity, flaunted untenable pretensions to infallibility. It is quite wrong to represent romanticism as a movement of religious and political *reaction*. Its disciples were not the least bit in the world cowards whom the excesses of a reason that had become too audacious terrified, and who wished to go back and find refuge in the faith of the past and in historic tradition. They were, on the contrary, spirits who were courageous to the point of rashness, freed from prejudice to the point of nihilism, and impregnated by the highest culture of their day. They were intrepid explorers who aimed at penetrating into regions of the human soul to which their mediocre predecessors had no access. They never denied the triumphs of rational science, but they avowed that theoretical reason was not the only instrument by means of which man could grasp reality.

In the domain of science they opposed prudent empiricism and the analytical method by intuition and idealistic speculation. They aspired to know the Cosmos in all its prodigious unity, and constructed a philosophy of nature which was independent of experience and which saw unconscious spirit everywhere in nature, conceived of natural forces as the organs of hidden wills, and aimed at showing in everything the mysterious mingling of the conscious and the unconscious. In the religious sphere we have already seen how they denied the competence of reason and founded religion upon the direct contemplation of the universe, and upon the emotion which fills the soul in the presence of the infinite. In the domain of politics they agreed with Fichte in opposing the cosmopolitanism of the eighteenth century by patriotic enthusiasm. For the individualistic conception which made the State merely an " undertaking for public security " which safeguarded the citizens against foreign invasions or attacks on the part of their fellow citizens, they substituted a *social* conception according to which man as an individual could not attain liberty, but could only realise it in society through the medium of the State. With the example of revolutionary France before their eyes they were full of scepticism with regard to the organising powers of reason, and insisted upon the importance and the rights of history and tradition. They professed the greatest respect for all institutions which had developed gradually in the course of centuries, and appeared as the normal fruit of historical evolution, like the English constitution in distinction to that of the republic of Berne. Such institutions, if we are to believe the romanticists, had by their very antiquity an intrinsic value, and were infinitely superior to those which sprang from the brain of a legislator or the debates of a constituent assembly. They reinstated the Middle Ages, which had been decried by the rationalists as an era of obscurantism and barbarism. They extolled its institutions, its civilisation, its literature, and its arts. Like Hugo and Savigny, they represented right not as the result of a conscious act of will, a social contract, but as an unconscious and necessary action on the part of the national soul, of the *Volksgeist*, which lives and breathes in all the individuals who form part of the same community.

In the sphere of art also, they combated the rationalistic conception according to which the work of art was the product of the reasoned and conscious industry of man. They did not consider the intellect or technical knowledge as by any means the essential elements of genius, but rather creative imagination on the one hand and the gift of emotion on the other.

In the first place the romanticists had the highest opinion of the creative faculties of the artists. Their æsthetic was based, as we have already seen, upon the idealism of Fichte. It identified the artist with Fichte's ego, which found its position by standing

in opposition to the non-ego and finally recognised
the identity between the ego and the non-ego. It
thus made the poet a kind of creator whose conscious
fictions were scarcely less " real " than the unconscious fictions of the ego, that is to say, of the external
world, the non-ego, to which we attribute an independent existence only by virtue of an illusion which
is destined to disappear with the progress of consciousness. In the eyes of Friedrich Schlegel, therefore, the most profound theorist of romanticism, the
artist was supreme. " Romantic poetry," he proclaimed, " is infinite ; it recognises as its supreme
law that the arbitrary fancy of the poet should
submit to no law above it." The artist was as free
in the face of the universe as the independent and
autonomous ego, and should become conscious of
his liberty with regard to the non-ego.

From this sovereign independence of the artist
there also arose the famous law of *romantic irony*.
Fichte's " absolute ego," the primordial and original
ego, the point of departure for all society and all
speculation, *was* not, but eternally *became*. There
was and always would be an everlasting antagonism
between the " absolute ego," which only existed as
an ideal that was never realised, and the " empirical
ego," which was always realised, but also constantly
appeared in an individual, limited, and, as such, imperfect form. The romantic artist, therefore, according to Schlegel, ought to realise the necessary dis-
crepancy which existed between his " absolute ego "—
that is to say, his creative imagination—and his
particular manifestations. In other words he ought
to feel himself superior to all the works of art he
produced. And this contrast would find expression in
irony, that supreme irony which Schlegel admired

so much in Goethe's *Wilhelm Meister,* and which in
his opinion no really superior work should be without. The romantic poet should not deceive himself,
and should prove that he did not. He should aim with
whole-hearted sincerity to communicate himself as
much as possible and to put himself entirely into
his work. But he should also know that no partial
creation can ever be an adequate expression of the
ego. He must therefore remain sufficiently free in
spirit to " raise himself above his highest creations "
and prove, by means of irony, that he did not take
them altogether seriously himself.

Lastly, romantic poetry as well as being " ironical "
should also become a " poetry of poetry." In
Fichte's eyes the transcendental philosopher did
not restrict himself to taking cognisance of himself
and to attempting to give an explanation of the
system of his representations. He also reflected upon
the attempt itself—in other words, he philosophised
about philosophy. At the same time as he produced
a work of art he should describe himself in his
capacity as poet. He should exercise his poetic
activity, and also reflect upon that activity at the
very moment when he was exercising it. This is
what Schlegel called making poetry raised to the
second power, or the " poetry of poetry."

Thus romanticism resulted in an absolute subjectivism with respect to art. It proclaimed in
theory the sovereignty of creative fancy, its independence with regard to all conventional rules, and
even with regard to external reality, and its right
to destroy by irony the fictions it creates. In
practice it gave birth to strange and sometimes disconcerting works, in which the subjectivity of the
artist spread itself out and overflowed in all direc-

tions, whether he conjured up before men's imaginations a more or less fantastic dream-world, whether he amused himself with his own creations and suppressed illusion by means of irony, or whether he obtruded his own personality into his fictions and wove confessions, philosophical reflections and æsthetic dissertations into his tale. Works like Schlegel's *Lucinde*, Novalis's *Ofterdingen*, Wackenrode's *Outpourings of an Art-loving Monk*, and Tieck's *Geneviève* may be cited as typical productions in this respect.

Another essential characteristic of romanticism was, that full of contempt as it was for intellectualism, it attached the highest importance to pure emotion and thus tended towards music and lyricism.

The deep feeling for nature and its diverse aspects, the cult of friendship and love were more and more strongly developed during the second half of the eighteenth century. The life of the soul grew ever richer and more complex, and men learnt to feel its various shades more and more. This faculty was manifested by a rapid and colossal development of the musical instinct. The beginning of the nineteenth century appears in this respect as a period of marvellous fruitfulness. It witnessed the advent of Beethoven and the resurrection of Bach, whose immense value began to be understood after a long period of eclipse. It brought the growth of the song in the person of Schubert, and the efflorescence of romantic opera with Weber. With Beethoven especially music became conscious of the extent of its domain and the greatness of its task. It felt that it was able to express in a different form, but quite as well as poetry, the most profound aspirations and the highest emotions of the human soul.

Now the romanticists foresaw the fresh popu-

25

larity which music was destined to enjoy. They felt that in order to describe the psychic emotions of the new era which was being inaugurated, in order to express all the world of more or less vague and hovering impressions which can be divined above the level of clear thought, and which has such a strong fascination for the modern mind, tired out by the excess of rationalistic common sense, there was perhaps no more suitable vehicle than music. And from that moment there developed in them a growing cult of music, an ever more marked tendency to pure lyricism. Music was in their eyes " the most romantic of the arts "—that which best taught us to " feel emotions." They loved to give descriptions of types of musicians. Thus Wackenrode introduces us to his Joseph Berlinger and Hoffmann to his celebrated Johann Kreisler. Some romanticists, like Hoffmann, were both musicians and poets. Others like Tieck insistently proclaimed the supremacy of music over the other arts, declared that a symphony was superior to the richest drama, tried to vie with music by means of poetry and words, amused themselves by writing poetic " symphonies," and sought to produce in their lyrical verses purely musical effects by the accumulation of certain rhymes and the repetition of certain sonorous sounds. Many, without going to the lengths of this somewhat superficial and fictitious imitation of musical processes, were profoundly lyrical natures, whose chief preoccupation was to express states of the soul and pure emotions, to discharge, in floods of lyrics, that *Sehn-sucht*, that indefinite longing, at once sweet and painful, made up of regrets, expectation, vague aspirations, despair and enthusiasm, which vibrates in romantic hearts. And it is in this lyricism which is

entirely impregnated by music that Romanticism, from
Novalis's *Hymns to the Night*, to Heine's *Intermezzo*
and Nietzsche's *Zarathustra*, found its happiest inspirations and produced its most perfect masterpieces.

There remains for us to draw attention to one last
characteristic necessary for the understanding of
German romanticism ; and that is the evolution by
means of which, after starting out from the Hellenism
of the classicists, it resulted gradually in the conception of an autochthonous national and popular art.

The romanticists, as we have already pointed out,
posed at first as the heirs of classicism and as the
disciples of Goethe and Kant. Schlegel began by a
brilliant apology for Hellenism. Its historical evolution seemed to him the logical development of the
Beautiful, which, taking its rise in the naturalism of the
Ionic School, rose in Attic art to sublimity and perfection, only to founder in the end in the anarchy and
barbarism of the Alexandrians. Thus the Greeks
were the fairest example of humanity that had ever
existed in the world, and their history showed us not
only the destinies of a privileged people, but the most
admirable type which men of all ages could realise
in accordance with their various degrees of development. Greek poetry produced in every department
and at every stage of its history the most perfect works
to which the human genius had ever given birth.
Taken in its entirety it was, according to Schlegel,
" the ideal and the canon of poetry itself in its natural
evolution." Thus budding romanticism began by
pushing to its extreme the Hellenic "legend" as it was
elaborated by classicism. I doubt whether any German
poet ever experienced such an intense longing for
the beauty of antiquity as the unfortunate Hölderlin,
who is often classed in the earliest Romantic School.

But romanticism did not remain long in this first phase. Schlegel, after having at the outset sacrificed the " characteristic " and " individual " poetry of the modern to the " objective " poetry of the Greeks, was not slow to confess that modern art was not inferior to Greek art, that at bottom they were both of equal value, and that the duty of the critic was to realise " the absolute identity between ancient and modern art." And thus he claimed for " romantic " art the same degree of grandeur as for " classical " art. Born in Germany, where in the bosom of a young and pure race there existed a fine store of heroic legends, romantic poetry was developed by contact with the old Latin culture or the civilisation of the East, in Italy through Dante, in Spain through Cervantes, and in England through Shakespeare. And after a period of eclipse which was manifested by the classical epoch in France and England which Schlegel regarded as " a system of false poetry," it reached its culminating point in Germany. There the torch of Greek culture was once again rekindled. It was Winckelmann who revealed to his contemporaries the splendours of Greek art, and Goethe who, as a new Dante, appeared as the restorer of poetry, and brought about the reconciliation of the ancient and the modern. And lastly it was the romanticists who realised the unity between poetry, philosophy and religion, and who, by raising the translation of foreign poets and the imitation of their metres to a fine art, made a science of criticism and paved the way for a regular " history of poetry." Wilhelm Schlegel, in his celebrated Berlin lectures, which are recognised as the most authoritative exposition of the doctrines of German romanticism, does scarcely more than develop that species of the " Legend of the Ages " of poetry which had been sketched out by his brother.

From being *classical* romanticism became *cosmopolitan*. It consciously set itself the task of initiating Germany into the literatures of other lands. It vaunted as one of the typical virtues of the Germans that gift for assimilation which allowed them to partake freely of exotic masterpieces and proclaimed that it was precisely this quality which was destined to raise them to the highest rank among the nations of Europe. " We aim at nothing less," wrote Wilhelm Schlegel, "than at uniting in ourselves the various merits of the most diverse nations, at assimilating them by means of intelligence and sensitiveness, and thus constituting ourselves a cosmopolitan centre for the mind of man." Numerous translations—of which the most celebrated, that of Shakespeare by A. W. Schlegel, was a masterpiece of its kind—adaptations and imitations of all kinds from that moment familiarised the German public with the literatures of the " united Europe," of the Middle Ages, of Italy and Spain, ancient France, and England in the time of Shakespeare, and even with the poetry and civilisation of the East, which Friedrich Schlegel, in his famous book *On the Language and Wisdom of the Indians* (1808), presented to the reading public as a document of the first importance for the study of human thought. Without fear of losing her own originality, romanticist Germany endeavoured to assimilate the treasures of universal art and to enlarge the field of German thought to such an extent as to make her, in a way, the spiritual and artistic conscience of civilised Europe.

And, at the same time as it explored exotic literatures in this way, romanticism, by reviving and continuing the tradition of Herder and young Goethe, became devotedly absorbed, on the other hand, in the study of the past history of Germany. And this was perfectly natural. The hatred of the romanticists for intellectualism, their religious and mystic aspirations, their suspicion of the organising power of reason in the sphere of politics, their aversion for " artificial " art, their worship of Nature, necessarily led them to reinstate the Middle Ages, which had been decried by rationalism as the era of obscurantism and barbarism. They were enamoured of the Middle Ages because they saw in them an epoch in which a glowing and simple faith was supreme, in which the Holy Roman Empire shone with incomparable lustre under the Ottos and the Hohenstaufen, in which poetry found a magnificent expansion on the lips of popular jugglers, or of the noble *Minnesinger*, and in which the arts, in the persons of Albert Dürer and Peter Vischer, shed a marvellous brilliance. In 1793 Tieck and Wackenroder discovered in the course of a summer's journey, the picturesque and unconventional beauty of the old city of Nuremburg. And from that moment they fell in love with ancient German art. And this enthusiasm, which spread from man to man, was shared by almost all the romanticists.

Poets, writers, philologists, painters and artists, all went for inspiration to the Middle Ages. They published or adapted old poems, which till then had been buried in dusty libraries. Tieck reinstated the *Minnesinger* in a place of honour; and Schlegel recalled the attention of the public to the *Nibelungenlied*. People studied the old traditions, they made collections of folk tales—the *Volksbücher* and the *Volkslieder*. They raved about anonymous and impersonal popular poetry and all works which seemed

to proceed from a collective impulse. They placed
the creations of the poetical instinct that lived in the
masses above the artificial productions of conscious
art. They extolled the incomparable civilisation of
the Middle Ages ; they were full of admiration for the
marvellous enthusiasm of the Crusades ; they tried
to defend the custom of tournaments ; they found
beauty even in the religious wars, and discovered a
certain poetry even in heraldic science. The poets
showed a predilection for subjects drawn from German
history, and took particular delight in resuscitating
the old epic and heroic traditions. The legend of
the Nibelungen alone gave birth to a whole host of
adaptations and imitations. Or else they depicted
the life of the people in its characteristic aspects, the
existence of the humble and simple souls who were
very near to Nature.

Painters as well as writers were involved in the
Romantic movement. Some like Overbeck and
Ph. Veit tried to restore a " Christian " art and aimed
at attaining beauty by means of fervid religious
feeling and a deep mysticism which impelled some
of them to find refuge in the bosom of the Catholic
Church. Others, like Steinle and Schwind, found
inspiration in the traditions of the Middle Ages, and
gave form and colour to all the legendary or fantastic
world called into being by the poets and tale-tellers.
In architecture there was a revival of the taste for
the Gothic, which was considered to be the national
art of Germany (which is historically incorrect) as
well as the religious art *par excellence*, an art which
" scaled the skies " and raised the soul to God.
Great enthusiasm was shown for the completion of
Cologne Cathedral. Sculptors extolled the simple
perfection of the Gothic art of the end of the Middle

Ages, and endeavoured to give their statues a really Christian expression. The cult of Germany's past showed itself even in the dress of the men and women, and an attempt was made to revive the old German costume !

Thus, after its worship of Hellenism and its voyages of discovery through the art of the world, romanticism returned to its native land. It aimed at becoming national and religious, and sought its inspirations in the past of Germany, and in the religious art of the Middle Ages.

## II

Nevertheless, romanticism clearly contained the germs of dissolution. When it discarded its original revolutionary character and became decidedly reactionary, when it made itself the ally of feudal absolutism and clericalism, when its subjectivism degenerated with certain enthusiasts into a sort of mystic folly and ended in some cases in clearly pathological symptoms, and when its anti-rationalism became studied eccentricity or affected puerility, it gradually lost its hold on men's minds. Immediately after 1830, Heinrich Heine, though he was still half a romanticist himself, nevertheless denounced with a cruel irony the weaknesses and faults of his old leaders, and covered them with floods of ridicule. It was, moreover, clear that the development of the system of enterprise was hardly compatible with the essential tendencies of romanticism. How could people who were aiming at material power and wealth, who were toiling with all their might for the advancement of natural science, and for the gradual rationalisation of technical processes—how could such people have continued to pay homage to men who placed reason below imagination and emotion, who despised all useful activity, spent their lives in defending " the divine art of idleness," found pleasure in the eccentricities of mysticism or spiritualism, professed a fantastic philosophy of nature from which up-to-date men of science turned aside with contempt, and reduced art to the level of a frivolous pastime as meaningless as the capricious outlines of an arabesque ! How was it possible for the middle and lower classes of Germany, who were marching to the conquest of political liberty and social emancipation, to avoid protesting against the apologists of the Middle Ages, the champions of the Holy Alliance, Catholic clericalism and orthodox pietism, the sworn enemies of the Revolution and democracy ? It is obvious that the table of values of the representative of capitalistic enterprise could not be the same as that of romanticism. Theoretic and practical reason was in their eyes superior to poetic fantasy, or reverence for the past, and the minute and patient study of objective reality had greater value than the brilliant and inconsistent constructions of the artistic imagination.

And thus a more realistic spirit came to light in literature and art. Out of romanticism realism gradually sprang up. People still continued to take an interest in the Middle Ages and in the past history of Germany ; but they were not content with an approximate and fantastic reconstruction. The historical sense became more exacting and demanded a more rigorous correctness and a greater precision than before. With the brothers Grimm and their successors, scientific philology took the place of romantic dilettantism and set itself to make a methodical examination of the nation's past. At the same time, the historical novel and historical paintings endeavoured to reproduce with accurate sincerity the spirit of the old days and the great moments in the evolution of humanity. And thus in the spirit of the rising generation enamoured of accurate observation, the mediæval conventions brought into fashion by romanticism gave way to ever more objective restorations of historical reality.

And with a similar avidity for truth and sincerity literature and art turned on the other hand to the reality of the present, and applied themselves to describing the life of the nation. This was studied in its most diverse manifestations, in all the degrees of the social scale, in all its local variations, either in descriptions of the life of the upper classes, of the cultured minority, of the working middle classes, the peasant and the urban masses, or by conjuring up before our eyes the various aspects of provincial or local life, from Pomerania to Switzerland, and from Swabia to Styria.

And at the same time as art became impregnated by realism it also allied itself on occasion with tendencies of a practical nature. Whilst romanticism inclined towards conservative or reactionary traditionalism, realism seemed, on the whole, and in spite of certain exceptions, to show an affinity with the various shades of democratic opinion from middle-class Liberalism in its most moderate form to the extremes of Socialism.

Lastly, whilst from the point of view of form romanticism frequently resulted, through its excess of subjectivism, in works of a somewhat amorphous nature, in an entirely musical lyricism or an unbridled fantasy, realistic art reacted against this tendency. From the literary point of view, the increased attention paid to form had the happiest results, particularly for the drama, in which romanticism had proved itself quite inferior. In the history of painting its influence was even more important. The romanticists willingly subordinated technique to ideas. They made religious images, symbolical paintings, and colossal theatrical scenery ; they recounted episodes from history, or daubed pictures of a humorous or touching nature. The essential point in their eyes was not so much the real pictorial interest of a picture as its sentimental and historical interest, its symbolical value and its story-telling power. This fundamental misunderstanding of the importance of form in matters of art had fatal results for romanticist painting, and every one to-day is agreed that the works of men like Overbeck, Cornelius, Piloty, and Makart, are of very little value. But with the development of realistic tendencies, German artists gradually corrected this mistake. They endeavoured to give a sincere representation of reality, and at the same time to interest the public not by some beautiful " thought," but simply by means of the resources proper to their art, and by their technical excellence.

It is obviously impossible for me to attempt, within the limits of this work, to give an outline sketch of this evolution towards realism which in literature as well as in the fine arts was prolonged throughout the whole of the nineteenth century, without it being possible, of course, to draw a distinct line of demarcation between the romanticists and the realists. In this connection it is enough to recall the case of Kleist, in whom the realistic and the " classical " sides are both so much developed that the critic sometimes hesitates to classify him as a romanticist.

Conversely there are a number of realists like Gottfried Keller, in whom it is easy to discern a very
strong romantic vein.  And one of the greatest artists
of the century, Heine, fluctuated all his life between
romanticism and realism, equally attracted and
repelled by these two conflicting principles—an un-
repentant romanticist through his gift of imagination, an incorrigible realist through his reason, and,
moreover, conscious of occasionally suffering by this
dualism in his nature.  Nothing, then, could present
a more delicate task than to describe in detail the
transition from romanticism to realism.  Without
undertaking any such analysis we will confine ourselves to pointing out the fact that the outburst of
realism in Germany was almost contemporaneous
with the development of German imperialism.  The
culminating point of the curve it described might
be marked in painting by such a man as Wilhelm
Leibl, whose scrupulously realistic work, with its
unimpeachable command of technique, is one of the
most distinctive creations of modern German art.
In literature, the naturalistic drama of Gerhard
Hauptmann and his imitators seems to be the most
characteristic effort to depict with the utmost
possible objectivity the real life of the present day in
its most minute details, and that without adulterating
it by any philosophical or æsthetic considerations.
And we must not forget, in passing, that this " con-
sistent naturalism," in spite of its conscious objectivity, has been realised by the popular mind to be
a democratic production, and that the Socialist
working-classes have " by the free choice of their
own inclination " welcomed naturalism in literature
just as, in the domain of speculation, they made
straight for materialism.

## III

At the same time as the German art of the nineteenth century evolved from romanticism to realism
it also developed in the direction of *impressionism*.

There is no doubt that the nervous sensitiveness
of the modern man increased considerably during
the course of the last century. Lamprecht sees in
the wealth, the complexity, and the growing intensity
of elementary nervous life the great psychic fact
which dominated our era. And, whatever may be
our opinion of the ingenious hypothesis by means of
which he lays at the door of susceptibility (*Reizsam-
keit*) all the economic, political, and artistic phenomena
of modern German life, the fact itself of the intensification of nervous activity is indisputable. It is also
certain that the history of art in the nineteenth
century reflects this acceleration in the rhythm
of existence, that over-excitement of the emotional
faculties, that gradual refinement in the sense per-
ceptions, which everybody regards as one of the
characteristic features of the world of to-day.

The earliest and perhaps also the most striking
manifestation of this evolution towards impressionism
is apparently to be found in the history of music.

Whatever opinion one may have upon the much-
disputed question as to the significance of music, it
seems, in the first place, an incontrovertible fact that
if one examines its development since about the
sixteenth century, it has become more and more a
subjective art which expresses or reflects more and
more finely shaded states of the individual soul.
During the Middle Ages, when the psychic life of the
individual had not yet separated itself from that of
the community, when everywhere, in literature as

well as in art, in the moral as well as the religious life, and in the law, the same impersonal character was always to be found, and the same conventional faithfulness to a type, music also was an impersonal art. In the period during which counterpoint flourished, that art of complex rules which Wagner called "the arbitrary game that art plays with itself, the mathematics of feeling, the mechanical rhythm of selfish harmony," musical composition obeyed mathematical and architectonic principles. It formed combinations of sounds by means of objective and purely formal rules without troubling for a moment to make them *express* anything, a state of the soul, a passion, a desire or a will. What the musician required in order to be able to create was technical skill and *savoir-faire*. His works sprang from his brain rather than from his heart. They had, as a rule, for their elementary principle no subjective emotion which, by virtue of an inner necessity, tended to overflow and find expression in the language of sound.

In modern music, on the contrary, we find a constant increase in the importance of this emotional and sentimental element. Pure beauty of form in music ceased to be an end in itself. The musician is no longer merely an industrious craftsman ; he is moved himself and wishes to move others. He finds the fundamental inspiration for his works in a certain state of the soul, in certain vibrations of his nervous sensibility—vibrations which may be and certainly are unconscious or semi-conscious, in the sense that the artist is as a rule incapable of analysing them in speech, or of defining their meaning and various degrees of intensity. And these vibrations he instinctively endeavours to translate into the language of sound, and then to communicate to his hearers and to arouse in them, by means of this language, vibrations similar to those which he has himself experienced. The evolution of music is thus to a large extent determined by a factor of a psychic nature. The more intense the psychic life of a particular era is the more will men be susceptible to feeling emotions, delicate, refined, and differentiated nervous impressions, and the more also will music endeavour to renovate and perfect its technique in order to reproduce these impressions in all their various shades of intensity. The capital importance of music, not only in the history of art, but also in the history of the modern soul, and especially of the German soul, thus becomes clear. It is the eloquent witness to the development of the nervous life. By means of music and through the divining effort of the musician, the elementary psychic life, which till then had been obscure and confused, tended to leave the domain of pure unconsciousness in order gradually to blossom out into conscious clarity.

And thus the aim of music in the nineteenth century tended towards translating as adequately as possible, and by ever more perfect technical processes, the complexity of the modern soul. And conversely, the increasing complexity of the nervous life of the modern man was attested by the very fact of the progress made in the language of music. If one compares the language of the musicians at the beginning of the century, such as Beethoven, Schubert and Weber, with that of the great artists of the middle and the end of the century, a Liszt, a Wagner and a Strauss, one is immediately struck by the thought of how much richer and more complicated the latter are. Musical composition became at once a more complex organism and one that was more differentiated in its elements and also possessed a more rigorous unity. Harmony became more scientific and more refined owing to the substitution of an ever bolder use of the chromatic in the place of the diatonic upon which the existing system is still, at least in theory, founded. Polyphony grew more and more complex in consequence of the increasing importance given to the accompaniment, which had for a long time been subordinated to the melody. Rhythm constantly gained in liberty and variety, and became ever more supple and natural and less subservient to the schematism of the time. Thus the elements forming a musical composition became more complicated, and were differentiated in such a way as to be able to express more and more subtle, delicate, tenuous, and fugitive nervous impressions—impressions which the consciousness of an earlier age would have been incapable of seizing and fixing.

And these elements, at the same time as they became differentiated, tended also to form organisms of a more rigorous unity. To use Herbert Spencer's expression, there was a *differentiation,* and at the same time a growing *integration* in the elements of a musical composition. Harmony became more complex, and the use of the chromatic bolder than ever. But the sense of tone unity was also sharpened and refined in similar proportions ; and it has been pointed out that in *Parsifal,* for instance, the unity of the general tonality (A flat major) is perhaps stricter than the tone unity of many symphonies of an earlier period. Rhythm became infinitely more subtle than before, the divergencies between rhythm and time were of ever more frequent occurrence, and yet the ear perceived and appreciated the unity of the most extensive and complicated systems of rhythm. But, above all, the need of organic unity in composition became infinitely stronger than it was in the past. There had once been no difficulty in admitting that a symphony or a sonata was an aggregate of perfectly distinct and occasionally frankly incompatible parts. People were not scandalised by the fact that an opera was an arbitrary succession of isolated pieces, but faintly connected with each other by the slenderest threads, an agglomeration of overtures, airs, duets, concerted numbers, choruses, ballets, and intermezzos. To-day the strictest unity of impression and construction is demanded. In the symphony as well as in the sonata this unity is sought by binding the different parts together in various ways; and it is hardly necessary in this connection to point out the care with which Wagner, in his dramas, abolished the traditional divisions of opera in such a way as to endow his works with the strictest unity. It is, for instance, a well-known fact, that the whole of the *Flying Dutchman* is only the development of *motifs* contained in the ballad of *Senta*. The harmonious symmetry of the plan of *Tristan* has often been observed, and one ingenious critic has endeavoured to prove, without laying himself open to a charge of absurdity, that the whole score of the *Meistersinger* might be regarded as founded upon one single theme —that known by the name of the " spring " theme, in which the " organic-*motif* " of the whole work was to be found.

To sum up, it is clear that musical language, in the course of the last century, became infinitely richer, more scientific and subtle than before. It is possible to hold the opinion that this evolution was not

26

progress, and that the musicians of the past were quite equal to those of our own day. I must not enter into any discussion on this subject. But it is at all events certain that they do not say the same things. If one compares an opera or a symphony by Mozart, or even one of Beethoven's early symphonies, with the great musical works which reflect the tendencies of modern Germany, with Wagner's latest operas, with symphonic poems, or with Strauss's *Salome*, one sees at once the radical change which has taken place in the depths of the soul of modern Germany. For these new works to have been conceived, and for them to be understood by the public, it was not merely necessary for the specifically musical sense to become extraordinarily refined. It was requisite for the emotional faculties to be fundamentally modified, and for the modern soul to become susceptible to ever more subtle, more refined and more intense vibrations than in the past.

And the same thing holds good in the case of painting as with music. Visual sensitiveness increased in the same degree as auditory sensitiveness. Lamprecht gives an ingenious explanation of the evolution towards *impressionism* which, in the domain of the fine arts, appeared first in England and France, and afterwards in Germany also. Instead of simply reproducing the external outlines of objects and afterwards colouring these designs by means of more or less arbitrary processes, painters gradually accustomed themselves to note down directly the impressions produced by coloured light upon the optic nerve, and thus ended by no longer reproducing the *external* world, as we represent it to ourselves by virtue of our acquired habits, but the instantaneous pictures which are reflected upon our retina—that is to say, a phenomenon which is in reality *internal,* neurological and psychological. Whatever may be said for this curious interpretation, it is clear that artists also have learnt to see things they did not perceive before, or which they instinctively over- looked. They have learnt, for instance, to see and to paint light in its variegated play and reflections, whilst the artists of the old school used to declare the impossibility of fixing light upon canvas. They became conscious of subjective impressions which in their predecessors did not get beyond the threshold of consciousness. And if, among modern German im- pressionists, such as Liebermann, Stuck, Exter, and Hoffmann, there was apparently no genius to com- pare with Wagner or Strauss, and if, on the whole, visual sensitiveness is perhaps less developed in Germany than musical sensitiveness, it has none the less evolved in the same direction.

Poetry also followed the same path, as is at once obvious if one compares the sensitiveness of a Goethe with that of Heine or Nietzsche. Goethe's was a healthy, normal and harmoniously balanced nature. Heine's was an excessively nervous temperament, whose manifestations quickly assumed a character of excessive and abnormal intensity ; he suffered from an acute hyperæsthesia which made him able to analyse down to the smallest details of their com- plexity the apparently most simple states of the soul ; a capacity for emotion so great that all his feelings of joy or sadness, love or hate, were ex- aggerated beyond measure, and filled his whole being with painful vibrations ; a cruel irony which con- demned him never to feel simple emotions, but obliged him to scoff while he was suffering and to suffer in the midst of happiness. In Nietzsche we may also observe a singularly complex and many-sided personality, who united the very diverse gifts of the artist and the thinker, the philologist and the musician, an ardent and passionate nature who *lived* his thoughts with an unheard-of intensity, and pushed them to their most extreme and most tragic consequences ; who aimed at perpetually " surpassing " himself, who knew the most unspeakable agonies of solitary meditation as well as the most extraordinary ecstasies of fruitful inspiration, and pursued his path without stopping or resting with the energy of despair, until the day when his overwrought nervous system, stretched to breaking-point, suddenly became unhinged and was engulfed in the night of madness. He is a particularly typical example of modern sensitiveness. And if among our contemporaries we can apparently no longer find such *extreme* natures, yet even now there is no doubt that men like Richard Dehmel, Stefan George, Hugo von Hofmannsthal are, in spite of all the individual differences that separate them, highly nervous temperaments. Their impassioned and refined lyricism, subtle and full of mystery, shows into what depths of the human soul they attempt to plunge and what obscure regions of our elementary nervous life they delight to explore.

Lastly, it must be pointed out that just as realism superimposed itself upon romanticism, impressionism in its turn came and planted itself upon realism and romanticism without, however, ousting them. Modern men are at once romanticists, realists, and impressionists. These tendencies are to be found among them in different degrees, and are mingled in various proportions without excluding each other. And the greatest are precisely the " problematical natures " who resist all attempts at simple classifica-

tion. In men like Wagner, Nietzsche, Böcklin,
Klinger, and Gerhard Hauptmann, the most diverse
elements are to be found. They are *at once* true to
nature, idealists, realists, and symbolists, but above
all impressionists ! " The symbol of the modern
soul," says Nietzsche, " is the labyrinth." When the
present day is defined as an era of neo-romanticism,
when it is asserted that Germany is now entering
upon a period of emotional culture in which the most
important part will belong to art, certain characteristic features of the time are undoubtedly explained.
Romanticism is enjoying a fresh popularity, and the
writers and thinkers belonging to that category are
being studied with redoubled energy. To-day just
as was the case before, doubts are being raised with
respect to " the little sagacity." [1] People are plunging with sympathy and curiosity into the study of
religious phenomena. Spiritualism and even the
occult sciences are rejoicing in fresh favour, as they
did at the beginning of the last century. Music and
lyric poetry are held in high esteem, and symbolism
flourishes in literature and art. But contemporary
Germany is none the less enamoured of realism,
which is the classical ground of imperialistic rationalism. And this characteristic is to be found in
artists and thinkers as well. Nietzsche is, perhaps,
a romanticist, but he is also one of the greatest
realistic observers that Germany has ever known.
Gerhard Hauptmann is the romanticist of *The
Sunken Bell*, but the realist of *The Weavers*. And
it is difficult to decide whether in the work of a man
like Klinger one should admire the realism and the
impeccable technique or the intense lyricism and
profound symbolism most.

[1] See note on p. 232..—Tr.

406 EVOLUTION OF MODERN GERMANY

Is this rich and complex culture really healthy ?
Does it not present some rather morbid features ?
German critics have asked themselves this question,
and occasionally display some anxiety in this respect. The menace of " decadence " to which some
chosen spirits like Heine and Nietzsche succumbed,
is clearly a danger for the society of to-day. The
same symptoms as are to be found in the victims
of this evil, nervous over-excitability, enthusiastic
emotion, weakness of will, the undermining of the
unity of the personality, are to be observed in various
degrees in a large number of individuals. And we
may, perhaps, be allowed to feel some anxiety on
this account. If the attacks against Nietzsche, for
example, have been exceedingly violent, and if even
to-day a certain amount of adverse criticism against
him has not died out, it is probably because he is
hated as a type of " decadent," and a tendency in
him which is regarded as dangerous for the psychic
health of the nation is opposed. Generally speaking,
however, fears of " decadence " are not apparently
very widespread in Germany to-day. People have
faith in the somewhat ponderous robustness of the
race, in the powers of expansion it has shown in
the domain of economics, in its military instinct and
its sense of discipline and solidarity. It is willingly
admitted that the excesses of present-day impressionism are only due to a crisis of growth, and an
overbalancing of equilibrium which is necessary for
the realisation of future syntheses and superior
harmonies. And it is hoped that this crisis will
result in a renaissance of Goethean classicism and
scientific rationalism, and an era of renewed health
in which will flourish a type of man as rich, but more
subtle and harmonious, than his ancestor of to-day.

# CHAPTER III

## SYNTHETIC ART

### I

EVOLUTION, to quote once again Herbert Spencer's expression which we have already used, is not only carried out by means of *differentiation*, but also through *integration*. Natural development in the first instance goes from the homogeneous to the heterogeneous, from unity to diversity. The law of gradual specialisation is as true in the domain of art as in natural and physical science. It is thus that the " integral " work of art of primitive times with which one meets at the dawn of human society, which is a combination of dancing, poetry, music, and religious worship, tends to split up. We find art gradually becoming separated from religion, the various arts which were at first intermingled becoming differentiated, and ever more numerous subdivisions growing up in each of the branches of art. But the fundamental law of evolution is none the less integration. In every department of natural phenomena, in astronomy as well as in natural history, in biology and in language, progress is made by the birth of ever more complex organisms and ever vaster unities. The history of art forms no exception to this rule. At the same time as it shows us the disintegration of the primitive " communion " of the arts, it presents us, on the other hand, with various attempts to produce synthetic works of art resulting from the collaboration of several distinct arts. Germany of the nineteenth century affords us, in the domain of poetry and music as well as in the plastic arts, extraordinarily interesting examples of this effort towards synthesis.

One may perhaps be tempted to find an explanation for this integrating movement in a curious and well-established phenomenon of our psychic life— that phenomenon of the correspondence of the various kinds of sensation with each other by virtue of which waves of sound, for instance, can summon up impressions of light, feelings of touch result in impressions of sound, waves of light engender sensations of smell, etc. This phenomenon would obviously belong to that general development of nervous sensitiveness which we described above as one of the essential characteristics of modern times. And this is certainly to be found in Germany, especially among certain romanticists in whom nervous life seems to have acquired an extreme intensity which is somewhat abnormal. Thus Tieck makes various instruments, violins, hautboys, and horns, sound in his verses; he composes poetic symphonies, sees the sound of the flute as a blue sound, or gives us a picture in which the song of the nightingale is set upon canvas. In a man like Hoffmann, who suffered from alcoholic and neurotic hallucinations, these correspondences were still more frequent and strange. He proclaimed that for the musician sight was an external sense of hearing, that colours, perfumes, rays of light, were like sounds to him, and that their combination was a marvellous concert. The scent of a red carnation roused in him the sensation of

hearing hunting horns in the distance. He per-
sonified musical intervals. His fantastic creation,
Kreisler, says without blinking that he is wearing a
coat the colour of which turns upon C sharp minor,
and that it is finished by a collar in D major, and
moreover he threatens to stab himself with a dagger
in the augmented fifth. And after Hoffmann phenomena of this kind were multiplied among artists—
from the painter Feuerbach, who always connected
colours with musical impressions, to the dramatist
Otto Ludwig, in whose case the thought of Goethe
and Schiller was always connected with impressions
of colour, or the *Kapellmeister* Hans von Bülow,
who used to implore his orchestra to play such and
such a passage in a more " red " or more " green "
way. These extreme and doubtless somewhat morbid
cases were probably the excessive and exaggerated
manifestations of a much more common phenomenon.
If to-day we find the technical processes of the
various individual arts drawing nearer together, if
more than ever before we see artists excelling in very
different branches of art at the same time, this is
perhaps an indication that in modern man the
different psychic and physiological functions tend
to react more and more upon each other, and to
vibrate simultaneously in a kind of mysterious sympathy as soon as any one of them is brought into play.

However this may be, it is at all events certain
that we find in the nineteenth century more than
ever before the tendency for music to approach
poetry and poetry to approach music. In the magnificent development of the symphonic poem from
Liszt to Strauss, in the addition of words set to
the symphony from Beethoven to Mahler, the
attempt made by pure music to be completed by

words and thoughts is already marked. We have
also pointed out in another connection how, in
the case of the romanticists more particularly, the
attempt to express pure emotion impelled them to
exalt the art of sound and to solicit the help of the
musician in some form. The union between music
and the word seemed realised, though still in an
elementary manner, in the song, which from Schubert
and Carl Löwe to Schumann, Brahms and Hugo
Wolff, attained a marvellous artistic perfection. And,
finally, it was also manifested with incomparable
richness and brilliance in the domain of drama by the
extraordinary works of Wagner.

The conception of a lyrical drama which would
not, like the opera, be merely a more or less incongruous aggregate of pieces of pure music, of
singing and dance tunes, but which should be the
veritable result of the sincere collaboration of all the
arts, made its appearance long before Wagner in
the history of German civilisation. It was formulated
from the eighteenth century onwards by æstheticians
like Sulzer or poets like Wieland. It played a part,
which was exact to the smallest detail, in a celebrated
passage in Herder's *Adrastäa*. And from that time
it never disappeared from the literary horizon. It
has often been observed that Schiller's drama, " with
its internal melody and its musical rhythm," tended
of its own accord to find its completion in music, and
that a work like *The Bride of Messina* was an opera
without music. Similarly the second part of Goethe's
*Faust* would demand, in order to produce its full
scenic effect, the help of *all* the arts, and contains a
large number of regular opera *motifs*. And so also
Wagner himself attached great importance, especially
in the second part of his life, to connecting his work

with that of the classicists and to establishing the
fact that the art of the future, which was so loudly
scoffed at by his contemporaries, should be nothing
more than the blossoming out of certain seeds which
were already to be found in *The Bride of Messina*
and *William Tell*. And he delighted to prove that
his artistic idealism was descended in a direct line
from the idealism of Schiller.

Musical drama was also the form of art towards
which romanticism gravitated. Romanticist thinkers
like Schelling, Solger, or Schleiermacher had a presentiment of this, or else endeavoured to define it.
Hoffmann, who was both a musician and a poet,
formulated with perfect lucidity the programme of
the work of art of the future, and himself laboured
to carry it out, without, however, meeting with
much success. And even among the contemporaries
of Wagner two of the most celebrated masters of the
German theatre, Otto Ludwig and Friedrich Hebbel,
also conceived the idea of musical drama previous
to 1850, quite independently of Wagner, and during
the years that the latter was producing his first great
composition. The idea of " the complete work of
art, " therefore, was not the isolated fantasy of one
artist of genius, but the necessary and normal product of centuries of evolution. It was the realisation
of a programme formulated long before the days of
the master of Bayreuth, and made its appearance as
the successful outcome of the converging efforts of
numberless generations of poets and artists.

It was not, of course, and could not be, the only
form of art or the final one. Profound as was the
influence which Wagner exercised over modern art,
the epoch of his exclusive predominance has already
for some time past ceased to exist in Germany.

Musicians and dramatists are trying to emancipate themselves from his formulæ, and critics are endeavouring to determine his precise historical importance. The first of these was Nietzsche, who, after having in his *Richard Wagner in Bayreuth* hymned Wagner in almost lyrical accents as the Dionysian artist *par excellence*, afterwards, as we all know, denied with incredible violence this god whom he had adored, and proclaimed his grievances against Wagnerism with exasperated passion to his contemporaries. He described Wagner as an essentially romantic genius. He saw in him a marvellous mime, an incomparable actor, who knew how to utilise the resources of all the arts to produce a colossal whole, who turned himself into a poet, a musician, a scene-painter, and a mime, in order to get a firmer hold over his audience. By his superior understanding of theatrical effect, by his religious aspirations, his sympathies for a mystic and vaguely Catholic asceticism, by his resigned pessimism, his mistrust of conscious will and reflective action, he was the genial representative of the neo-romanticism of his day. But, in Nietzsche's eyes, this neo-romanticism had its roots to a large extent in " decadence " and in physiological degeneracy. If the influence of Wagner were allowed to grow and the evolution of culture to progress indefinitely in the same direction, the inevitable result would be pessimistic nihilism, and subsequently practical nihilism, and the downfall and death of modern civilisation. The time had come to confront the romantic ideal with the classical ideal, the religion of human suffering with the worship of life and the will to power, Richard Wagner with Bach and Beethoven—or even Bizet—Sophocles, Racine and Goethe.

And contemporary critics, whilst they render full homage to the most powerful artistic genius that modern Germany has produced, frequently agree with Nietzsche in realising that the Wagnerian ideal could not be an artistic and philosophical creed for the men of to-day. They hesitate to place Wagner on a level with the real heroes of German culture, men like Luther and Goethe, Bach or Beethoven. The latter were robust and healthy natures, full of admirable vitality, in whom energy seemed concentrated, and as it were summed up in a single point in order to develop itself harmoniously in all directions. Wagner's, on the contrary, was an extreme and discordant nature, which was swayed between a strong instinct for power and a religious mysticism which aspired to Nirvana. His art, which vibrated and shook with emotion, did not take its source, as was the case with the other great geniuses of German culture, in the richness of a personality which was overflowing with life, but in the terrific discords of a torn and tortured nature. He could not therefore be the prophet of a new era. In his integral drama he melted into one marvellous whole all the creations of those fruitful epochs in which religions, cosmogonies and myths had been born. His work summed up the productions of primitive ages, and with prodigious intensity suggested the idea of the energies which created German and European culture in the past. It was not a forecast of the future, it was not a prophetic vision of the latent forces which lay dormant in the heart of the nation and determined the task of future generations. By the all-powerful magic of its accents, it was, according to Max Graf, the swan-song which accompanied the twilight of the old gods, the death-sigh of a culture which was drawing to its close.

It would seem that the ideal towards which modern Germany is tending is no longer Wagnerian romanticism. She endeavours no longer to realise the integral work of art, the great mythical drama which by its symbols expresses the most profound ideas of philosophy and religion. She would prefer, as we have already pointed out, to conjure up by her prayers the advent of a Goethean art, an ideal of proportion and harmony, of self-mastery, and a valiant and virile acceptance of the realities of life. She must therefore seek outside Wagnerism for the formula, as yet undiscovered, of that art for which she longs, but has not found as yet.

## II

In the domain of the plastic arts as well, Germany endeavoured to produce synthetic works of art with the help of architecture, painting, and sculpture. In other words she attacked the difficult task of creating for modern houses a harmonious style which should be strictly suitable for the needs of the life of to-day. It is, moreover, only quite latterly that German artists seem to have gained a clear idea of the exact form in which this problem was posed and began to draw near to a solution.

The economic evolution which took place during the course of the nineteenth century obviously brought in its train profound modifications in the conditions of material life. In the construction of public buildings or private houses, in the arrangement and decoration of houses and flats, architects found themselves confronted by fresh demands. Moreover, technical innovations of prime importance had been introduced. The use of iron and glass as

constructive materials increased every day, and gave
rise to new architectonic possibilities. In a large
number of cases, too, and especially in the production
of furniture and utensils, mechanical machinery
took the place of the craftsman's handiwork. Thus
the modern artist found himself faced by fresh requirements, and to meet them had new technical
resources at his disposal. And consequently the
very force of circumstances imposed upon him the
task of creating an original style in harmony with
the conditions of modern life.

Germany endeavoured at first to get out of the
difficulty by imitating the old styles. Artists copied
the Greek or the Gothic, and found inspiration in
the Italian or the French Renaissance. In short, they
reproduced the forms of the past instead of frankly
tackling the problem of finding new ones. Thus they
frequently sank into conventionality and artifici-
ality. They produced works devoid of architectural
" truth," works whose form was fictitious and not
the necessary outcome of the use to which the edifice
was to be put or of the materials used in its construction. They also frequently employed inferior
material instead of the genuine stuff—plaster and
stucco, for instance, in the place of stone—without
deigning to consider that the nature of the materials
employed should determine the architectonic forms,
and that any kind of " imitation " was to the last
degree inartistic.

From this point of view, the industrial art which
was developed in the new German Empire just after
the war of 1870 marks the acme of bad taste. It
raised to the position of a principle the machine-
made imitation, in cheap materials, of external
ornaments which had been shaped by hand in good

material at the time of the German Renaissance, when the " Baroque " and " Rococo " styles were in fashion. As it was proud of producing cheap manufactured articles within reach of the most modest purses, it dumped its appalling stock in enormous quantities over all the houses in Germany, even the most humble, and thus really perverted the taste of the public belonging to the middle and the lowest classes of the population. Owing to its influence there were to be found everywhere sham-bronzes, made of zinc covered with a patina, imitation leather made of paper, windows of transparent paper stuck on to ordinary glass to represent the leaded lights of real windows, beer pots overladen with renaissance ornament or adorned with rustic scenes, crockery heavily decorated with printed pictures or patterns, mouldings in papier-maché, and painted imitations of wood and marble. And the manufacturers who exploited this branch of industry, not content with inundating the home market with their goods, exported their shoddy art wares abroad, more particularly to England and America, where they naturally excited the contempt of all who had the smallest artistic taste, but nevertheless found a market owing to their cheapness. Yet this speculation was not altogether a profitable one. If even at the present moment the public opinion of other countries is very sceptical with regard to German " taste," and somewhat disposed to despise the artistic output of Germany *en bloc*, this state of mind can certainly be largely explained by the fact that in foreign countries German art is chiefly represented by this pretentious and shoddy stock of goods, which the cultured public of Germany itself hates and condemns with the utmost severity.

It would be exceedingly unjust at the present day to continue to judge contemporary German art by the mediocre productions of an unscrupulous industry. It is true that Germans still export their trashy art wares, and adorn their houses with pretentious " imitation " atrocities. But among the cultured *élite* there has been developing, for about ten years past, a vigorous movement of reaction against the errors of the past. The promoters of this movement, drawing their inspiration from the principles of decorative art in England, have endeavoured to revive a sincerely modern Teutonic art in Germany. They resolutely turn their backs upon the imitation of ancient forms, believing that it is the duty of our age to create original forms which are suited to it. Above all, they proscribe without mercy the cheap imitation of external ornaments borrowed from the art of the past. They proclaim the principle that the use of good material and honesty in execution form a *moral* condition indispensable for the production of any work of an artistic nature. They desire that an object should by its form express the use to which it is to be applied and the material of which it is made.

And at the same time as they are making a distinct rupture with the errors of their predecessors and loudly proclaiming the fundamental principle of " truth " and loyalty, without which no art worthy the name is possible, they also lay down the general principles which should govern the creation of new forms.

Instead of limiting their attention to isolated objects, they take as their unit the room, the inside or the whole of a house. Their aim is to create synthetic works of art, *aggregates* which are entirely

27

adapted to the use for which they are destined, in which the architectonic arrangement, the general scheme of colour, every decorative feature, and each piece of furniture combine to produce a whole impression of perfect convenience, harmony, and light. They do not confine themselves, moreover, to creating expensive interiors for the use of the rich, but also endeavour to do work suitable for more modest purses. And, in this connection, they have succeeded in producing suites of furniture entirely made by machinery, but of good quality and irreproachable workmanship, which can compete in price with the pretentious rubbish which still for the moment encumbers the large furniture warehouses of Germany.

German critics based the greatest hopes upon this artistic movement, which is barely ten years old and which may be destined to a brilliant future. Even to-day the promoters of this renewal of the art industry, who were isolated at the beginning, have founded a school. Important local centres have been established—notably in Darmstadt, Dresden, Vienna, and Munich. The new German art, which was very much discussed and criticised at first, has vindicated its value not only at local exhibitions like the Darmstadt Exhibition of 1901, which was the first imposing manifestation on the part of the new school, but also at International Exhibitions, especially at St. Louis, where it had a very distinct success.

It would no doubt be premature to attempt to prophesy the fate of so recent an undertaking. But, on the other hand, there is now no doubt that it draws its inspiration from a fruitful source, which in some shape or form will certainly be realised in

time. Our era is obviously aiming at producing an
honest, practical, and sober art, which will banish all
superfluous ornament, which aims through the collaboration of technical knowledge and artistic taste
at creating forms which are at once rational and
æsthetically satisfactory, and which does not limit
itself to building homes of sumptuous luxury for a
few rich persons, but also knows how to descend to
the people and endow with a little beauty the surroundings in which the life of the humble is passed.
From this point of view the birth of the new synthetic art, which tries to make the whole modern
house into a work of art and to give it a style in its
entirety as well as in detail, may perhaps be a more
important fact than the rise of some fresh tendency
in painting and sculpture. The Germany of to-day
clearly understands the new duties of art towards
life, and has formulated the most interesting principles
of artistic reform. It now remains to be seen to
what extent artists will be able to realise the programme which they have set themselves, and also
to what degree the public, whether at the top or the
bottom of the social scale, will second their efforts,
and prove themselves capable of that aspiration
towards the beautiful without which no synthetic
and collective art can ever be developed.

# CONCLUSION

IF, now that we have reached the end of our sketch, we endeavour to formulate the general impression made upon our minds by the spectacle of the evolution of modern Germany, I think there is one sentiment that will impress itself upon us and take precedence of all others, and that is a feeling of astonishment in the presence of the prodigious development which German power underwent during the course of the past century.

At the beginning of the nineteenth century Germany as a great Power did not exist. The Holy Roman Empire was merely a ruin which was falling lamentably to bits in the midst of the general indifference. There was no longer any Germany. There were only German princes, widely separated from each other and mutually jealous, whose sole care was their own petty dynastic interests, who were capable of every meanness and every crime for the protection or strengthening of their precious sovereignty, unable to subordinate their selfish ends to the good of the nation, but always ready, on the contrary, to treat with the foreigner and even on occasion to make war on their own countrymen if they thought they could derive any profit from their treason. In this disunited and powerless nation there was no political life. Everywhere there reigned supreme a monarchical absolutism which was fre-

quently a depressing despotism accepted by the
people with a docility which bordered upon servility.
Rigorously excluded from public matters, the peasants
and citizens, artisans and townsmen submitted pas-
sively to the imperious and officious tyranny of the
State and its officers, took not the smallest interest
in the national life, and confined themselves to the
narrow circles of their private occupations. The
economic life of the nation, moreover, was narrow
and petty ; the population was sparse, the country
poor, capital small, and industry almost non-existent.
To escape from this poverty only one path remained
open—that of thought and art. The intellectual
minority threw themselves into it in a magnificent
outburst of enthusiasm. And in this partitioned,
humiliated Germany, half ruined by wars and invasions, there blossomed a literary and philosophical
culture which perhaps constitutes the nation's
greatest title to glory. From that time forward Germany had the reputation of being the classic ground
of idealism and dreams. Just as England had made
herself mistress of the seas, and France of the land,
all that remained for Germany was, according to
the well-known proverb, the kingdom of the air.
And she created for herself an empire of incomparable splendour in this domain.

When, lo and behold! in this backward nation,
which from the point of view of earthly realities was
disinherited and apparently absorbed in dreams and
mirages, the spirit of enterprise began to develop !
And soon it became evident that, of all the Western
nations, the German people were perhaps the most
happily endowed to succeed in the economic struggle.
In her prodigious stride Germany not only caught
up but left behind the Latin races who had had a

long start upon the path of material progress, and to-day she even menaces the old industrial and commercial supremacy of England.

It has been discovered that this somewhat slow and heavy, though robust and healthy nation, provides an exceptionally favourable basis for the development of a capitalistic civilisation. Germany is not by any means artistic, voluptuous and passionate, like the Latins. She is not, like the latter, enamoured of *far niente*, leisure, and a life of beauty and gay sociability. She is serious and strong, a stubborn and conscientious worker, who from the earliest days has been adapted to severe moral discipline, and subjected to rigorous military training. And lo ! in this nation devoid of grace and brilliance, but solid and long-suffering, there sprang up a vigorous, patient, and methodical will to power, which was capable of pursuing with untiring perseverance the end it had set itself, without once being distracted by a caprice or a passion, without once being rebuffed by a difficulty or an obstacle. The German wishes for power, not so much from any personal desire to push himself forward and make himself respected, and not even for the sake of the material advantages he may procure ; he wants power *for its own sake*, because it is the measure of the true value of a man, a group, a party, or a people.

He is impelled towards enterprise by an economic law and by virtue of a necessity imposed upon him by fate. The German, as we have already shown, is extraordinarily prolific. The annual increase in the population of the Empire between 1816 and 1900 was 1·01 per cent. ; between 1900 and 1905 it reached 1·50 and 1·45 per cent. The population increased from almost 25 million inhabitants in 1816 to over

36 millions in 1855 and over 60 millions in 1905. About 1820 France had four million more inhabitants than Germany. Shortly before the middle of the last century the two countries each had about $34\frac{1}{2}$ million inhabitants. To-day Germany has 20 millions more than France, and the difference between them is increasing daily. These figures are an eloquent testimony to the extent in which the birth-rate of Germany exceeds that of France, and to the fact that large families are consequently more frequent in Germany than in the Republic.

Now this is a circumstance which is in the highest degree favourable to the development of capitalism. The annual increase of population has furnished Germany with the army of workers which is required for the development of industry. And in the well-to-do classes of the population the spirit of enterprise has developed enormously. The German father of a family has not the ambition that is prevalent among French parents of leaving a ready-made position and a secure income for his children. He gives them a good education, equips them well for the struggle of life, and then leaves it to their own efforts to make a place in the sun for themselves. Under pain of sinking and falling below the level attained by his parents it is necessary for a young man to work hard and exert himself. Thus the fecundity of the race has in the case of Germany been one of the strongest stimuli in the rush for wealth and power.

And this desire for power is growing and getting stronger in all ranks of life in Germany and in all domains of human activity. It is to be found in individuals, in political parties, in social groups and in States. It asserts itself in the breast of the whole German community in the shape of imperialism and a universal policy. It tends towards military, naval, and diplomatic supremacy, towards economic, industrial and commercial hegemony, and scientific preeminence—for science also is a form of human power, and it is certainly to German science that Germany owes a large share of her success. The will to power is gradually ousting from the German mind the aspiration for culture, and is imperceptibly pushing the latter into the second place. The cult of art is cooling down, or rather is changing in character; art is no longer regarded as an end in itself, but merely as an accessory to life. And the worship of force is increasing in Germany. But it must be confessed that the power the Germans revere is not brutal, tyrannical, capricious, and arbitrary force, which delights in stupid oppression and denies all rights. They worship intelligent and deliberate power which imposes itself lawfully through its own virtue ; because it is not only inevitable, but also useful, wise and normal for strength to take the lead of weakness and for the superior *monad* to hold the inferior one in subjection. They revere that Might which is *at the same time* the Right, because it is the expression of a real superiority which *should* in all justice be recognised and respected.

It must, moreover, be pointed out that the effort to gain power is as orderly a process as possible among the Germans.

The system of unrestricted competition, by instituting war on the part of each individual against all the rest and thus stimulating private selfishness to the highest degree, certainly contained within itself an anarchical and dissolving principle. It was capable of exciting, as it once did in Italy at the time of the Renaissance, exasperated individuals to fight desperately against each other for supremacy, and to destroy each other without mercy. Yet it is a very remarkable fact that the development of the system of free enterprise in Germany has not entailed consequences of this nature. The competition among individuals or bodies is very keen, but it never degenerates into disordered convulsions.

The struggle between the German States for political hegemony was very long and fierce, and it was finally decided by war. But once the verdict of force had been given, antipathies were calmed after quite a short interval, and hatreds died out. And instead of wasting time in useless grudges, or squandering her power in vain rebellions, Germany rapidly accepted the new order of things imposed upon her, and united all her forces with a view to political and economic struggles in Europe or the world. Similarly the struggle between political parties was obstinate and persistent. But it hardly ever ended in any serious trouble. The conflict between the classes was perhaps more serious than anywhere else. But it was not of a revolutionary character. Even among the Socialists, the irreconcilable adversaries of the capitalistic state in Germany, the reforming type of mind tended more and more to gain the upper hand. They condemned without exception all appeal to violence, all attempts to gain their ends by force ; they openly repudiated anti-militarism and recourse to general strikes. Industrial and commercial competition is very keen and private initiative exceedingly bold and vigorous. Yet Germany, the classic ground of cartels and great associations of masters and men, is certainly also one of the countries where the most has been done to regulate production, to institute control over the rate of exchange, and consequently to restrict competition, limit the frequency of crises, and diminish their severity when they do occur.

To sum up: personal enterprise is very strong in Germany, but it does not result in anarchic individualism. And the explanation of this fact is to be found in a well-known racial characteristic. The German has less need than men of other countries to develop his *complete* personality. He willingly confines himself to some special occupation, to which he delivers himself up unreservedly. He gladly sacrifices a part of his individuality and limits himself, to use the expressive German word, to being merely a *Teilmensch*, a fraction of a man, a specialist who performs with conspicuous superiority some particular task, without troubling his head about anything that exists outside the carefully bounded domain in which he barricadés himself. And for this reason too he loves to join associations and to be a subordinate. He takes delight in becoming a member of the innumerable *Vereins* of all kinds that have sprung up in Germany, and enjoys the feeling that he is an integral portion of a vast organisation of which he is a more or less essential wheel. He is pleased to associate his private destiny with the fate of some vast enterprise, to the success of which he is ready to devote his life. In a word he has the instinct of discipline. He knows how to *obey* and also how to *command*; he knows how to execute punctually the orders he has received, as well as how to display initiative in the sphere assigned to him. The German nation thus provides admirable human material wherewith to build up the colossal organisms of all kinds which go to constitute the system of enterprise : national armies, great admini-

strative bodies, vast financial, industrial and commercial enterprises, syndicates and cartels. There
is no department of life, even to the domain of art,
in which he does not aim at producing a synthetic
work, either in the shape of musical drama or an
edifice with a style in all its various parts. And this
taste for association and subordination is innate in
the German. He is not obliged to *resign himself* to
discipline. He practises it with joy. He becomes a
specialist by desire, and feels no regret for the things
which will for ever remain beyond his horizon. He
shuts himself up within the limits of his means, in
his *Fach*, with a certain austere joy which is often
mixed with a slight disdain or amused irony with
regard to the dilettante who meddles with matters
he knows little about, and who professes to discuss
*de omni re scibili* and boldly tackles the deepest problem of politics or religion, art and morality. His
serious side, his *Gründlichkeit*,[1] instinctively despises
improvisers, bunglers, Jacks-of-all-trades, who touch
upon every subject with an audacity only to be
equalled by their incompetence. He takes pride in
not transgressing beyond the bounds of things he
knows. Or, to put the matter more simply, he is
lacking in curiosity and for him the universe ends
with the limits of his own speciality.

This instinct for discipline, this sense for an order
of rank which is so widespread in Germany, has as
its first consequence the conservative attitude of the
nation as a whole. Individual thought in Germany
is extremely bold ; it recoils from no problem, and
examines them one and all with complete independence. But at bottom it detests radical solutions.
In religious matters Germany is neither " atheisti-

[1] Thoroughness.—TR,

cal " nor " clerical." She repudiates none of the
conquests of scientific rationalism. But she still
preserves a sincere veneration for the instinctive
wisdom which finds its expression in the religious
evolution of humanity. And she tries her best to
reconcile science and faith, rational truth and traditional truth. Similarly in politics she endeavours
to unite the principle of authority with that of
democracy. She would no longer tolerate despotic
absolutism. Yet she keeps a spontaneous respect for
monarchy, for the established hierarchy and for
" qualified " authorities. German democracy does
not arrogate to itself the position of being the *only*
mistress of the nation's destinies, but willingly
shares its power with a supreme head it has not
chosen but whom tradition has provided.

Moreover, it seems that, thanks to her sense of
discipline and order, Germany is gradually raising
herself to a conception of life as a *unity* which is
little by little correcting and completing the combative idea of unrestricted competition. And it is
in this respect that, in my opinion, her evolution
most deserves our admiration. The development of
political parties, social groups, syndicates of masters
and men, and the tremendous extension of social
insurance schemes prove the continual progress made
in the idea of solidarity. The unchaining of universal
competition, and the war of each man against his
neighbour, have gradually given place to the realisation of the necessity for a *united* struggle for power.
After a period of great upheavals, of instability and
insecurity, caused by the development of the system
of free enterprise, Germany expects and hopes for
the advent of a more secure economic and social
order, a more stable hierarchy, and a less uncertain

moral "faith." After the colossal struggle for political supremacy and material wealth, she aspires to a renaissance of the idealistic impulse towards culture and art. These are certainly beautiful aims. However uncertain they may be, it is enough for them not to appear impossible of realisation for Germans to have the right to look with legitimate pride at the road already covered, and to gaze with some optimism into the future towards which they are marching.

It now remains for us to point out that for the moment the consciousness of unity among Germans remains almost exclusively *national*. The German feels himself more and more at one with other Germans. But in connection with other nations he generally holds the combative idea of unrestricted competition. The fundamental strength of German nationalism to-day forms in this respect a striking contrast with its generous cosmopolitanism a hundred years ago. Pan-German imperialism which is so robust and combative, so confident in its power and in the star of its fate, so energetic in its enterprises, and moreover so vigilant and inclined to take alarm, so prompt to threaten on occasion, and so decided in repelling all solicitations on the part of peace-advocates and internationalists, is certainly an example and a warning to other nations. It shows that the era of competition is not even to-day at an end, either in the case of individuals or of nations, and proves moreover that a country should in any case still keep its strength intact.

Is the present nationalism of Germany destined to be the end of her evolution for some time to come ? There may, perhaps, be some reason to hope that she will not stiffen herself indefinitely into this pugnacious attitude, and will not prove herself an obstacle to the realisation of a less anarchical state of things in the civilised world. And why, indeed, should not the country, which in her own national development showed such a clear understanding of the necessity for competition *and* combination, of fruitful emulation *and* unity, why should she not gradually raise herself from the point of view of national solidarity to that of the unification of Europe and of the human race ? There are numerous symptoms which indicate that from many points of view, but especially in the domain of science and economics, as well as in scientific and artistic culture, this evolution has long since begun in Germany as well as in other countries. Perhaps it is not altogether chimerical—and it is with this hope that I would end this study—to think that the twentieth century will see the growth and spread of the modern religion of unity, and that we shall gradually approach the ideal of the " good European " which, during the height of the nationalistic enthusiasm, Nietzsche had the courage to preach to his countrymen.

# INDEX

28

Printed by Hazell, Watson & Viney, Ld., London and Aylesbury, England.